MESSAGE OF THE FATHERS OF THE CHURCH

General Editor: Thomas Halton

Volume 17

MESSAGE OF THE FATHERS OF THE CHURCH

DIVINE PROVIDENCE
&
HUMAN SUFFERING

by

James Walsh, S.J.
and
P. G. Walsh

Michael Glazier

Wilmington, Delaware

ABOUT THE AUTHORS

JAMES WALSH, S.J. was founder and editor of *The Way* for twenty years. With Edmund College OSA he has edited Julian of Norwich in the Toronto *Studies and Texts* series, and Guigo II in the *Sources Chrétiennes* series; his editions of *The Cloud of Unknowing* (Paulist Press 1981) and of *Revelations of Divine Love* (1973) have reached a wide public. He is now on the staff of the Jesuit Centre of Spirituality, St. Beuno's, St. Asaph, N. Wales.

P. G. WALSH is Professor of Humanity (Latin) in the University of Glasgow. His publications on Classical subjects include *Livy* and *The Roman Novel* (both Cambridge University Press). He has translated the letters and poems of Paulinus of Nola (ACW vols 35-36, 40), Andreas Capellanus on Love (1982), and (with A. Ross O.P.) Aquinas, *Courage* in the Blackfriars series.

First published in 1985 by Michael Glazier, Inc.
1723 Delaware Avenue, Wilmington, Delaware 19806

Distributed outside U. S., Canada, Australia, and Philippines by Geoffrey Chapman, a division of Cassel Ltd., 1 Vincent Square, London SWIP 2PN.

Library of Congress Catalog Card Number: 84-48852
International Standard Book Number:
    Message of the Fathers of the Church series:
        (0-89453-312-6, Paper; 0-89453-340-1, Cloth)
    DIVINE PROVIDENCE AND HUMAN SUFFERING
        (0-89453-328-2, Paper)
        (0-89453-357-6, Cloth)

Cover design: Lillian Brulc

Typography by Susan Pickett

Printed in the United States

CONTENTS

IN MEMORIAM PATRIS NOSTRI
VIRI FORTIS IN FIDE
DIE PALMARVM MCMLXXXIV
IN PATRIAM TRANSLATI

EDITOR'S INTRODUCTION

The *Message of the Fathers of the Church* is a companion series to The *Old Testament Message* and The *New Testament Message*. It was conceived and planned in the belief that Scripture and Tradition worked hand in hand in the formation of the thought, life and worship of the primitive Church. Such a series, it was felt, would be a most effective way of opening up what has become virtually a closed book to present-day readers, and might serve to stimulate a revival in interest in Patristic studies in step with the recent, gratifying resurgence in Scriptural studies.

The term 'Fathers' is usually reserved for Christian writers marked by orthodoxy of doctrine, holiness of life, ecclesiastical approval and antiquity. 'Antiquity' is generally understood to include writers down to Gregory the Great (+604) or Isidore of Seville (+636) in the West, and John Damascene (+749) in the East. In the present series, however, greater elasticity has been encouraged, and quotations from writers not noted for orthodoxy will sometimes be included in order to illustrate the evolution of the Message on particular doctrinal matters. Likewise, writers later than the mid-eighth century will sometimes be used to illustrate the continuity of tradition on matters like sacramental theology or liturgical practice.

An earnest attempt was made to select collaborators on a broad inter-disciplinary and inter-confessional basis, the chief consideration being to match scholars who could handle the Fathers in their original languages with subjects in which they had already demonstrated a special interest and competence. About the only editorial directive given to the selected contributors was that the Fathers, for the most part, should be allowed to speak for themselves and that they should speak in readable, reliable modern English. Volumes on individual themes were considered more suitable than volumes devoted to individual Fathers, each theme, hopefully, contributing an important segment to the total mosaic of the Early Church, one, holy, catholic and apostolic. Each volume has an introductory essay outlining the historical and theological development of the theme, with the body of the work mainly occupied with liberal citations from the Fathers in modern English translation and a minimum of linking commentary. Short lists of Suggested Further Readings are included; but dense, scholarly footnotes were actively discouraged on the pragmatic grounds that such scholarly shorthand has other outlets and tends to lose all but the most relentlessly esoteric reader in a semi-popular series.

At the outset of his *Against Heresies* Irenaeus of Lyons warns his readers 'not to expect from me any display of rhetoric, which I have never learned, or any excellence of composition, which I have never practised, or any beauty or persuasiveness of style, to which I make no pretensions.' Similarly, modest disclaimers can be found in many of the Greek and Latin Fathers and all too often, unfortunately, they have been taken at their word by an uninterested world. In fact, however, they were often highly educated products of the best rhetorical schools of their day in the Roman Empire, and what they have to say is often as much a lesson in literary and cultural, as well as in spiritual, edification.

St. Augustine, in *The City of God* (19.7), has interesting reflections on the need for a common language in an expanding world community; without a common language a man is more at home with his dog than with a foreigner as far as intercommunication goes, even in the Roman Empire, which imposes on the nations it conquers the yoke of both law and language with a resultant abundance of interpreters. It is hoped that in the present world of continuing language barriers the contributors to this series will prove opportune intepreters of the perennial Christian message.

Thomas Halton

INTRODUCTION

It would be a fair summary of the patristic teaching on divine providence and human suffering to say that none of the ancient Christian writers ever experienced more than a passing difficulty in accepting the two concepts as perfectly compatible with one another. The neo-Platonists among them might feel called upon to offer philosophical disquisitions on the nature and existence of evil in the face of the divine attributes; but this would only be to help us to delve deeper into the mystery of sin, and to distinguish it from its painful effects. In the fourteenth century we even find an apostrophe to sin which adequately reflects the earlier tradition, in the *Book of Showings to the Anchoress Julian of Norwich*, who writes: 'Ah, wretched sin, what art thou? Thou art nought. For I saw that God is all things; I saw thee not. And when I saw that God has made all things, I saw thee not. And when I saw that God is in all things, I saw thee not. And when I saw that God does all things that are done, the less and the more, I saw thee not. And when I saw our Lord Jesus sit in our soul so worshipfully, and love and like and rule and govern all that he has made, I saw thee not. And thus I am sure that thou art nought, and all that love thee and like thee and follow thee and wilfully end in thee, I am sure that they shall be brought to nought with thee and endlessly confounded. God shield us all from thee. Amen, for charity.' (*Short Text*, ch. 23).

Evil, then, poses no particular problem in respect to the divine Wisdom, which 'reaches from end to end mightily, and orders all things sweetly' (Wis 8:1). The book of Wisdom, the first Old Testament treatise to link unambiguously the afterlife with its joys and retributions to this passing life, is the model for patristic praise of divine providence: 'Intelligent, holy, one, manifold, subtle, eloquent, mobile, undefiled, sure, sweet, loving what is good, quick, keen, irresistible, beneficent, all-powerful, all-watchful, gentle, kind, steadfast, assured, unanxious, penetrating,......the breath of God's power, pure emanation of the glory of the Almighty......the reflection of the eternal light, the spotless mirror of God's working and the image of his goodness. Being one, she can do all things, and remaining the same in herself she renews all things' (Wis 7:22-29).

Universal, too, is the view that the greatest harm ever done to humankind was Adam's sin. And if death entered the world by the devil's envy, after God had created man incorruptible (Wis 2:23-24), the common doctrine of the Fathers was the corporate solidarity of all human nature with the first man, Adam. The Pauline principle, and indeed the entire anthropology flowing from it, was accepted by all without question: 'By one man sin entered into this world, and by sin, death; and so death passed into all men, and in him all men have sinned' (Rom 5:12). St. Basil of Caesarea writes of the first and second Adam and in terms that are generally acceptable and representative, that 'the providence of our God and Saviour with regard to humankind consists in our being raised from the fall and the return to intimate communion with God from the alienation incurred by our disobedience. This was the purpose of Christ's dwelling among us in the flesh and of the pattern of his life as portrayed in the gospels — his passion, cross, burial and resurrection. It was so that man could be saved, and could once again receive the adoption by the Father through assimilation to Christ.' (*On the Holy Spirit*, XV, 35).

These are no more than half-hearted attempts to share out responsibility for the introduction of evil into our world between the serpent and Eve, and between our first parents. Augustine, in his short treatise *On The Literal Meaning of Genesis (De Genesi ad Litteram)* cites the proverb from Paul's first letter to Timothy, that the root of all evils is cupidity (*radix omnium malorum est avaritia*). But he insists that avarice is used in a larger sense than the inordinate love of money. It was the root of evil in Lucifer as well, who had nothing to do with money. Later it was the unbridled desire for knowledge and power which was shared by Adam and Satan alike (P.L. 34, 346). The sin of the Angels is always portrayed analogously with that of Adam. It was left to the medieval writers to try to put the fear of the devil in the hearts of their readers, and with gusto. John Chrysostom in one of his *Homilies on Matthew*, tells us how reluctant he is to speak at all about the pains of hell. The Fathers who write about Job make observations similar to one another about the person and influence of the devil. In the memorable phrase of Julian of Norwich, 'the power of the fiend is locked in God's hand.'

If the modern problem concerning the reconciliation of the pain of this world and the providence of God is the suffering of the innocent, this was taken as solved by the sacred writers from the time of the Wisdom of Solomon and the Maccabean Wars; and their solution is wholly acceptable to the Apostolic writers and to the Fathers as a whole. Job's suffering is presented as an exemplary test of virtue; that of the servant of Isaiah as the supreme love of God and of the neighbor. In Job, it is clear that the justice of God is never brought into question, and the protagonist is certain that God recognises his integrity and judges him accordingly (Job 31:6). It is not possible for man in his powerlessness and ignorance to take issue with the all-Powerful and all-Wise in his moral government of his Creation. This is Gregory's standpoint in his *Moral Reflections on Job*, and he speaks for all. It is the modern commentators, not the Fathers, who would argue that the Epilog, with its lauding of Job's restored prosperity, is a letdown and strikes a discordant note. Patristically, its significance is anagogical as well as moral. Virtue is triumphant, and Job's reward is everlasting bliss.

The identification of the Servant of Isaiah with the beloved Son to whom God the Father testifies at the river Jordan and on the Mount of the Transfiguration is taken as absolute. There is no patristic suggestion of this Servant having a corporate personality. It is always Jesus, who has received the Spirit to prepare him for his mission. 'In Jesus' writes Leo the Great 'the promise of the prophetic images and the Law's purposes are fulfilled; one covenant reinforces the other' (*Sermons* 51:4). Pope John Paul II has recently resumed this tradition by reminding us that Isaiah on the Suffering Servant has been called the fifth evangelist (Isa 52:13-53, 12). 'These verses of Isaiah shed such light on Christ's passion that it is thrown into greater relief and touches our hearts more effectively than the narratives of the evangelists themselves' (*infra*, Appendix II, p. 236). Here we have the climax of the Old Testament teaching on the value of suffering. In the view of the Fathers it is equally and exactly that of the New Testament, especially when suffering unto death is emphasized. Cyril of Alexandria, in his *Commentary on St. John's Gospel* (IV,2), imagines Christ as saying from the Cross: 'I am dying for all humanity so that all may have life through me. I have redeemed the flesh of all in my own flesh. In my death, death itself will die, and fallen human nature will rise again with me.'

The reason why the Fathers so rarely pose the question 'Why does God permit such suffering in his world?' is because, in their view, the Christian religion, as in the New Testament, rests on the belief in the future life, 'the bright promise of immortality.' Christianity is nothing if it is not other-worldly. Its faith is no less solid when the ancient writers come to the realization that the *eschaton* is probably not going to take place tomorrow or the day after. The Pauline text is echoed very frequently, particularly in respect of such dominant patristic themes as the Paschal mystery and the Last Things: 'I reckon that the sufferings of this time are not worthy to be compared with the glory that is to come which shall be revealed in us' (Rom 8:18). But it is repeated by the Fathers without eschatological immediacy; and the same is true of the 'little time' in the first letter of Peter (1:6).

The treatise on the spiritual advantages of suffering by the twelfth-century schoolman, Peter of Blois (*infra*, pp. 141-162) may be considered as the formal treatment of the extensive and general tradition from early apostolic times. All suffering, no matter how intense or widespread, every calamity, no matter how dreadful, is in no sense a reason for regret, much less for questioning the merciful designs of an all-loving Providence. In our age, however, large-scale natural disasters or the terrible havoc wreaked or threatened by modern warfare such as the conflict between Jew and Arab, the American adventures in Southeast Asia, and the British in the Falkland Islands, have become cast-iron arguments for agnosticism or even atheism. Documentaries on the appalling violence in El Salvador and the North of Ireland, like *Roses in December* or *The Steel Shutter*, and the frequent news items on television and in the tabloid press which highlight the suffering and death of little children, have shifted the theological and pastoral focus of the average Christian churchman from heaven to earth. Many of them are no longer at odds with Karl Marx; it has become all too obvious that religion can be and often is the opiate of many.

Though Vatican II's Pastoral Constitution on the Church in the Modern World is persistently at pains, in its methodology, to maintain a fruitful tension between concern for the here and the hereafter, we would hunt in vain amongst early Christian writings for such unambiguous statements as the following: 'Whilst rejecting atheism outright, the Church sincerely professes that all people, believers and unbelievers alike, ought to work for the betterment of the world in which we all live' (*Gaudium et Spes*, 21). Nor is it likely that the Fathers would draw the same conclusion as does the Council document from the gospel saying, 'the Sabbath was made for man and not man for the Sabbath' (Mk 2:27).

This, implies the Constitution, refers to the social order and its development, which 'requires constant improvement. It must be founded on truth, built on justice and animated by love; in freedom it should grow every day towards a more humane balance' (*Gaudium et Spes*, 25). The Fathers would expect this from the newly converted Christian community in their relationships with one another, as indeed did the Apostolic writers; they would certainly never have expected it from the world. It might be looked upon as an ideal belonging to the prophetic millennium, or even to a fictional order such as that propounded in Virgil's *Georgics* (cf. *infra*, p. 214), but not to the here and now. Patristic writing hardly envisaged the pluralistic society to which the modern Church must address itself; only the black and white of "he who is not with me is against me" (Mt 12:30). And though our spiritual forebears might agree in the abstract that extreme poverty cripples human freedom (*Gaudium et Spes*, 31), they would be much more likely to remind us of the basic Christian duty of almsgiving, and of the Psalmist's assurance that the Lord himself listens to the cry of the poor. Both the Council document (41) and the second-century anonymous *Letter to Diognetus* (chs. V-VI) speak of the Church, or Christians, as the soul of the world, or of human society. But their concepts are vastly different. According to the Constitution, for the Church to live in the world means not only being present in it, but 'living and acting with it,' whereas the *Letter to Diognetus* insists that Christians dwell in the world without being part of it. They are aliens and prisoners in it, persecuted and dishonoured by it. They are heaven's, not the world's, citizens.

It is true that some were witnesses of the bloody persecutions under the Roman Empire. But martyrdom was a blessed lot. And even one of the most bloodthirsty of the barbarian invaders was called God's scourge, chastising those whom God loved. The Fathers had less experience of the incredible violence, genocide, exploitation, famine and the rest which are modern man's constant companions. The Book of Revelations has nothing to compare with the horrors of Kampuchea or El Salvador —or even the Falklands and Grenada. The traditional answers to the problem of evil which a perennial Christian humanism still offers (cf. *infra*, pp. 208-217) seem to force us today to beseech our God to provide us with better ones, such as will help us truly to assuage human grief, particularly for the suffering of the innocent. This, in fact, is the task Pope John Paul recently set himself in his Apostolic Letter on the Christian significance of human suffering, *Salvifici Doloris*. In the belief that no fuller nor more competent assessment of the relationship between divine providence and human suffering has ever been attempted by the *Magisterium*, we have thought it well to present our own translation of the Latin text. We think that it provides a fitting conclusion to this book.

Easter Day 1985

J. W.

ABBREVIATIONS

CCL   Corpus Christianorum, series latina

CSEL   Corpus Scriptorum Ecclesiasticorum Latinorum

OECT   Oxford Early Christian Texts

PG   Patrologia Graeca

PL   Patrologia Latina

PST   Patristic Studies, Washington, D.C.

SC   Sources Chrétiennes

SLH   Scriptores Latini Hiberniae, Dublin

Chapter One

PROVIDENCE AND EVIL

All accept that suffering is integral to the human condition, since it is part of our daily experience; we both witness it in others and endure it ourselves. The biblical account, from the moment that our first parents are expelled from Paradise, reflects this human experience. We therefore expect to learn from scripture the origin and meaning of suffering, of the spirit in which it should be confronted and borne, of the rewards which attend an authentically Christian endurance of suffering. We learn that suffering was never intended by God to be part of human life. The myth of Genesis suggests that after triumphing over a divinely-appointed test or temptation, during which fidelity to the Creator was to be established in a serene and fulfilled life of unknown duration, the human creature was to pass into an even more wonderful and harmonious existence with his Maker. Yet though the whole of creation had as its end the harmony and happiness of human creatures, Adam and Eve were seduced by the first temptation to sin. Man was punished for his rebellion against God; he lost his immortality, and the qualities of life and being which accompanied it. This changed the conditions under which the human race inhabited the world which God had created for it.

This was the theological framework within which the Fathers sought to refute the sceptical objections of later Greek philosophers, for whom the problems of living had become the leading preoccupation.

THE SOURCE OF EVIL

1. Athanasius

> The philosophical problem which is central to the issue
> of suffering is the problem of evil: what is the source of
> evil, and how can it exist in a providentially ordered
> world? Athanasius, bishop of Alexandria from 328 to 373
> and the leading defender of orthodoxy against the Arian-
> ism of his day, confronted the problem in his early work
> *Against the Pagans.*

Against the Pagans, 2-3[1]

"Evil did not exist from the beginning, and even today it is
not present among the holy angels, for it does not exist at all
there. It was later that men began to think of it and to
fashion it within themselves. Hence they formed for themselves the notion of idols, accounting as existent non-
existent things. God, the Creator and King of all, who lies
beyond all being and beyond all human concepts, has
through his own Word our Saviour Jesus Christ made the
human race in his image. Because he is good and surpass-
ingly noble, he made man observe and become aware of
reality by making man like himself; he gave him also awareness and knowledge of his own immortality, so that by
preserving his likeness he might never forsake his vision of
God, or recoil from the company of the angels. Rather, he
would retain the grace of God who had endowed it, and the
peculiar power of the Father's word, and be happy and
converse with the divine, and live an immortal life, painless
and truly blessed...

This was how the Creator fashioned the human race, as I
have said, and this was how he wished it to remain. But men
belittled the better things, and were chary of their vision of
them. Instead they sought what was closer to themselves.
And what was closer was the body and its sensations. So
they diverted their minds from observable things, and began
to regard themselves. From this self-regard and from laying

[1]Text: OECT, ed. R.W. Thomson, 1971, 4

hold of the body and the other sensible things, they deceived themselves in regard to their own affairs, and became eager for themselves, preferring their own qualities to the contemplation of the divine. So they wasted their time with these matters, not wishing to turn from things close at hand. They confined their own souls within bodily pleasures; they were now turbulent and foul from all their desires, so that finally they forgot their power which they had initially received from God.

You can realize this truth from the account in holy scripture of the first created man. Whilst he kept his mind on God and on contemplation of him, he turned away from thoughts of the body. But when at the serpent's instigation he turned from thoughts of God and began to contemplate himself, both Eve and he turned to bodily desire, realizing that they were naked, and feeling shame from that knowledge. They realized that they were bare not so much of clothing as of the contemplation of divine things, and they directed their attention to the opposite. Renouncing the contemplation of, and longing for, the one Being, God, they turned henceforward to different beings, and to the separate desires of the body. As usually happens, in laying hold of their desire for each and everything, they began to develop the fear of losing it all, and so apprehensions, fears, pleasures, preoccupations with mortal things have become attached to the soul. Through its unwillingness to abandon these desires, it fears death and separation from the body."

2. Athanasius

This account of the origin of evil offered by Athanasius is presented against a background of conflicting opinions offered by earlier Greek philosophers and dissident Christian sects. Particularly influential was the notion of dualism, that there exist in the world two powers or principles of good and evil. Amongst the Greek philosophers the idea is as old as Pythagoras, who flourished in the sixth century BC, and Plato's differentiation between the world of ideas and the material world from which the soul longs to escape gave it wide currency in the early Christian centuries. The idea was strong also in certain of the mystery-religions, for example that of Isis, which became particularly influential when the Middle Platonists like Plutarch and Apuleius preached a reconciliation between the Platonist philosophy and the Isiac religion. This dualism was taken up by Christian gnostic groups and by the Manichees, who actively evangelized amongst Christians. Athanasius was accordingly anxious to refute the notion that evil had an independent existence, or was attributable to the Christian God, and in this same treatise *Against the Pagans* he stresses that these are heretical views, and that evil is non-substantial, an argument resumed by later authorities in this chapter.

Against the Pagans, 6[2]

"Certain Greeks who have wandered from the truth and are unaware of Christ have stated that evil exists in reality and independently. This assumption is wrong on two counts. Either they strip the Craftsman of his title of Creator of all that is, for he would not be Lord of all things if evil had an independent existence and substance, as they believe; or in wishing him to be the Creator of the whole reality, they will of necessity grant that he is the Creator of evil as well, because in their view evil is one of the existing things. But this seems extraordinary and impossible, for evil does not come from good, or exist in good, or through good. For the good would no longer be good if its nature were adulterated, or if it were the cause of evil.

Some heretics too who have forsaken the Church's teaching and whose faith has suffered shipwreck wrongly believe that evil has a positive existence. They fabricate for themselves in addition to the true Father of Christ a second god, an unbegotten creator of evil and founder of wickedness who is also the craftsman of creation. We can easily refute them from the scriptures and from human reason itself, which they have abandoned in fashioning this lunatic view.

[2]Text: OECT, ed. Thomson, 14

Our Lord and Saviour Jesus Christ in his gospels underlines Moses' teachings when he says 'The Lord God is one' and 'I acknowledge you, Father, Lord of heaven and earth' (Mark 12:29, Matt 11:25). If God is one, and he is Lord of heaven and earth, how could there be another god as well, and where will the god they invent be, since the one true God fills everything within the confines of heaven and earth? How could there be another creator of the things over which God the Father of Christ is Lord, as the Saviour says, unless they were to suggest that the vile god can also be lord over the good God's creation in equal partnership? But if this is what they say, note into what impiety they fall; for when power is shared, there cannot be a higher or better element...

Since then this attitude appears unsound, we must present clearly the truth of the Church's judgment: that evil is not from God nor in God; it did not originally exist and it has no substance."

3. Basil the Great

St. Basil the Great (c. 330-79), one of the three Cappadocian Fathers and the formative figure of Eastern monasticism, elaborates upon the nature of evil outlined by Athanasius. The definition of evil as the privation of good is adopted from Plotinus; Basil synthesizes this Neoplatonist notion with the biblical explanation of its origin, that man of his free will turned away from God and thereby forfeited his natural and healthy condition.

God is not the author of evils, 5[3]

"In short, do not regard God as the cause of the substance of evil. Do not imagine that evil has a substance peculiar to it. Wickedness does not exist like some living thing. We cannot set it before our eyes as something existing. Evil is a privation of good. The eye was created, and blindness came into existence with the loss of eyesight. So if the eye had not been destructible by nature, blindness could not have come

[3]Text: PG 31. 341

into the world. In the same way evil does not exist in its own right, but comes into existence through the mutilation of the soul. It is not unbegotten, as impious people state who accord to an evil nature equality in degree with a good nature on the grounds that both have no beginning and transcend birth, nor is it begotten. If all things are from God, how could evil come from good? The base does not come from the noble; vice does not come from virtue. Read the account of creation, and you will find there: 'Everything was good, and exceedingly good.' (Gen 1:31). So evil was not created together with good things. This holds good for the unseen creation; when it was fashioned by the Craftsman, it did not come into being with an admixture of wickedness. If physical things had no evil associated with their creation, how could spiritual things, which excel the physical in purity and holiness, have had a joint existence with wickedness? Yet evil exists, and its power shows that it is diffused through the whole of life. So the question is: from where does its existence come, if it has no beginning, and has not been created?

Those who ask such questions must be asked in return: What is the cause of diseases and defects of the body? Sickness is not without a beginning, but it is not the creation of God. Living things were made with the natural equipment appropriate to them; they came into existence fitted with the physical parts which life required. They grew ill when they were diverted from their natural state. They suffer ill-health through either defective diet or some other cause of sickness. God created the body, not sickness; God too created the soul and not sin. The soul became wicked when it was diverted from its natural state. What was its preeminent good? Its proximity to God and its union with him through love. When it abandoned that love, it was vitiated by sicknesses of diverse kinds. Why in short was it receptive of evil? Because it was endowed with free will, which is especially appropriate for a nature endowed with reason. So the soul is freed of all constraint, and obtains from the Creator a life at its own discretion; and because it was made in God's image, it understands the good and knows its joys, and has the possibility and power of maintaining its natural life by continuing to gaze on the good and to enjoy the life of the spirit. But it has also the possibility on occasion of abandoning the good. This happens to it when it is sated with blessed joy, and weighed down, so to say, with sleep; it tumbles down from heavenly things and mingles with the flesh to enjoy base pleasures."

4. Augustine

The classic statement of this Neoplatonist view of the nature and origin of evil adapted to a Christian framework is enunciated by St. Augustine (354-430) in his *Confessions*. This account of Augustine's quest for philosophical and theological truth, and for the solution to the nature of the happy life, has as one of its main strands the author's sustained investigation into the problem of evil.

Confessions 7.111.4[4]

"But though I said and staunchly believed that our Lord, the true God, who made our bodies as well as our souls, who made all men and all things as well as our souls and bodies, is incorruptible and unchangeable and suffers no transformation in any way, I still did not unravel and disentangle and grasp the cause of evil. But I saw that, whatever the cause of evil was, I must not seek an explanation which forced me to believe that the unchangeable God was changeable, for if I did that, I should become the cause of evil which I sought. So without anxiety I investigated the problem; and I was certain that the truth was not the teaching of the Manichees, whom I shunned wholeheartedly, because I saw that in their search for the source of evil they were themselves full of malice, and this made them believe that your existence suffered evil rather than that their existence inflicted it.

I concentrated on examining the view which I heard, that free will is the cause of our doing evil, and that your right

4Text: CCL 27.94

judgment is the cause of our suffering it. But I could not see this clearly. I tried to draw my mind's eye up from the depths, but I was again submerged, and often though I tried I repeatedly sank back. But what raised me some way to your light was my knowledge that I had a will as I had life. So when I willed or refused something, I was absolutely certain that it was none other than I who willed or refused it, and I was at the point of realizing that this was the cause of my sin. But what I did unwillingly, I regarded myself as suffering rather than inflicting, and I considered this a punishment rather than a fault. But I readily admitted that my affliction was not unjust, for I thought of you as just.

But again I asked: Who made me? Was it not my God, who is not only good but Good itself? So what is the source of my willing evil and refusing to do good, that I should justly pay the penalty? Who set and implanted in me this root of bitterness, since I was wholly made by my God who is most sweet? If the devil is responsible, where does he originate from? If by his wicked will he has changed from a good angel into the devil, from where did the wicked will in him come to make him a devil, since he was made wholly an angel by the Creator who is most good? These reflections cast me down again and stifled me, but I was not reduced to that hell of error where none confesses you and where it is believed that you suffer evil rather than that man inflicts it. . . .

I sought the source of evil, but my search was defective, and I did not see the flaw in my search. I set before my mind's eye the whole creation, both the things we see like earth, sea, air, constellations, trees, mortal creatures, and the things which we do not see in it, such as heaven's firmament above and all its angels and spiritual powers. These too I pictured as apportioned in different places as if they were bodies. I visualized one huge mass of your creation which I divided according to kinds of bodies, both the real bodies and those which I had pictured as spirits. I made the creation huge; not the size it is, which I could not assess, but the size of my fancy, bounded on every side. And you, Lord, I pictured as encompassing it on every side and entering it, but as One wholly infinite; just as if there were sea everywhere, nothing but boundless sea on all sides through space immeasurable, and it had within it a sponge which was huge but finite, and that sponge was wholly filled in every part with the boundless sea. This was how I envisaged your creation as finite and You as infinite, and I said:

"See, this is God, and this is what God created; and God is good, and he is most mightily and by far superior to that creation. Yet he is good, and what he created is good, and see how he encompasses and fills it. So where is evil and its source, and where did it creep into the creation? What is its root and its seed? Or does it not exist at all? In that case why do we fear and take precautions against what does not exist? If our fear is unbased, fear itself is an evil by which the heart is vainly agitated and tortured. The less valid the cause of our fear, the more oppressive that evil is. So either there is an evil which we fear, or our fear is itself an evil.

So where does it come from, seeing that the good God made all these things good? The greater, highest Good made all lesser goods. But Creator and created things are all good; so where does evil come from? Was there some evil stuff from which he made these things, and did he fashion and arrange it and leave something in it which he did not make good? Why should he do this? Was he, though all-powerful, unable to change and transform it all so that no evil remained? Finally, why did he decide to make something of it, rather than cause it to cease to be by his omnipotence? Could it have survived against his will? If it were eternal, why did he allow it to exist so long through the boundless lengths of past time, and then decide much later to make something from it? If he decided to do something on the spur of the moment, should he not in his omnipotence have caused it to cease to be, so that he himself alone might be the whole truth and the highest boundless Good? Or seeing that it was not fitting that he who was good should create and establish something not good, should he not have removed and reduced to nothing the evil matter, and created good matter with which to make everything? He would not be almighty if he could not establish something good without the assistance of matter which he had not made."

These were the thoughts which I pondered in my wretched heart, heavy with gnawing anxieties about the fear of death and a failure to attain the truth...

Then it became clear to me that things which suffer corruption are good. They could not be corrupted if they were the highest good, but they could be corrupted only if they were good; for if they were the highest good they would be incorruptible, and if they were not good at all there would be nothing in them to be corrupted. Corruption damages, and there would be no damage if it did not diminish the good. So either corruption does no damage, which is impossible, or all things which are corrupted are deprived of good, which is as certain as can be. If they are deprived of all good, they will not exist at all; if they continue to exist and cannot henceforth be corrupted, their state will be better because they will continue incorruptibly. But what could be more outrageous than to say that they have become better after losing all their good? Hence if they are deprived of all good, they will be absolutely nothing; so long as they exist, they are good. Thus whatever exists is good, and the evil whose source I sought is not an entity, for if it were it would be good. It would be either an incorruptible substance, an especially great good, or its substance would be corruptible, which it could not be unless it were good.

So I saw and it became clear to me that you have made all things good, and no substances exist at all which you have not made. And since you have not made all things equal, the totality of things individually good is collectively very good, for our God has made all things very good (Gen 1:31).

In you, and indeed in all your creation, evil does not exist, because there is nothing outside to break in and corrupt the economy which you imposed on it. But because some parts of it do not harmonize with some others, they are thought to be bad, whereas in fact they achieve harmony with yet other parts and are good, and good in themselves. All the things not in harmony with each other belong appropriately to the lower part of the world which we call the earth, and which has its own cloudy, windy climate appropriate to it. Heaven forbid that I should now say: 'These things ought not to be'; because even if I saw nothing but these, I should long for better things, but even for these alone I should have to praise you.

That you are deserving of praise is revealed by the things of the earth — snakes and all the pits, fire and hail, snow and ice, the gusts of the storm that fulfill your words, mountains and all hills, fruitbearing trees and all cedars, beasts and all cattle, creeping things and feathered birds; kings of earth and all peoples, princes and all judges of the earth; young men and girls, old and young praise your name (Ps 148:7-12). Since from the heavens all your angels praise you, our God, in the highest, and all your powers, since sun and moon, all stars and light, the highest of heavens and waters above the heavens praise your name (cf. Ps 148:2-4), I did not yearn any longer for better things because I pondered the whole. With a sounder judgment I assessed the higher things as better than the lower, but the whole as better than the higher things alone.

Those dissatisfied with any facet of your creation are unsound in mind, as I was when many things which you made displeased me. Because my soul did not dare to be dissatisfied with my God, it would not identify as yours whatever dissatisfied it. In this way it had strayed into a belief in two substances, and it got no rest, but recounted the opinions of others. Recoiling from that error it had made for itself a god inhabiting the boundless area of all space, and it had considered that God to be you, and had set it in its heart (Ezech 14:7), and had become again the shrine of its idol, deserving of your loathing. But after you stroked my ignorant head and closed my eyes so that they should not see vanity, I retired from myself a little and my madness was lulled to sleep. I awoke in you, and saw you infinite in a different way, and that vision was not with the eyes of the flesh.

And I looked upon other things, and saw that they owed their existence to you, and that all things are bounded in you, but in a sense different from the local. You hold all things in your hand, which is Truth, and all things in so far as they exist are true. Falsehood does not exist except when it is considered as what is not. I realized that all things are opposite not only to their places, but also to their times, and that you, who alone are eternal, did not begin to work after countless periods of time; for all periods of time, past and future, could not pass or come to be without your work and sustenance.

I realized through experience that it was not surprising that bread which tastes good to a healthy person is hard to swallow for a sick palate; again, the light which delights those with untroubled sight is an affliction to sore eyes. Likewise your justice annoys the wicked; much more so do the snake and the worm, which you have created as good things, suited to the lower realm of your creation, to which the wicked themselves are also suited in so far as they become less like you, though they are appropriate to the higher levels the more they become like you. I inquired into the nature of evil, and I discovered that it is not something that exists, but a perversion of the will which is wicked towards the lowest things and away from the supreme Substance, the God which you are."

5. Ps-Dionysius

We can round off this section on the nature and source of evil with an extract from Ps-Dionysius. This writer until the time of the Reformation was commonly but erroneously identified with Dionysius the Areopagite of *Acts* 17:34; in fact he was an eastern Christian, writing as late as 500 A.D. Ps-Dionysius has an immense influence on the mystical theology and spirituality of the Christian tradition; he seeks to achieve a systematic synthesis between the doctrines of Christian revelation and Neoplatonist notions of the relationship between man and God. *The Divine Names* is a treatise in which God's attributes are examined, and in this work he expounds the nature and source of evil, attempting to reconcile its presence in the world with the workings of Providence.

The Divine Names, IV 18-19, 31-4[5]

In fact, what is evil? Whence is its origin and in what things does it exist? And why did the One that is good wish to produce it? And why having so willed was he able to do so? and if evil does come from some cause other than the good, what other cause is there? And how, if there is a Providence, is there evil at all? How can it come into being, or not perish? And how do any of the things that are desire it instead of the good?

First of all we will not hesitate to say that evil is not from the good; and if it is from the good it is not evil. Just as it is not the property of fire to make things cold, so it is not characteristic of the good to make things not good. And if all things that are come from the good (for it is the nature of the good to produce and to conserve, and of evil to corrupt and to destroy), then none of the things that are, come from evil. And evil itself would not exist were it evil to itself. Unless this is so, then evil is not wholly evil but possesses some part of the good by which it has some being. And if the things that are desire the beautiful and the good, and do whatever they do for the sake of that which seems good to them, and if the whole purpose of the things that are has the good for the source and the goal — for nothing does what it does by looking at evil as such — how can there be evil in the things that are? Or how can evil be when it is wholly without the desire of the good? And if all things that have being have it from the good, and the good is beyond the things that are, then that which is not yet has its being in the good, but evil has no being; otherwise it is not all evil or non-being, for that which is wholly non-being is nothing unless we are speaking of the good superessentially. The good will therefore be set far above and ahead of that which has being entirely, and that which has not. But evil is neither in those things that are nor in those things that are not; and it is further removed from the good because it does not exist, being as it were alien and with less being.

[5]Text: PG 1. 716f., 732f.

'Whence then is evil?' someone will ask. For if evil is not, then virtue and vice are the same, both whole to whole and part to part, and even that which is in opposition to virtue will not be evil. Yet temperance is the opposite of intemperance, righteousness of unrighteousness. I mean not only in so far as they proceed from the righteous and the wicked man, or the temperate and the intemperate. I mean that even before the difference between the virtuous man and the reprobate has shown on the outside, virtues and vices are long before distinct in the soul itself, and the passions make war upon the reason. So we must assume something evil there which is opposed to the good; for the good is not opposed to itself, but since it proceeds from one Principle and one Cause, it rejoices in fellowship, oneness and harmony...

Evil in itself, then, has neither being nor goodness, nor is it productive. It lacks the power of creating things which have being or goodness... So evil is not anything.

There is a single cause of good things. If evil is the contrary of the good, then evil has many causes. But the efficient causes of evil are not reasons and powers but impotence and weakness and the discordant mingling of unlike elements. Evil things are not unchanging or forever the same, but indeterminate and indefinite, carried along by alien influences which are purposeless. So the good is the principle and the end even of all evil things, for it is the final purpose of all things, bad as well as good. For even when we do evil it is with desire for the good; no one acts with a view to his own evil. Therefore evil has no substantial being, and is no more than a shadow of it, existing only for the sake of the good and not for itself.

Evil, then, must be given no more than accidental being, existing for something else and not from its own principle; so that when it is done, it seems right because it is done for the sake of the good, yet it is not right because we think something is good when it is not. Clearly in this case one thing is intended and another results... So evil is a privation, a defect, a weakness, a disproportion, an error without purpose or beauty, life or understanding, without reason or perfection, reality or cause; it is indeterminate, sterile, inert, impotent, disordered, confused, indefinite, dark, unsubstantial, having no kind of subsistence whatever.

How then can evil possess any power at all in its admixture with the good? For what is entirely without the good is nothing, nor could it be anything. And if the good is existent, and possessing will and power and action, how can its opposite have any power against the good, lacking as it does existence, will, power and action?. . .

How can there be evil things at all, if there exists a Providence? Only because evil as such has no being, and does not inhere in things which have being; and nothing of those that have being is independent of Providence, for evil has no being at all except that it is mingled with the good. And if nothing among all that exists is without a share in the good, and evil is a privation of the good, and nothing of all things that are is wholly destitute of the good, then divine Providence is in all things that are, and nothing that is can be without Providence. Even those who become evil are exploited by Providence for a beneficent purpose, for the common or individual help of themselves or of the community. And thus it is that Providence provides for each thing that exists. So we will not pay heed to the false saying, often heard, that Providence leads us to virtue even against our own will; Providence would never operate against our nature. Rather it is on this account that Providence preserves the nature of everything, and seeks out the independence and freedom of all things, providing collectively and individually for them according as their nature can receive the providential benefits which are bestowed upon each appropriately and according to their capacity by such universal and manifold providential goodness.

So evil has no being, and evil is in nothing that is. Evil as evil is nowhere; and it comes about not through any power but through weakness. Even the evil spirits, in so far as they are, derive their being from the good, and as such are good. Their evil results from their fall from their proper goodness.

And they long for the good in so far as they reach after being, life and understanding; and in so far as they do not desire the good, they long for that which has no being. And this is not desire, but a mistake for true desire."

EVIL AND HUMAN CORRUPTION

6. *Athanasius*

> In these philosophical formulations of the nature and source of evil, the biblical portrayal of the ancient corruption of the human race, and the continuing projections of that corruption, are implicitly present. This theme of human guilt and responsibility for the evil in the world is pervasive in the Fathers; a few examples will suffice to demonstrate this.
>
> Though Athanasius' writings *Against the Pagans* (no. 1 above) and *On the Incarnation* (no. 6 below) are traditionally cited separately, they in fact comprise a single work: on the one hand, a rebuttal of pagan theories of life's nature and purpose, and on the other, the exposition of Christian claims centering on the Incarnation. This explanation of Christ's redeeming presence in the world necessitated a preliminary account of the death-dealing corruption which had overtaken mankind.

On the Incarnation, 4[6]

"...God made man and willed him to remain incorruptible. But men belittled and turned away from the contemplation of God. They thought out and invented evil for themselves; so they obtained the sentence of death with which they had been threatened. Henceforward they did not continue as they had been, but they suffered destruction in accordance with their machinations. Death conquered them and was their king. Transgression of the Lord's command consigned them to the realm of nature; as they had come

[6]Text: OECT, ed. Thomson, 142

into being from non-being, so now they were reasonably to undergo in the course of time annihilation into non-existence. In their state of non-existence they were called into being by the presence and kindness of the Word; and it followed that since men were emptied of awareness of God and had turned to things which did not exist (for evil is non-existent, whereas good exists, brought into being by the existent God), they should be emptied of eternal existence. In other words, once they were dissolved, they would abide in death and annihilation, for man is by nature mortal since he came into being from non-being. But his likeness to him who does exist meant that if he had preserved that likeness through the contemplation of God, he would have thwarted natural annihilation and remained indestructible. As Wisdom says, 'Observance of the law is the assurance of incorruptibility' (Wis 6:18); and being incorruptible he would henceforward have lived as God. Divine scripture indicates this, I believe, with the words: 'I said you are gods, and all sons of the most High, but you die like men and fall like one of the princes' (Ps 81:6f.).

Not only did God make us out of nothing; by the grace of the Word he bestowed on us divine life. But men turned away from eternal things, and at the devil's prompting turned to annihilation and so were themselves the cause of their destruction in death. As I said before, they were in their nature destructible, but if they had remained virtuous they could have avoided the consequence of their nature through the grace of the Word's communion with them. By reason of the presence of the Word in them, even natural corruption would not have encroached on them. As Wisdom says: 'God created man for incorruption, and made him the image of his own eternity; but by the envy of the devil, death entered the world' (Wis 2:23f.)."

7. Cyprian

Athanasius' account of man's first disobedience implicitly suggests how through the corporate solidarity of the human race the pains endured by our first parents are imposed also on their posterity. The reason for this is that we have inherited a propensity to sin; the hardships which we bear are attributable to our personal guilt and to the corporate guilt of the race. This idea of our personal sinning as the cause of suffering is strongly present in the writings of Cyprian, bishop of Carthage 248-58. The years of his episcopate were marked by an era of savage persecution launched by the Roman emperor Decius in 250-1. Cyprian's treatise *The Lapsed* was written in 251, and in the course of pastoral exhortation to the many who had renounced the faith in the face of Decius' fierce persecution, he offers this explanation of the privations which African Christians have had to endure.

The Lapsed, 4-7, 11[7]

4. Who could be so hard and unbending and forgetful of brotherly love as to be able to remain dry-eyed amidst the diverse disasters of his own people, amongst the mournful, foul and shabby remnants of what they had been? Tears at once well out, and one's lamentation issues forth in weeping rather than in words. I grieve with you, brothers, I really do: my own immunity and personal well-being does not entice me to seek respite in my grief, for when the flock is attacked the shepherd feels the pain more than the sheep. My heart is joined with each one of you, and I share the grievous burdens of your pain and desolation. I mourn with the mourners, shed tears with the tearful, feel myself lying prostrate with the prostrated. My body too was struck by those darts of the rampaging enemy; their savage swords pierced my entrails as well. The mind could not be untouched by or free from the impact of persecution; when my brothers were brought low, I was brought low as well by my feelings.

5. None the less, dearest brothers, we must take account of the truth. The murky fog of savage persecution ought not to have so blinded our intelligence and our vision that no

---

[7]Text: OECT, ed. Bévenot, 6-10, 16

clear light enables us to see God's commands. If the reason for our calamity is acknowledged, we light on the remedy for our wound. The Lord wanted his household to be tested. Because long peace had corrupted the ordered life bestowed on us from above, God's judgment bestirred our faith, which was supine and virtually sleeping. Though we deserved still worse for our sins, the Lord in his great mercy so tempered the whole process that what occurred seemed to be a trial rather than a persecution.

6. Each of us was concentrating on increasing his family possessions. Forgetting what believers had done in the time of the apostles, and what they should always do, each of us showed an insatiable, burning greed to redouble his wealth. Bishops abandoned their devoted piety, priests their untarnished faith. There was no compassion in works of mercy, no self-control in our habits. Men wore effeminate beards, and women painted their bodies; their eyes, God's handiwork, were touched up, their hair deceitfully tinted. There were crafty tricks to beguile the hearts of simple people, clever designs to trap our brethren. Marriages were made with pagans, Christ's limbs prostituted to heathens. People not only swore at random, but even took lying oaths. They treated their superiors with proud arrogance, cursed each other with poisoned tongues, fell foul of each other with unremitting hatred.

Many bishops who ought to have been an encouragement and example to the rest despised God's stewardship, and turned to worldly business. They abandoned their sees and forsook their flocks; they wandered through the territories of others, sniffing out markets for profitable transactions. Whilst their brothers in the Church were hungry, they sought to have money in plenty. They grabbed farms by crafty trickery, their profits by loans at compound interest. For sins of this kind there is no punishment that people like us do not deserve to suffer. God's judgment long ago warned us with the words: 'If they forsake my law and walk not in my judgments, if they profane my justice and keep not my commandments, I will visit their iniquities with a rod, and their sins with stripes.' (Ps 88:31-3).

7. This had already been foretold to us by way of warning. But we were heedless of the law given to us and its observance. By our sins and by our scorn of the Lord's commands, we were forced by harsher remedies to endure correction of our sin and proof of our faith. Even then at that late hour we did not turn back to fear of the Lord, and bear patiently and bravely this correction and testing of us by God...

Brothers, we must not conceal the truth, we must not suppress the matter and cause our illness. Blind love for their property beguiled many. Their wealth bound them like chains, so they could be neither ready nor unburdened to abandon it. Their possessions were the bonds of those who remained; these were the chains which hindered their courage, confined their faith, bound their minds, choked their souls. So they became the plunder and food of the serpent, who by God's judgment devours the earth, because they clung to the things of earth. It was of this that the Lord, the teacher of the good, forewarned us: 'If you will be perfect, sell all you have and give to the poor, and you will have treasure in heaven. And come, follow me.' (Matt 19:21). If the rich did this, they would not perish through their riches. If they stored up treasure in heaven, they would not now have an enemy and a violator in their homes. Their hearts, minds, feelings would be in heaven; if their treasure was there they could not be overcome by the world if they had nothing in the world to cause their downfall. They would follow the Lord free and unfettered like the apostles and many of their followers. People since then have often abandoned possessions and parents, and bound themselves with the bonds of Christ which cannot be sundered."

8. Basil

Amongst the Greek Fathers, Basil preaches a similar message in *God is not the author of evils*, the treatise cited earlier (no. 3).

God is not the author of evils, 3[8]
    "We must keep this firmly fixed in our minds: since we are
the creation of the good God and are kept in being by him,
and our affairs large and small are governed by him, we
cannot suffer anything unless God wills it; and nothing
which we suffer is harmful, or such that we can imagine
anything better. Deaths come from God, but death is in no
sense evil — except the death of the sinner, for when he
leaves life, it is the beginning of his punishments in hell...
    Again, we call evil what is burdensome to us and painful
to our senses — illness and physical punishment, lack of
life's necessities, ill-repute, loss of money, bereavement of
relatives. Each of these is imposed on us by the wise and
good Lord for our benefit. He removes wealth from those
who use it badly, so as to destroy their means of injustice. He
inflicts illness on those for whom it is more profitable to
have their limbs impeded than to have uncontrolled
impulses towards sinning. Death is visited on us when the
limits of life are reached; this the just judgment of God has
assigned to each from the beginning, as he looks forward
from afar at what is profitable for each of us. Famine and
hunger, torrential downpours are stripes, as it were, inflicted
on cities and races in common as punishment for their
unlimited wickedness. Just as a beneficent physician may
inflict sufferings and pain on the body as he grapples with
the sickness and not the patient, so the good God dispenses
salvation for the whole by punishment of the parts.
    You do not rebuke the doctor when he cuts or cauterises
or wholly removes part of the body; you pay him, I imagine,
and pronounce him your saviour because he confines the
illness to a tiny part, before the suffering spreads to the
whole frame. But when you see a city in an earthquake
collapse on its inhabitants, or a ship wrecked with its crew at
sea, you do not hesitate to blaspheme against the true
Physician and Saviour. Yet you should have realized that
when men's illnesses are mild and can be healed, beneficial
treatment is applied; but when the sickness appears too

[8]Text: PG 31.332

serious for healing, the useless part must be removed so that
the disease may not advance to the vitals. Just as the disease,
not the doctor, is the reason for surgery and cautery, so the
destruction of cities takes its cause from the monstrous
nature of our sins, and acquits the Lord of all blame."

9. *Augustine*

Just as Cyprian's *The Lapsed* had been written in the
wake of savage persecution, so Augustine's *City of God*
was composed at a period of severe trial in 413-26, immediately after the fall of Rome to Alaric in 410. This
momentous event sent shock waves of fear and outrage
through the whole civilized world, and many traditional
Romans claimed that the fall of the city was to be laid at
the door of Christianity for extirpating the old pagan
ritual. Augustine seeks to rebut that accusation. In this
long work he links man's corrupt behavior with his inheritance of sin from Adam; and then he attributes the
privations which all must corporately endure to the sinful
condition in which we live, and from which we can be
delivered only by divine grace.

In this first passage, Augustine stresses that life itself is
a trial and a punishment, and he instances this with a
favorite theme, familiar also from the *Confessions*, of the
misery endured by schoolchildren.

The City of God, 21.14f.[9]

"Very few people suffer punishment only after this
life and not during it. We know from both our own experience and that of others that there are some who have not
experienced the slightest sickness but live an untroubled life
to a ripe old age. But the whole of human life is a punishment, because it is all a trial. Sacred scripture declares this
with the words: 'Is not the life of man on earth a trial?' (Job
7:1).

Lack of wisdom or experience is itself no small punish-

[9]Text: CSEL 40.543

ment; we rightly judge that it should be avoided, to the point of our compelling children to learn the various professions or to undergo literary training through painful chastisement. The very process of learning to which children are forced to submit by punishments is so painful for them that sometimes they prefer to suffer the punishment enforcing the learning rather than to do the learning. Who would not feel apprehensive and choose death, if he were given the choice of suffering death or a second childhood? Infancy enters life not with laughter but with crying, and this is a kind of prophecy of the ills which it has embarked upon in ignorance. They say that Zoroaster was the only child ever to have laughed at his birth, and this unnatural laughter did not presage any benefit for him; for he is said to have been the inventor of magic arts, but they could not aid him to obtain even the empty happiness of this life in the face of his enemies; for as king of the Bactrians he was overcome in war by the Assyrian king Ninus.

The words of scripture are certainly true: 'A heavy yoke lies on Adam's sons, from the day they leave the mother's womb to the day they are buried in the mother of all' (Eccl 40:1). These words must be fulfilled to the point that even babies freed at the font of rebirth from the bonds of original sin, which alone bound them, suffer in many instances numerous ills, on occasion enduring even attacks from wicked spirits. But we must not regard this suffering as an impediment to them, even if they quit this life at that point through the pressures of the suffering driving the soul from the body.

It is true that a heavy yoke is imposed on Adam's sons from the day when they emerge from their mother's womb to the day of their burial in the common mother of all, but even this ill is found to have marvellous effects. It makes us sober, causing us to realize that this life has been made punitive for us because of that most wicked sin committed in Paradise. We are to understand that all that happens to us through the New Testament applies solely to our inheritance in the new world; once we have received the promise in this life, we may attain it at the appropriate time. But now we are to walk in hope, and we must mortify the flesh as we make progress in the spirit from day to day" (Rom 9:23).

10. *Augustine*

> In a subsequent passage in the same work, Augustine again links human misfortunes and sufferings with the sinful lives which men lead; and the sins which men commit are the direct result of the legacy which has been bequeathed to us by our first parents.

The City of God, 22.21-2[10]

"To these first origins our present life is relevant. This immediate life — if it deserves the name life by reason of such numerous and profound evils — is full proof that man's entire mortal progeny is condemned. What else is spelt out by that dreadful abyss of ignorance from which all error has its rise, and which takes into its cavernous clutch all the children of Adam, so that none of them can be free of it without hard labor, sorrow and fear? What else does our love of the trivial and the positively harmful make manifest? That love begets gnawing anxieties, agitations, sorrows, fears, lunatic joys, dissensions, altercations, wars, treacheries, persistent anger, enmities, deceit, flattery, fraud, theft, robbery, treachery, arrogance, ambition, envy, homicide, patricide, cruelty, savagery, wickedness, licentiousness, wantonness, shamelessness, lewdness, fornications, adulteries, incest, and so much unnatural debauchery and impurity with both sexes, even the mention of which is a foulness; sacrilege, heresy, blasphemy, perjury, oppression of the innocent, calumnies, cheating, collusion in court, false witness, iniquitous judgments, violence, brigandage, and other similar evils which do not now come to mind but which are never absent from human life. Truly these are the doings of evil men, which grow from the root of error and perverse affection, which every child of Adam brings with him into the world. Who does not know what depths of ignorance of the truth come with a man into this life? We see it in infants; what an abundance of empty desires! We see it begin to show in young people, so much so that if a person were left to live and act as he chose, he would fall into all or many of the criminal and shameful deeds we have mentioned.

But the divine governance does not altogether desert the lost, nor does God in his wrath hold back his mercies (Ps 76:10). The forces of law and learning work against the darkness in which we are born and which permeates the faculties of the human race, and oppose its inroads. And yet in those mercies toil and trouble abound. What do those various terrors signify with which we check the empty pursuits of the young? What of escorts and teachers, ferula and strap and cane, and the discipline which holy scripture says is to be applied to the person of a beloved child (Eccl 30:12), lest he grow up to be ungovernable and impossible, or almost impossible, to manage? What is the point of all these punishments except to wear down our rude behavior and bridle our wicked desires? These are the evils in whose company we enter the world. Why is it that we toil to remember, yet effortlessly forget, that we struggle to learn yet are ignorant without trying, that diligence requires application and sluggishness none? Does it not all show how prone our nature is to vice, and what resources are needed if we are to be free of it? Sloth, dilatoriness, laziness, indifference — these are the vices by which we avoid taking pains; for efficacious effort is a form of punishment.

But forget the pains proper to childhood, without which we cannot learn what our elders require of us — not that they aspire to anything useful; think of the great variety of punishments which afflict the human race, not as the outcome of the malice and wickedness of evil men but simply as the native condition and common lot of human misery. Who can tell their tale or comprehend them in his mind? What fears and catastrophes inflicted by bereavement and mourning, by losses and convictions, by false dealings and human swindles, by false accusations, by all the crimes of violence and hostile villainy! Sometimes we are the victims of plundering and enslavement, of fetters, prison and exile, of torture and loss of limbs, of deprivation of our senses, of exposure of our bodies to the foul lust of the oppressor, and to many other dreadful misfortunes. What, too, of those innumerable accidents which threaten our lives from without? Of heat and cold, tempest, cloudbursts, floods, lightning, thunder, hail, thunderbolts, earthquakes, subsidence, collapse of buildings; of the stumbling or panic or even wilfulness of our mules; of widespread poisoning from plants, contaminated water, noxious air, animals, the deadly bites of wild beasts; from rabies caught from a mad dog, so that the animal fawning and friendly to his master is sometimes to be more keenly feared than lions and snakes, for it infects the person whom it bites with so furious and deadly a madness that he becomes a worse menace to parents, wife and children than any wild beast?

And what miseries men endure who go to sea or journey by land! Who can travel anywhere and not be liable to unexpected accidents? A man came home from business sound in limb; he slipped, broke his leg, and died of it. Who looks safer than a person sitting in a chair? Yet the priest Eli fell off the chair he sat in, and died on the spot (1 Kings 4:18). Farmers, or rather the whole population, worry that their harvests may suffer grievous loss from the depredations of heaven and earth and harmful beasts, but once the grain is gathered in the barns they usually rest secure; yet, as we know, the best of harvests gets swept out of the barns and away by a sudden flood from which the people take flight.

Who can depend on his innocence to protect him from innumerable attacks of evil spirits? Sometimes even baptized babies more innocent than anyone are sorely afflicted by them. God allows it especially in their case to demonstrate the tearful miseries of this life, to show how desirable is the happiness of the world to come. Then there are so many evil diseases which can infect the body that they are not all listed in the medical books. In the case of most or nearly all of them the very remedies and medicines are a torment, so that people are delivered from painful destruction only by painful means. Extremes of heat have led thirsty people to drink men's urine, even their own;

extremes of hunger have made men unable to refrain from eating human flesh, and where corpses were not at hand they have killed others — and not simply strangers, for mothers with incredible cruelty caused by mad hunger have consumed their own children.

Finally, our very sleep, which we properly term rest, is so unquiet that what is seen in its dreams often cannot be put into words; the ensuing terrors experienced by the spirit, though they relate to things of fantasy, are so immense that we cannot distinguish the true from the false, so distraught is the wretched soul and its feelings. Those who lie awake suffering from certain poisons and diseases are more wretchedly disturbed by these hallucinations. Equally, evil spirits will often deceive even healthy people with a great variety of deceitful tricks and with similar illusions, so that even if they cannot draw them to their own way by these stratagems, they delude their senses solely by the attempt to persuade them to falsehood in whatever way they can.

Nothing liberates us from the hellish condition of this miserable life but the grace of Christ the Saviour, our Lord and God; for Saviour is what the name Jesus means. He will surely see to it that after this life we do not fall into the clutches of a more wretched and eternal existence, which is death rather than life. For though in this life we have great consolations of healing through holy persons and holy things, these blessings are not always given to those who ask for them. This is so that we may not aspire to religion for these motives, when it should be sought rather for that other life where there will be no evil whatsoever. Moreover, grace helps better persons to cope with these evils, so that the more enduring the heart is, the greater the fidelity with which trials are borne. It is to meet these trials that the learned of this world aver that their philosophy (which Cicero says the gods have given as truth to but few men) is profitable. Cicero said that there was never a greater gift, nor could there be, given by them to mankind. So even those with whom we dispute are in some sense compelled to confess the presence of divine grace in the possession not of any philosophy but of true philosophy. Further, if this single help of true philosophy has been divinely given to a few in face of the miseries of this life, then it is clear enough that the human race has been condemned to suffer the pains of this wretchedness. And as they confess that there is no greater gift of God, so we must believe that it was given by no other God but him than whom the worshippers of many gods declare that none is greater.

PROVIDENCE IS UNIVERSAL

11. Origen

The explanation of the presence of evil in the world as attributable to the sinning of our first parents, and to our own propensity to turn away from God, is complemented in the Fathers by a positive vision of God's benevolent dispensation to men. In spite of our sinning God does not disregard our true welfare. All that befalls each individual in this world is foreseen and lovingly observed by him.

It is a favorite argument to demonstrate the clear signs of the working of Providence in the natural order, and to claim that God has designed the world preeminently for man's benefit. This is not an original insight; Christian apologists are able to adapt here the traditional Stoic arguments as marshalled, for example, in Cicero's *On the Nature of the Gods*. The great scriptural scholar Origen (c. 185-254) argues this thesis in his treatise *Against Celsus*. Celsus was a distinguished pagan philosopher who about 178 A.D. in a tract called *The True Discourse* attacked in a rational and dispassionate spirit the exclusive Christian claims; Origen, equally dispassionately, demonstrates that Christians are at one with Stoics in proclaiming a providential order in the world which establishes the human race as lord of creation.

Against Celsus, 4.74[11]

"Celsus next on many grounds makes the charge against us that we claim that God made the whole world for man.

[11]Text: SC 136.366

He seeks to demonstrate from the history of animals, and from the sagacity clearly residing in them, that all things were made as much for unreasoning creatures as for men. This comment seems to me to be equivalent to condemning the praiseworthy deeds of one's closest friends through hatred of those who dislike us. Just as people blinded by hatred fail to see that they are accusing their dearest friends of charges which they think they are leveling against enemies, so Celsus is confused in his reasoning, and has failed to see that he is inveighing against the Stoic philosophers. These thinkers rightly set men and preeminently their rational nature before all creatures without reason, and say that Providence has created all things chiefly for the benefit of that rational nature. The creatures endowed with that reason are preeminent and have the status of children safely delivered, whereas things without reason and without life have, so to say, the role of the womb created along with the child.

In my view the situation resembles the administration in cities, where those in charge of the corn-market exercise their job for human beings alone, though dogs and other brute animals incidentally enjoy a share of the abundant produce. In the same way Providence takes thought chiefly for creatures with reason, but animals without it come in their wake to enjoy the things created for men. Just as the person is mistaken who claims that market-superintendents are concerned as much for dogs as for people just because dogs enjoy a share of the abundant cereals, so Celsus and those who think like him are much more impious towards God who provides for creatures with reason, when they say that the world is created for shrubs and trees and herbs and thorns as much as for men.

First of all, he thinks that 'thunder and lightning and rain are not the works of God'; he is here more clearly playing the Epicurean. Secondly, he says that 'Even if it were conceded that these are God's works, they do not nurture men any more than they do shrubs, trees, herbs and thorns.' Like a true Epicurean he is arguing that such weather occurs not by Providence but by chance; for if these things are no more useful to us than to shrubs, trees, herbs and thorns, they clearly do not proceed from Providence, or else they proceed from a Providence who cares no more for us than for the tree or herb or thorn. Both arguments are self-evidently impious, and it would be foolish to oppose such contentions emanating from one who is charging us with impiety, for all can see from the arguments who the impious one is. His next statement is: 'Even if you say that these things — trees, shrubs, herbs, thorns — grow for men, why will you claim that they grow for men rather than for the wildest animals bereft of reason?' Celsus should say clearly that the great range of plants growing on the earth is not the work of Providence but that a chance collision of atoms has made so many varieties; and that it is by chance that so many forms of shrubs and trees and herbs are similar to each other, and that no rationale of artistry underlies them all, and that they do not have their beginning from a Mind that transcends any wonder-worker.

But we Christians who dedicate ourselves to the one God who has created these things, are thankful to the Craftsman of this world because he has prepared such a dwelling for us, and on our behalf for the creatures which serve us. 'He brings forth the fodder for the herds, and the grass for those who minister to men, so that they may bring forth bread from the earth, so that wine may delight the hearts of men, so that their faces may exult with oil, so that bread may strengthen the hearts of men' (Ps 103:14-16)."

12. John Chrysostom

Amongst the Fathers St. John Chrysostom (c. 347-407), earlier a student of rhetoric under Libanius and of theology under Diodore at Antioch, and later bishop of Constantinople, was most prominent in proclaiming this message of God's surpassing providence for men. Chrysostom ('The Golden-mouthed') was especially celebrated for his eloquent preaching. His homilies on the gospels and on the Pauline epistles reflect deep study of the scriptures and the ability to direct them towards moral instruction. This knowledge of the scriptures is manifest in the treatise which he devotes to the subject of divine Providence; his highly rhetorical presentation of the kindly dispensation of God is underpinned by apposite citations of scripture.

On Providence 5.2 ff.[12]

"The providence of God is clearer than the sun and its rays. On every occasion and in every place you will see clear and abundant evidence of this providence — in the desert, on cultivated and uncultivated land, on land and sea, wherever you go. This evidence is old and new. Voices are raised from every side which sound more clearly than the voices of our reason, and they tell of God's care to him who wishes to hear. This is why the prophet in demonstrating the outstanding nature of these voices said: 'There are no speeches nor languages in which their voices are not heard' (Ps 18:4). Our tongue is known only to those who share our language, not to those of other tongues; but the voice of creation is audible to all peoples who dwell in the inhabited world.

Those of good judgment regard as sufficient God's proclamation, without the demonstration of deeds. It reveals not only his providence but also his abundant love for us; for he does not merely take thought for us, but is also our lover, and he loves us boundlessly with an inconceivable love. It is a love that knows no emotion, but it is most warm and intense, noble, insoluble, unquenchable. Divine scripture wishes to bring this love before our eyes, and presents us with human images of it, offering numerous examples of his love, providence and care. Scripture wishes us not to remain content with them, but to transcend these examples by reflection. She does not adduce them as being merely sufficient to demonstrate his affection, but as things well-known to those who listen, and as things better able than all else to show that affection.

My message is this. In reply to the lamentation and grief of individuals who claim 'The Lord has forsaken me, the

---

[12]Text: SC 79.92, ed. Malingrey

God of Israel has forgotten me,' the prophet argues: 'Will a woman forget her child, or cease to pity the offspring of her womb?' (Isa 49:14f.). By this he means that just as a woman could not forget her children, so God could not forget the human race.

Next the prophet wanted you to realize that he made this comparison not because he wished to show that the measure of God's love is commensurate with a mother's for the offspring of her womb, but because he considered it well-known that the measure of her love transcends that of all other humans. In fact God's affection is much greater than that, so the prophet added: 'Even if a woman were to forget her children, I will not forget you, says the Lord' (Isa 49:15). You see how he surpasses the measure of maternal love? And so that you may know that he far excels a mother's love and a father's longing for their children, the prophet says: 'As a father pities his sons, so the Lord has compassion for them that fear him' (Ps 103:13). He again introduces this image of love because he knew that it has a quality surpassing all others.

The Lord of prophets and of all things shows that God's care transcends by far the measure of this fatherly love. The difference between the bounty and providence of God and the affection of a human father is as great as that between light and darkness, between wickedness and goodness. Hear what he says: 'Which one of you will give his son a stone when he asks for bread? Or if he asks for fish, will give him a serpent? If you who are wicked know how to give good gifts to your children, much more will your Father in heaven give good things to them that ask him' (Matt 7:9-11). He shows that the goodness of God rises above the loving care of fathers with a gulf as great as the difference between wickedness and goodness.

I have offered these examples so that when I come to other forms of love you may not confine your thoughts within the limits of the prophets' words, but with this criterion you may soar further in your thoughts and discern the ineffable extent of his love. He is not content with the limitations of nature; these he disregards, and with a more distant aim he offers still further examples. This is the nature of his love; he wishes to demonstrate his love to the person he loves with further examples. This is what he does when he speaks of distances. He does not want you to think that his love is measured by these dimensions, but he knows that extent of distance is preferable to other images, and is understood by his listeners. So he says through David: 'According to the height of heaven above the earth he has strengthened his mercy towards them that fear him' (Ps 102:11). Again, 'As far as the east is from the west, so far has he distanced our iniquities from us' (Ps 102:12). Through Isaiah he says: 'My plans are not your plans, nor my ways your ways. As far as heaven is distant from earth, so are my ways distant from your ways, and my thoughts from your thoughts.' He did this after having earlier spoken of the remission of sins: 'I shall forgive your transgressions to a great degree' (Isa 55:7).

Since some of you have feet of clay, are hard to guide and to persuade, and are subject to the flesh, let me show to such as you, in so far as I can, the Lord's providence through his deeds. It is not easy to describe all or indeed the greater part of it; for it is boundless and beyond telling, brilliant in its small facets as in its great, in its invisible as in its visible content. But let us prove the point initially from things which are seen.

God has made this marvellous and wholly harmonious creation for no other than for you. It was for you that he made it so beautiful, great, varied, rich, self-sufficient, useful, advantageous in every way for nurturing and sustaining the body, and suitable too for promoting the love of wisdom in the soul, and its journey towards knowledge of God.

The angels had no need of it, for they existed before it came into being. That they are much older than the world, you can grasp from God's conversation with Job: 'When the stars were made, all my angels praised me and made loud melody' (Job 38:7). In other words, they were astonished by the number, beauty, order, usefulness, diversity, brightness, clarity, harmony, and all the other aspects which angels descry more keenly than we do.

God has not merely beautified the creation with stars, but has also adorned it with sun and moon, and in both instances he has brought you great pleasure and filled a great need. What is more benevolent than the heavens which now gleam under the sun's rays, and now light the earth with myriad stars which are like winkings of human eyes, and which provide sailors and travellers with guides to lead them by the hand? He who cleaves the sea, seated at the rudder, takes heart from the guidance offered by the sky, and entrusts himself to the onset of waves, the violence of wild waters, the force of powerful winds and the moonless darkness of night. The star in the heavens, so hugely distant, guides him accurately as though it were at his elbow, and brings him to harbour with no word spoken. It indicates the course to the sailor's eye, allows him to cleave the sea with safety, and shows him the opportune time to keep his vessel in harbour and when boldly to steer it into the open sea. Thus he does not encounter stormy weather through lack of foresight and ignorance of what is to come, and he does not suffer shipwreck.

The stars do not merely mark the measure and the seasons of the years in their course; they also provide for those with eyes a closely accurate knowledge of the hour and moment of each night; that is, when most of it is past and the lesser part remains, and the opposite. This is useful not only to sailors but also to travelers to deter them from setting out at an unfavorable hour of night, and to prevent their sitting at home when the hour is ripe for their journey. As well as the stars the course of the moon can be trusted to give accurate bearings. As the sun governs the hours of day, so the moon regulates those of night, and it provides many other services...

If you were alert you could ascertain his providence from other signs as well; from clouds, seasons, heavens, winds, sea and the varied creatures within it, land and the quadrupeds upon it, reptiles, winged birds, land creatures, amphibious animals in lakes, brooks and rivers; from cultivated and uncultivated land, from germinating seeds, trees, and plants which grow in both desert and in arable land...

All this, man, is for you. So are skills, customs; cities and villages; sleep and death; life, growth, and all the great manifestations of nature. So too the universe in its present condition and in its future development. That it will become better for your benefit you must realize by listening to Paul's words: 'Creation itself will be set free from the slavery of corruption' (Rom 8:21), that is, from being corruptible. He showed how it will enjoy such great honor for you, when he added: 'For the freedom of the glory of the children of God.'

If I had not already discoursed too long beyond the proper limit, I should have spoken of death, and shown in death above all the wisdom and providence of God. I would have said a great deal about corruption — putrifying matter, worms and ashes, which are the object of particular lamentation and grief by the majority, because our bodies will dissolve into ashes, dust and worms. From this I would have demonstrated his ineffable providence and care. It is because of that same providence and goodness by which he created us from nothing that he has bidden us die and come to such an end. Created things differ from each other, but they emerge from the single Goodness. The one who has departed suffers no harm from this; and the one who lives on will derive the greatest profit from it, for he reaps his own advantage from the other's body."

13. *Titus of Bostra*

Titus of Bostra, a shadowy fourth-century figure who was bishop in that Arabian city in the 360s, is chiefly known for his surviving treatise, *Against the Manichaeans*. In the first section of it he attacks the Manichaean dualism with traditional Christian arguments, accounting for the presence of evil in the world through man's free capacity to sin. In his demonstration of the role of Providence in the world, he seeks to demonstrate that even those animals and plants which endanger the lives of men have their own beneficial purpose.

Against the Manichaeans, 2.7, 2.14, 2.22[13]

"Next we must discourse as best we can on God's most wise government of the world, and on the empty and denigrating criticism of his workmanship by Mani. He finds great disorder in our human affairs to criticise. He upbraids the inequality of riches and poverty, health and sickness; the fact that the evil-doer often escapes the vengeance of the law while the innocent is punished; and the fact that sometimes men of mean spirits exercise dominion over the rest.

We must state that man has been established by his Creator in this life to obtain nothing but piety and virtue; acquisition of these would win approval for the conduct of his life, but neglect of them would cause him to stray and to be unhappily submerged. God has given him physical nourishment and clothing and shelter, not as preeminent gifts but as necessary ones to sustain his life here, so that whilst he is in the body he may live by means of these, undertake work diligently, and obtain these benefits.

Man has procured light appropriate to his nature, and air to breathe, and water, and all such necessities, for these come from God and are naturally common to all men. No one could say that the poor man gets a smaller share of light and water and breath which is nature's way of maintaining life. . .

There is another kind of happening against which the Manichaeans inveigh most harshly, namely earthquakes, plague, famine arising from barrenness and locusts, and such things. They assume that these too stem from a first Principle which is hostile. But it is clear to all that with few exceptions the human species in times of excessive prosperity and success relaxes and indulges its passions, and totally forgets virtue and the piety engendered by labors. In a sense this is natural; for once we enjoy plentiful satisfaction of food and drink through their ready availability, our bellies become swollen and consequently our minds are blunted and our powers of reasoning are affected. Then the soul is weighed down and becomes susceptible to irrational emo-

13Text: PG 18. 1146-47, 1160-61, 1177-79

tions. But if any one of the disasters we mentioned occurs, we pay less attention to our bellies, we are less enslaved to pleasures, and we pursue temperance and piety to the best of our ability. We amend our ways all we can when we are afflicted rather than prosperous.

So what experiences by the Manichaean's book will we say are evil? Those that are painful to undergo but useful in their effect? And which shall we say are good? Those which are pleasurable but on occasion most harmful? In that case evil will seem to school us better than good towards virtue, for often the assault of grief and misfortune converts those whom prosperity failed to attract to better ways. Men need reminders such as these at vital moments to awaken their minds, and to rid themselves of the soft living which is excessive.

If it were possible to observe those in prosperity eschewing great injustices and committing only peccadilloes, it would be reasonable to inveigh against natural calamities on the grounds that they were pointless. But if the outcome of their obtaining perpetual abundance of necessities results in total forgetfulness of their Provider, at some time they must be roused by disasters to remembrance of God, to whom they should acknowledge unremitting gratitude for his care of us. So God arranges these events to instruct men. He is not possessed by the emotion of anger, but he acts out of solicitude and attention to what is necessary. It would not be an act of the greatest and sensitive love to play down human weaknesses out of softness of heart, and to permit them to grow by failing to rebuke them. This in fact would be an act of inhumanity if in his desire to maintain an appearance of soft-heartedness he treacherously allowed men to plunge totally into the annihilation of wickedness. What I mean is that he provides what is useful, and of necessity he inflicts what is apparently painful. When a father beats his erring son, he is not being inhuman; the opposite is the case, for if he did not induce him to mend his ways, he would not seem to demonstrate a father's compassion. Likewise the surgeon, when he cuts and cauterises spreading sores, is not inhuman; indeed, the more he exercises the technique of his profession, the more pain he inflicts from the harsher remedy which heals the patient. The invalid would die from his ulcers unless this aid were accorded him, whereas he will be saved if surgery and cautery are applied as necessary....

Moreover we can often observe that what is most harmful in snakes, their venom, is used for healing by the most accomplished doctors, and that sometimes when mingled with counteracting drugs it can clear away the most oppressive illnesses. Moreover, snake's flesh when mingled with other substances and plants makes an excellent cure for human bodies. The same is true of other wild beasts, of which some organs or limbs or blood often themselves benefit the sick. So how can they come from an evil source, when they are in part beneficial? We must consider them as beneficial to men alone. We must not call them good or evil, for they implant fear in men alone with the necessary aim of converting them to a better life. Their idle role is to prevent men becoming idle. They lie there as a whip does in a household, to ensure that the servants take care not to be idle or delinquent in domestic affairs.

If we observe that wicked persons are not harmed by them, we must marvel at the Lord's forebearance, but we must none the less note the whip lying there. If on the other hand good men encounter such beasts, we must realize that when a good man errs the Lord is sparing in his severity, but not in the case of one who is wholly rejected. The good man's sin can be healed, whereas the other man is kept for ireversible punishment. We can see and read many examples of this in divine scripture. So God shows great care for men, and has accordingly ordered things in every way to rouse him to take precautions, so that even his sleep is not free of most frequent apprehensions, but this too is hindered by monstrous beasts, and pricks our conscience like a spur. There are many things which marvellously aid our human weakness to make us keep God in mind. Through them we suffer physically but are freed from illnesses of the soul, and even if we do not suffer, the possibility that we may do so makes us careful. Man necessarily endures bodily suffering so that he may escape sin, which is the harshest and indeed the only true sickness. Lack of experience of pain induces indiscipline, and sinning which goes unpunished leads to destruction."

14. Hilary of Poitiers

In this pervasive consideration of God's providential care for mankind, the Fathers repeatedly turn to the *Book of Psalms* for inspiration, because in that book the writers resoundingly proclaim that God hearkens to the cries of the oppressed, defends the widows and orphans, and comforts those in affliction. Hilary of Poitiers (c. 315-67), who returned to Gaul after a period of imposed exile in Asia during which he deepened his knowledge of scripture, was the first of the western Fathers to essay systematic commentaries on the psalms, and in this exegesis of Psalm 140 he lays particular stress on God's recognition of each individual, and his loving care for each of us.

Commentary on Psalm 146[14]

3. *The Lord builds up Jerusalem ... he heals the broken of heart, and binds up their bruises. He tells the number of the stars, and calls them all by their names.* After the proclamation of healing broken hearts, we come to the celebration of the divine goodness. If praise is given to God because he builds up Jerusalem materially, what has this numbering of the stars and giving them names to do with the special praise of the divine work? Why is it more worthy of praise that God should have numbered and named the stars than that he should have created them, when creation established their number, bestowed their names, and distinguished names and number by means of words? Yet here are numbered the stars which Abraham contemplated in the heavens, which Isaac counted in terms of living seed, and which Paul saw as differing in glory. To know what it means to be called by

[14]Text: CSEL 22. 846

name, let us listen to him who will summon us. He says in the gospels: 'Do not wonder at this; for the hour comes when all those who are in graves shall hear his voice and come forth' (John 5:28-9). They are called, and they will come forth. They are counted by God to the extent that even the hairs of their heads, which are reckoned to be countless in each of us, fall under this numbering when the Lord says, 'Are not the very hairs of your head counted?' (Luke 12:7). The Lord healed the broken-hearted and bound up their wounds; but what is worthier of him, deserving the greater acknowledgment as a mark of his mercy, is that he calls them by their names, numbers them according to their individuality, and glorifies them with the light of heaven.

Because of this the Psalmist lauds his wonderful and glorious deeds: 'Great is our Lord and great is his power, and there is no counting his wisdom. The Lord lifts up the meek, and humbles sinners down to the earth.' This is the speciality of the meek, to be found worthy before God to be called, counted and glorified; for according to the gospels, the meek shall inherit the earth (Matt 5:4). The Lord is great when he gathers what is scattered. His power is great when he glorifies those who are bruised. His wisdom is beyond counting when he distinguishes out all things by naming and numbering them. But he who lifts up the meek brings sinners to the ground. The punishment for wickedness follows upon the reward for holiness. The meek are lifted to the shining of the stars; the sinners are brought down to the ground, destined for the sanction of the infernal law.

So it is that when we hold back and hesitate, the prophet urges us on to praise, and says: 'Sing to the Lord with praise, sing to our God upon the harp. He covers the heaven with clouds, prepares rain for the earth, makes grass to grow on the mountains, gives their food to the beasts and to the ravens' young that call upon him.' The word of the prophet often warns us to believe that the Lord of this universe is he whom the entire Law has called God, he who has desired that he be called the God of Israel, as in this psalm when he spoke of the Lord 'building up Jerusalem and gathering

together the scattered of Israel.' When he had urged us to
praise him, he added: 'He covers the heavens with clouds,
and prepares rain for the earth,' this was so that we could
realize that the God of creation is none other than the God
who brought the Law. In all this, then, God's providence
and goodness is shown forth.

15. Augustine

St. Augustine, who also composed a commentary on
the psalms, approaches the problem of God's providential care for us at a more philosophical level when he
writes on the historical interpretation of the Book of
Genesis. He is concerned to refute a contemporary view
of the creation and progress of the world which has
affinities with the 'Death of God' thesis of our own day:
that God, having created the world, has stepped aside, so
to say, and allows it to proceed as it will under the impulse
of human endeavour or the whim of chance. Augustine,
like Hilary, cites the psalms as well as the New Testament
in support of the view that God's providence continues to
work in the world.

On the Historical Interpretation of Genesis. 5.20ff.[15]
"Let us then separate the works of God which have been
and are being performed up to the present time from those
over which he rested on the seventh day. There are some
who think that only the world itself was made by God,
whilst everything else comes to being from the world
according to his command and ordinance, and that he
himself does nothing further. The Lord's own saying stands
against them: 'My father works until now,' and lest anyone
should think that he is working in his own domain and not
in the world, he adds: 'The father dwelling in me performs
his works; and as the father raises the dead and gives them
life, so the son gives life to whomsoever he will' (John 5:17,

[15]Text: CSE1 28, 1.163

20-21). Furthermore, it is not merely the mighty and preeminent works that he performs, but also the earthy and meanest ones. As Paul says, 'Foolish man, what you sow is not quickened into life unless it first die, and what you are now sowing is not the body to be that you sow, but merely the grain of wheat or whatever. It is God who gives it the body in whatever way he will, and to each of the seeds its proper body' (1 Cor 15:36-8). So let us believe and understand, in so far as we can, that God is performing his works even until now; so that if his operation were withdrawn from the things fashioned by him, they would perish...

We therefore need to be reminded how to consider those things which are formed and brought to birth in the course of time. It is not for nothing that it is written of Wisdom that 'she shows herself cheerfully in the streets to those who love her, and meets them with every providence' (Wis 6:17). We must not give any credence at all to those who considered that the higher parts of the world (those, that is, at the boundaries of this crasser air and above) are ruled by divine providence, but that the lower part which is earthy and moist, which is the province of this nearer air and is damp with the exhalations of earth and water where the winds and clouds arise, is set in motion by accidental and fortuitous stimulations. It is against these that the Psalm speaks out; after singing the praises of things heavenly, it turns to those lower in the order: 'Praise the Lord from the earth, you dragons and all the deeps; fire, hail, snow, ice, the breath of the tempest, all of you who fulfil his word' (Ps 148:7-8). For nothing seems so exposed to chance emergence as all those warring and turbulent elements by which the shape of this lower heaven appropriately designated by the name of earth, is turned and changed. Yet when the Psalmist adds 'who fulfil his word,' it is clear enough that these too are subject by divine command to the universal order of nature; they do not escape it. It is merely hidden from us.

To conclude then: it is the Saviour who says that not a single sparrow falls to the earth except by God's will, and that he himself adorns the flower of the field which is so soon to be thrown into the oven (Matt 10:29, 6:30). And so he confirms that it is not only the part of the world cut off from mortal and corruptible things which is governed by divine providence. The same is true of the vilest and most abject of bodies.

Those who deny this certainly repudiate the sacred words of the supreme authority. They insist that the lower part of the world is moved by the stirrings of chance rather than governed by the wisdom of the divine sovereignty. They purport to prove this by a twofold argument, either the one about the inconstancy of the weather mentioned above, or another about the fortunate or unfortunate lot of individuals which does not come about in accord with what a human life deserves. They tend to see order only as it appears in the limbs of animated flesh. I do not address doctors, the demands of whose calling bring them to careful analysis of exposed and numbered organs, but anyone of modest intelligence and reflection: would they not cry out that God never lifts his hands from his guiding work even for a second — he who is the yardstick of all measurement, the point in all numbering, the balance for all weighing? What in one's experience could be more absurd, more insensate than that the thing whose smallest and meanest dimensions are seen to be drawn by so powerful a force should be wholly devoid of the influence and direction of Providence; one which when given closer focus strikes us with ineffable awe and admiration? And since the nature of the soul surpasses that of the body, what is more outrageous than to consider that there is no judgment of divine providence concerning man's moral behavior, when in his physical activity there are so many clear indications and manifestations of its ingenuity? But because these little things are readily accessible to our senses, and it is easy for us to compute them, their natural order is apparent. But when we cannot see how things are arranged, those who think that nothing exists except what they can see consider that no such order exists, or if they think that things invisible do exist, they regard them as similar to regular objects of sight."

16. Boethius

A question-mark must hang over the claim of the Italian layman Boethius (480-524) to a place in the college of the Fathers. Few nowadays would question his authorship of the theological treatises which establish his Christian orthodoxy. But his general approach to the problems of life's purpose is that of the working philosopher rather than of the contemplative theologian. On the question of Providence, however, his contribution entirely squares with traditional patristic teaching. *The Consolation of Philosophy* was composed by Boethius when he was in prison and under sentence of death at Pavia; and its central tenet is that the course of the world, and the destiny of each individual in it, is under the control of the highest Good which rules all things firmly and disposes them sweetly (*Cons.* 3.64, citing *Wis.* 8:1). Once this lesson has been grasped, the so-called 'gifts of Fortune' — noble lineage, rude health, temporal power, wealth and the rest — lose any claim to value or significance.

The Consolation of Philosophy, 1.6 ff.[16]

"'Will you first allow me' asked Philosophy 'to probe and try out your mental condition with a few short questions, so that I may decide on the manner of your cure?'

'Ask whatever you want at your discretion' I replied 'and be sure that I will answer.'

Then she said: 'Do you think that this world proceeds by chance and at random, or do you believe that it is controlled by reason?'

'There is no way' I answered 'by which I have ever believed that so orderly a system is moved haphazardly by random chance; I know that God the Creator watches over this work. The day will never come when I am dissuaded from the truth of this belief.'

'Splendid' she said. 'What you proclaimed in your lament just now was that men alone are not subject to God's care;

[16]Text: CCL 94.14, ed. Bieler

you remained convinced that all else was governed by reason. But how distressing and surprising to me that you hold such a healthy belief and yet are sick in this way! But let us look at the matter further, for I suspect that something is missing. You are convinced that the world is governed by God. What kind of control do you believe he wields over it?'

'I can scarcely understand the drift of your question, let alone reply to what you ask.'

'I was surely right' she said 'to suggest that there was a chink in your armour, through which the canker of anxiety crept into your mind. Tell me, do you remember what is the end of all things which the whole of nature strives to attain?'

'I did hear it' I said 'but grief has blunted my recollection.'

'But you do know the source of all things?'

'Yes' I replied. 'God is the source.'

'Well, how can you fail to know the end of things when you know their beginning? But it is the way of these anxieties, which are so strong, that they can disorientate a person, but cannot wholly dislodge or uproot him. Now please answer this: Do you recall that you are a man?'

'Of course.'

'Can you define man's nature?'

'Are you asking if I know that I am a rational and mortal creature? I know it and I grant it.'

She replied: 'You do not know that you are anything more?'

'No, nothing.'

'Now I know' she said 'that other and greatest reason for your sickness. You have ceased to be aware what you yourself are. So I have fully ascertained the reason for your sickness, and the way to recover your health. Because you are confused and forgetful of your identity, you grieve that you are in exile, deprived of your own possessions. Because you do not know the end of things, you think that wicked evildoers are powerful and happy. Because you have forgotten the controls by which the world is steered, you think that changes of fortune are fluid and without a helmsman. These are causes enough to induce not only sickness but even death. But thanks be to the Author of health, for nature has not wholly abandoned you. The best poultice that we have is your true belief how the world is guided — your belief that it is subject not to haphazard chance but to divine reason. So do not be afraid. From this tiny spark rays of life-giving heat will break out...

If I have penetrated the causes and nature of your sickness, you are wasting away through the love and longing for your former fortune. It is the change of fortune which you rehearse in your mind that brings you low. I know the numerous counterfeit shapes which that monster assumes, and in particular the most seductive friendship she adopts towards those whom she strives to deceive, afflicting them with unbearable grief when she abandons them unexpectedly. But if you keep in mind her nature, behaviour and worthlessness, you will realize that in her you had nothing of value, and that you have lost nothing of value.'"

17. Prosper of Aquitaine

The extent to which the controversy about Providence dominated Christian minds in the anarchic years during which the Roman empire was being overrun by invading barbarians is reflected in a remarkable fifth-century poetic work, *A Poem on Divine Providence*. It is traditionally ascribed to Prosper of Aquitaine (c. 390-463), and the stylistic criteria certainly support the attribution. But alleged traces of Pelagianism in the poem have raised doubts, for Prosper was a warm supporter of Augustine's theology of grace, and a severe critic of John Cassian and Vincent of Lerins. These doubts may be too astringent, especially as Prosper in his later years is known to have toned down his anti-Pelagian polemic. This long poem certainly deserves more detailed attention from historians and theologians than it has received; it is the fullest and most systematic justification of the Christian doctrine of Providence to be found in the Fathers. Its full impact can be appreciated only if we recall the extent of the depredations caused by the presence of the Visigoths in southwestern Gaul throughout the period of Prosper's adult life.

A Poem on Divine Providence[17]

The months have slipped away, and the best part of a year is past, and not a page has been filled with your verses. What are the reasons for your long silence? What grief afflicts your saddened talent? Even if your cares are oppressive, poetry should still have its place; even if the wounds of this shattered world enmesh you, and the sea in turmoil bears you along in but one surviving ship, it would still befit you to maintain your enthusiasm for studies unimpaired. Why should lasting values tremble if transient things fall? Happy the man who by God's gift has the opportunity for free activity at such at time!

Who would not be shattered by the destruction and attendant slaughter, even if he were fearless amidst flames and floods? Beneath the great storm of evils we in our feebleness are cut down and fall. Whenever the picture of our smoking land comes before our minds, and the universal destruction stands before our eyes, we break down, and our cheeks are wet with abundant tears. Even as we show our devotion we turn to complaints. Then too some there are who do not refrain from attacking our troubled minds, who with darts of the tongue pierce our wounded hearts. Tell us, they say, the reasons for this, since you believe that the world's and men's labors stand and are governed by God's control. What crime has been done that all these cities alike have been destroyed? What evil have all these regions and people deserved? If the whole Atlantic had poured over Gaul's fields, more would have survived such raging waters. Our cattle, our seed-corn are gone; there is no place for vines or olives; the violence of fire and water has removed our farmbuildings, or more sadly still some of them stand deserted. If the taint of this evil is successfully borne, we are, alas, laid low in the course of ten years' slaughter by the

[17]Text: PL 51. 617-638; cf. M. McHugh, PSt.98, Washington, D.C., 1964

swords of Vandals and Goths. Strongholds perched on rocks, towns built on high mountains, cities on rivers as broad as the sea did not succeed in overcoming the wiles and arms of the wild barbarians; we have all endured the most extreme fortunes.

Let me not lament the indiscriminate slaughter of the common folk, or grudge the death of leading citizens, for perhaps those who are older or more wicked have endured what they deserve for offending God. But what have innocent girls or boys done, who in their short lives have committed no sins? Why were God's temples permitted to be plundered by fire, and the vessels of the sacred ministry violated? The distinction of vowed virginity did not protect the unmarried; love of religion did not save the widows. Those accustomed to spend their lives in solitary caves, praising God night and day, endured the same slaughter as any profane person. The same whirlwind removed good and wicked alike. No reverence for their cherished title shielded priests from the punishment endured by the wretched peasantry; they too were lashed by harsh whips and branded by fires; their hands too were bound and suffered pain. You too were dust-covered and heavily laden as you embarked on the hard road amidst wagons and the arms of the Goths, when that holy elder, driven from his fired city, led out his people like a shepherd in exile leading his battered flock.

But perhaps one should not dilate on things experienced in the gusts of war, for disorder reigned amidst those confused ills. Perhaps God's governing care may in times of peace deign to survey a world untroubled. But if we recall all the years of our early ancestors, and all that our own days have witnessed, we shall find that the loftiest ranks in the world were allotted to the unjust, whereas the good were oppressed and given hardly any standing. The violent, harsh, crafty, greedy, perfidious of heart and shameless of face are admired, loved, revered, honored by all. They get the highest offices, the greatest wealth. But the just man, who with different values prefers to live a chaste and blameless life, is dishonored, poor, hated by young and old alike, and spends his life in exile in all parts of the world. The wicked man remains joyful and healthy to an advanced age, whereas grim sores do not cease to afflict the good. Falsehood prevails in the lawcourts, and truth is in the toils; punishment attends the innocent, and immunity the guilty. The adulterer who mocks the holy liturgy goes scot-free. If God's care surveyed these events from his lofty citadel, if he controlled our affairs beneath his sway, sins would not escape avenging punishment, and virtue alone would be found on the earth.

When such complaints are diffused into the ready ears of the common folk, how many of the undiscerning are affected by such wilful talk! Destruction by Scythian troops is not so grievous as this gossip sown by faithless hearts. So ease out your heavenly weapons from their holy quiver, and dispatch the enemy with healing wounds. Perhaps some persons will be able to escape the darkness of error, to see the light, and return to the right path. The truth of these matters would be better ascertained as explained in the holy books, where it would be easy to give free sail to favorable winds on the open sea of the Law. But novices are fearful of entering the deep, so they must first learn to progress in shallow waters, where the land is lapped at the sea's edge, and where the race of human beings is widespread.

Whether you survey our own time or the early centuries, all men have sensed God's existence. Nature has left none without telling them of the Creator. If wicked waywardness has abandoned this truth by allotting to many the worship owed to the one God, all men have the innate capacity to acknowledge the true Father. He is unbegotten, outside time; he remains always the same, and neither ages nor regions enclose him. When no causes of the world existed, he had within him all that he desired, and when he thought it good he alone created all things as he wished, allotting forms, numbers, modes, species, lives and seeds to all things. All that is in heaven, on earth, in the sea, with any frame, whether alive or lifeless, hot or cold, wet or dry, all exist through the one Creator God, who through the richness of the Word which is God brought forth the nature of things and the elements; he is the Craftsman attentive to the highest and the lowest.

Some created things struggle with opposing causes, and some things impede others, but this movement of discord nurtures all opposites, for as things confront each other they are all stirred up, and obtain life-giving strength; otherwise they would be idle in inactivity, or would slide slippery down in headlong course, and would perish through lack of stability or through sluggish immobility. So the soft opposes the hard, and the thick the spare, the solid the liquid, the swift the slow; the dark wars with the bright, the bitter with the sweet.

It is not right for me to say that anything has been improperly created, and I would not presume to criticize any part of the world, for the Creator holds the dynamic of his own works, and governs their various uses separately for the good of the whole. In short, something which now hinders is of benefit, given a different cause or occasion. All things exist beneath twin hazards. He who endures the cold desires the sun, but when scorched by heat he prefers to shiver in arctic frosts. The traveler shouldering an iniquitous burden fears the rain for which the peasant in his thirsty fields prays. One man is fearful at beholding dark-blue snakes, but another man's table is happily laden with them served cooked. If you disapprove of the creation of wolves, lynxes and bears, cast an eye on Scythian princes and Gothic kings who despise purple and Chinese silks, and consider beasts' hides an outstanding adornment. It would take too long to recount each case, but Christ's kindness allows us to know that what the earth nurtures, what dwells in the sea, and all the varied growth in trees and plants exists for definite purposes to the Creator's praise.

151. God exists and is good, and whatever is done by him is wholly free of blame and complaint. He who created the whole mass of this world also governs it, and there is nothing which did not take its beginning from him. Likewise there is nothing which could endure if the Creator were removed. Those who assign to God an idle leisure are in my

view afraid that watchful anxieties and hard toils may exhaust him as he keeps close watch; they fear that one person cannot discharge simultaneously such great tasks. You who embrace these fears are plunged in darkness and empty of divine fire, seeing more with the eyes of the body than with those of the mind, for you dare to make the eternal God subject to your own nature and condition. Anything that you love you wrongly ascribe to his praise. You believe that he is blessed with your blessings, or that he bears your hardships. Is this because when you govern great cities and peoples it is a wretched business to divide your mind, sick with sleepless cares, on many tasks, and since oppressive worries from all sides oppress your fearful minds, your diligence is overthrown and cannot endure these pressing toils? Then, if worry is dispelled from sick minds, seductive repose begets pleasure for those who have obtained leisure. But is it properly religious to take this view of the Lord? He is always the same; nothing oppresses him; nothing at all preoccupies him. Years vanish and years come; begotten and begetter witness their end. But God remains, with firm grip on past and on future events. He lies beyond the future and before the past. He alone is present to all things, he alone is timeless as he creates the times.

Just as he precedes and outlasts all extent and count of time, so he is boundless and constrained with no limit of place. Nothing is so great that a fixed limit does not confine it. Sky, earth, the whole universe has boundaries; there is a limit to both heights and depths. But nowhere is God absent. He is wholly everywhere, freely penetrating and circling all parts of the universe. So his is the only power which can apportion control over nature, and continue unchanging with untroubled cares. Swift things cannot escape it, nor obstructive things delay it. It is never unaware or distant; when it moves to any regions, it is not absent from others. It does not need clear instruction on what is to be ascertained. It is the witness of the universe; it hears what is silent, sees what is hidden, gives life and removes it when given, saves what perishes, raises what is cast down, restrains the high-flying, both prolongs and diminishes length of years, transforms hearts, forgives sins.

195. But those who allow power of universal control to the Almighty may perhaps say that he lacks the will. They may think that his kingship is mighty, but that he has abandoned all care for men, who are born into times of scarcity, and abandoned beneath climatic extremes. Why is it your pleasure to be unmindful of your Father, and willingly to degenerate to the status of cattle or to attain the lot of wild beasts? Are the beginnings of our nature hidden and unknown, or does our present predicament confound the hope which resides in Christ? Cease to assault the high distinction of our eternal race with unworthy fear; instead mount the heavens, and lay hold of the immortal glory which remains for us. The path is known to us, since Christ our Master has opened it to all. He summons us and will lead us to himself.

So that we are not thought to be promising things uncertain with empty words, the situation demands that we reveal the origin of the human race from our first parents, and that we unfold the causes of our life which was lost and by Christ's gift recovered. The Creator had made his dispositions and had created the whole univese, and the world was green in its beautiful burgeoning. The sun divided its course into the appropriate hours, and moon and stars provided the night with light. The earth nurtured beasts, the sea fish, and the birds with their feathered wings floated in the clear air. But as yet there was no living creature on earth possessed of divine reason. The best of Creators gave this special distinction to man. Though he created all things by the word, he deigned to fashion man with his hands so that he would possess more attributes of the Father. A double substance was joined in him, so that opposites coalesced in a single existence. His soul, unlike the rest of him, was not begotten of anyone and does not experience death, save that it can be punished by God alone, and if guilty consigned beneath the title of death. It slips into the earthly home of the body, allowing the body to dwell as partner with itself, and to drink in the air of heaven as one.

But though the nature of the two components is dissimi-

lar, their status is not. A single end awaits both. Either the
higher is subjected to the law of the lower, or the weaker
raises itself to the power of the greater. Each can conquer or
be conquered, thrive or be reduced, reign or lose the kingship. This is not because the origin of their birth has bestowed more or less on each, or because any external power
draws them on once created, or drives them all unknowing
into different modes of behavior. It is because man is free
and wise, and can separate right from wrong, having the
capacity to make distinctions. He has the power of free will,
with which the mind governs the judgment as long as it does
not swell with self-importance amidst the blinding struggles
of life, but remains safe with moderate aspirations and
believes that its entire potentialities spring from its source of
being. The reflection of the Father's virtue, much practised
in the lengthy cultivation of justice, is implanted in us as if
reflecting God's light from a mirror. After it has passed a life
occupied in honorable pursuits, it may victoriously attain
the eternal citadel in lasting occupation. Having become
wholly God's possession, it may then undergo no battles,
nor fearfully engage in inner struggles. It would not have
desires which it would soon regret; it would have no knowledge of fear, ignorance, desire or suffering. It would not lack
growth in any increase, or be subject to any loss.

254. So that there may be trust in these great promises,
and certain hope of the crown set before him, man obtains
proof of the future life from the gift of our present existence,
and he learns to trust in future gifts from what he has
already obtained. To him are subjected the birds of the sky,
all living creatures on earth, the fish nurtured by sea and
rivers. He is granted knowledge of the changes of sun and
moon, and of the stars of night; the computation of days and
years; the powers of plants; the bestowal of names on things;
the development of his mental powers by various skills. He
alone is set above all living creatures, and is subject to the
service of God alone. He governs animals of superior
strength not by bodily force but by the resource of reason.

But if a person lacking full humanity believes that I am
exaggerating and does not yet recognize himself, he must

hear that our race has been driven far from the status of our first parents through sinning, and that through the widespread corruption of manners only a tiny seed of debased strength survives. To learn of the great glory of his nature he must return to the origins of his holy race, and assess himself as he was when the Lord's hands made him and the Lord's breath governed him, as Adam was before he was condemned to this world, when he was free of blame and possessed the world of lush Paradise, rich in the fruits of cultivated virtues. When God had bestowed such great gifts on Adam, the prince of the snaky band begrudged this. He had been cast down from the lofty quarter of heaven — for only pure goodness can dwell there — and had become changed in heart, and imbibed poison more deadly in its harm. He knew that Adam had been commanded not to touch one particular tree, and he persuaded that owner of such pleasurable possessions to pluck an apple from the forbidden branches in which lay the knowledge of good and evil. That knowledge was then beyond man's control, for he had not yet gained the power by which he could ascertain what things could be avoided without danger to himself.

289. Through these wiles death was ushered in; it was born through sin, and subdued man, for the blame seeped down to all Adam's descendants. Once they had been driven from that ancient citadel of virtue, death involved them in more than the one sin which was transmitted from their parents. Death thrived with the birth of nations, and spread manifold destruction and widespread carnage. But though death imposed destruction and controlled those who were carried off, every age brought forth men pleasing to the Lord, and every generation contained just men of diverse sorts. Though many blessings awaited them through their deserving lives, their vitiated nature dragged them to death. Human nature was not to be loosed from its attachment to its first parent until Christ was begotten in it with majesty undiminished, and could destroy the causes and seeds of death.

It is easy to observe by exemplars sought from the beginning that Christ's perennial care was at hand for all. The just

Abel, as he burdened the altar with holy offerings, did not escape his care, for when Abel chose the first fruits of the flocks he attracted the Lord's gaze to his pure gifts. Cain did not deceive the Lord with his appearance of religious devotion in the dedication of blameworthy gifts, when his envy unleashed bitter poison and his bile was stirred against his brother. The Lord did not forbear with kindly words to recall him from his wild conduct; he emphasized the depths of wickedness which Cain was perpetrating, and offered him the means of controlling himself and of governing his mad anger with greater restraint. But once his wickedness had been aroused, it carried through the cruel deed and plunged the newly-born world into crime. Could not God have preserved the just Abel, who was so pleasing to him, from this wicked slaughter? Yes, but a better life and the future conferment of the weighty crown of eternal glory transcended the final stage of his bitter death.

Again, the translation from the earth of Enoch while still alive shows that God was not contemptuous of earthly matters, for that was a profitable sign for all, enabling the fear of death to give place, and those in the flesh to preserve unshaken the hope of survival. Likewise in a later age subsequent generations deserved to obtain many proofs of the life which awaited them in Christ, when they saw Elias drawn up by fiery horses through the void, mounting the ether in his ruddy chariot. Was God's care remiss when men wholly abandoned religion and embraced every sin, begetting on forbidden beds grim and monstrous giants? God's care foretold the coming destruction of the world, and offered abundant time in which men could be restored to better behavior, and expiate by virtue their chain of sinning. But when delight in wickedness continued through the whole world, and sins could be obliterated only by a flood, the family of Noah alone was preserved. That family avoided disaster; they enclosed in the ark pairs of living creatures of every species, so that the empty earth could be repopulated with animals, and they survived unharmed, while the world perished. It was not that God could not have created fresh peoples, but so that the same race of men, subdued by many diseases, might be born from that seed into the body of Christ, and so that we might become aware that through God's just adjudication of men's deserts, there was rest for holy men amidst disasters imposed on the wicked.

Moreover, it is surely clear that the Lord's love was extended to our race at the time when the believer Abraham, who at faith's begetting became the father of many peoples, numbered the promised race as countless as the stars. Or when the fire descended in a shower on the Five Cities, the anger of the judging God surely came only after it had been delayed by long consideration? He who is ready to spare found no reasons for pardon. Amongst the polluted folk of Sodom he found one alone different from the rest; he excused Lot, and made him lord of a tiny township. When grim famine possessed Egypt and the kingdom of Canaan, and it had to be endured for seven full years, the ground was being laid for the emigration of the patriarchs; a home which would be pleasing was being prepared among foreigners which would sweetly nurture the growth of the future race. This was when the brothers of Joseph after he recounted his mysterious dream sold him into slavery, and deceived his father; when the wantonness of his mistress condemned that chaste man to prison; when the king was accorded an explanation of the riddle of his obscure dream, and he liberated Joseph, accounting him worthy of the second place in the kingdom; when the Jewish youth were deceived by kindly deceit, and rejoiced on recognizing the brother before whom they made obeisance as he pardoned them.

368. When Joseph though innocent was enduring many many evils, he might surely have rebuked God with empty complaints on the grounds that he was remote and disdainful of the affairs of men. But he knew that all things controlled by the just Judge stem from causes lying deep. Though these often trouble minds without faith, they cannot disturb those which are devoted. During our time on earth, the virtuous task set before us is that just men for a

brief period should bear with the unjust who have been given freedom, for God himself at present bears with them and postpones his anger.

The race dear to God and held in suspicion by a harsh tyrant endured the unjust dominion of that cruel king. The stronger offspring of sad mothers was put to the sword. The Jews provided bricks as bidden for the foundations of cities, so that grim toil and the harshness of savage death accounted for all those fearful years of that race. But God himself teaches that these trials were not imposed on our fathers in his absence; he demonstrates that he cares for his own. He bade his chosen one, Moses, to tell the Pharaoh that he should allow the Lord's people to quit Egypt; if he refused, he would in his arrogance suffer many blows. As long as the Pharaoh endured the darts of heaven, he acceded and pretended to obey. But once disaster was dispelled he became obstinate, and since God had spared him he wickedly sought the causes of destruction where he could have attained salvation. At last, overcome by force, the tyrant softened his harsh laws, and Moses advanced his column rich with barbarian treasure. A huge pillar pointed the way through the desert with its furrow; it changed its shape by day and by night, providing help to the marchers in alternating guise. By day it covered them, and by night it guided them, for it was both shade and fire, dissipating the sun's heat with cloud, and the darkness with flames. Why should I mention the parting of the sea before our fathers as they trembled at the pursuing enemy, how the waters were pegged back solid and stiff like a mountain, and abandoned the empty sea-bed? But where countless thousands of the Jewish people crossed unharmed, the Egyptians were overwhelmed by the closing of the waters. The whole of nature serves its powerful Creator; that which yields to proffer help serves also to fulfil his anger. But I have not leisure to recount all the forms of his powers, and my eloquence is not equal to his deeds. Who could enumerate such great and miraculous achievements, the shower of manna, all the dainties in the form of heavenly bread, the water from the dry rock, the sweetness of the bitter spring, the forty years spent in the desert which harmed neither limbs with age nor garments with wear?

It is my pleasure to have recourse to the example of the Law, and to ask those that say that the Lord shows no care whether from that time on God began to fashion men's minds to engage on a life-long covenant, and whether, unmoved by men's vices through countless generations, he then wrote down a just law. Go into the recesses of your minds, within your consciousness where law is inscribed, examine the written volumes of your hearts, and acknowledge the law which was born with you. Who is there except the beast of the field or the monster of the deep who takes such foolish delight in open vices that he would be willing to endure what he inflicts? The deceiver condemns lies, the plunderer thefts, the cruel man harsh behavior, the murderer bloodshed; the adulterer unsheaths the sword against the fornicator. There is one Father of all; no one is without the seed of right behavior; all have the identical origin. Before the Law was written down, how was it that men spent their lives peacefully in pious behavior, in awareness of the highest Father and in no need of law? So all of us were born and live the one life with law; we carry in our bones what is established in the books. This was no new care received when the writing entrusted to Moses condemned sins with imminent punishment. But an additional watch was set on the consecrated nation so that they might be mindful and continue with the glory of their ancestral faith, and succeed as heirs to the Lord's promises.

439. But when it became possible for anyone to share the same rites, and the temple-threshold did not repel outsiders, and when the prophets at God's prompting foretold the future, they often addressed also the different nations. So the queen of the south listened with reverence and eager ears to the utterance of the Lord from the mouth of Solomon. So Nineveh obeyed the warning of Jonah at a time of calamity, and after fasting for three days in mourning, it deserved by abandoning its evil ways to remain a kingdom. But we need not delay long over such scattered and varied warnings,

each delivered in its own time. None should claim that individual admonitions do not apply to all; the Lord's divided attentions cloak his general concern, and occasional manifestations of it are disregarded. State what people isolated in what part of the world, what men of what nation or condition God has neglected to save. We are all one in Christ — man and woman, slave and free, Jew, Greek, Scythian, barbarian. No individual, prince, lord or king comes first. We are all close to the one light, except that the employment of a mirror distances us. For the mind is, so to say, a mirror; the more it is cleaned by polish of faith and the more it is directed on the rays of heaven, the more it gleams with the image of the Christ whom we confess.

He is always God with God the Father. He abides in the Father's majesty but mingles with the human condition. The Word becomes flesh, the Creator of the world is born, the Founder of time follows upon a period of years. The Law, the revered books of the prophets, the certain hope of patriarchs fasten on to this: that when the final age of the world drew to its close, God would come to earthly things to destroy death and to loose the binding laws of hell, to relieve the lengthy fall of the human race with a better beginning.

473. But you who behold that the twin natures of man and God have assembled on the shore of a tiny land, be careful to maintain a firm course, so that error may not drive you in your fear off course into one of two extreme positions. When you behold the miracles achieved by God, you may regard him as God without flesh; or when you observe all the features of his human body, you may believe that he is man and not God. There is no life in man alone, and death subdues and possesses him; there is no means by which, once conquered, I can prevail if the true power of God is not joined to my humanity, or if the Saviour did not embrace me truly in the flesh. His unchanging majesty is not violated by the means of my redemption. He does not suffer diminution when I become changed in him. But my mortal existence yields, so that death dies so far as I am concerned because life cannot be held fast by death. It is not I, but Christ who will live in me, for he has joined himself to me in himself.

The earthly Adam was conquered and transmitted death to all men, for all are born of him and the condition of our sinning parent passes down to us. But a new Man was born from heaven in the womb of the holy virgin, and in his goodness he fashioned a fresh beginning for mortal men. He entered all men's flesh, and by sharing their nature delivered the dead, and by transforming life created the living. Just as grace embraced only those men of former times who beheld Christ in faith, so in our own time Christ renews only those in whose hearts he is welcomed.

500. Observe, man, what great power has been bestowed on you without cost. You can become the son of God if you wish; the almighty Spirit has formed and overshadowed you with the power of the Word. Do not now regard yourself as one born of the physical seed of your fathers; your enslaved beginning in the flesh must now be dissolved. Do not harness any of the old man to the new. This world, this life has not been bestowed on you; nothing here is yours, and you yourself are not your own. You have been purchased, and it is right to repay that price as best you can, so that by paying you may be richer, and so that the wealth which you bestow may accrue to you, so that the Redeemer himself may become your portion.

The harsh observance of the Law does not now bid you pass under its hard yoke. Your mind must be free, and embrace its holy obedience with the reason, which the fostering Spirit imprints on the tablets of your hearts with the blood of Christ. Whatever he expounded to us in words he established by example, matching his precepts with deeds. He is King and Lord of the universe, but his was the appearance of a poor man without splendid raiment or proud distinction. He was strong to the weak, a King to slaves, rich to the needy. His justice yielded to the unjust, his wisdom to the brute forces of unreason. Though beaten by sacrilegious hands, he did not try to return a blow, nor respond to any taunts of greedy tongues. The Judge was condemned, the Word was silent, the Light was spat upon. He himself imposed his own punishment. He drank the gall and vinegar which was sweeter than honeycombs. Though holy, he became the imprecation of the cross. Christ died whilst Barabbas lived. Wicked nation which dared such wickedness, are you aware of it now that the world condemns your madness? The sun fled from the world, and noon became night. The earth was shaken and trembled; when God endured death, the bodies of the saints were roused from their graves and became alive. The veil of the temple was rent, so that the unworthy nation might not retain any secrecy in its hallowed shrine, and the sacred vessels took umbrage and fled from their bloodstained priests.

534. But you, Jesus, trod underfoot the darts of death and destroyed it. You gained in the flesh a fresh trophy over the flesh, for the third day presented you to the stupefied disciples. They could recognise the Lord by undoubted signs when faith obtained its proofs, as with eye and hand it explored the traces of the nails and the wound of the spear, and when he fulfilled his promises for forty days in the full sight of many, and was often available to the touch.

We know you, Jesus, for that period in our own humanity. Subsequently our condition passes into yours. The two are no longer different, but one. There is life in life, light in light. Man's status is enhanced not ended. Man is glorified. You are man and God in such a way that the two are not separate. You bid us rise to you and in your company to attain your light, so long as we hasten on the same path, for we have been taught that we cannot attain heaven without the cross.

God's love is now surely established, and the care bestowed on all is now clear. We surely now realize that salvation is available to all? Yet man still engages in a war of prattling words in tones of complaint, implanting his darts in his own entrails. 'Why am I not good?' you ask; you do not wish to be so. 'Why am I evil?' This is what you want. 'Why do I desire what is evil, and not what is good?' You are free to choose, but though you can distinguish right from wrong, you choose the worse, and without forethought you cling to your choice. 'I sin' you say 'and only wish I could not.' There are two desires implied by this statement: either you desire total extinction, or to be deprived of reason.

Sinning is the activity of him who has abandoned the path of righteousness, and who can return to the right path under Christ's guidance. But the person who has never embarked upon a path does not leave it at any point; things which are not upright do not fear a fall. God's care is not for oxen; the word of the Lord is not addressed to any birds; the monsters of the deep are not constrained by law. When these beasts carry out the commands of the Almighty, they are unaware that they are so doing. Their willingness is only apparent; they believe that what they do for others is in their own interest.

570. Likewise inanimate things always remain in the mode of being in which they were fashioned. Level plains do not swell with hills; high mountains are not levelled into plains. The Alps do not become a sea, and the sea does not become fields. Rocks are immobile, rivers race down, marshes are stagnant. No reward accrues to these objects without sense; they accord to living creatures the benefits which they contain. But if the natural condition of these things seemed preferable to you, you would long to exchange places with an ox or a rock or a stream. I should not wish to fall below my present level, though I could wish to rise above it. Surely those who with their goodly ways have pleased the Lord are not displeasing to themselves? Are we not sprung from the one seed, or is the nature of good men different from ours? The rich man and the poor man have the same birth; slaves and kings have the one beginning. The best of men has not been given more than the most wicked. The Creator applies an equal measure, and enlightens all with the one light.

But when we have entered the world, we are greeted by the varying appearances of things, and all that is before our eyes enters our consciousness and is reviewed by human judgment. Countless shapes surround us; all can win approval in our sight. Crowded impressions enter our open ears — the errors of our earlier studies, the empty beliefs of our parents wearing the deceptive appearance of truth. Some things approach us with harmonious sound, some things are smooth to the touch, some are diffused far and wide with seductive aroma, some recommend different dainties with a thousand flavors. So man has to distinguish these things at great hazard. He must beware of excessive fear deterring him from launching into any sea, and he must not be carried along wandering and lawless with loosened reins. There is a pious employment of things; if we keep it within the proper limits of number and appropriate weight, we shall render honor to the Lord alone for all his gifts. All those goodly things he made not to inflame us to vices, but so that through them, once we have fought the contest of virtue in this world, we might obtain heavenly crowns. Do not the saintly men whom the world has brought forth and still brings forth seem to have endured the same experiences as ourselves — rebellious emotions and affections, and vices encompassing us with their besieging armies? But they conquered the bows of darkness and the darts of death with the sword of the Word and the powerful shield of faith. When they looked at this great and beautiful creation of the world, they did not reverence sea, sky, fire, or stars of heaven as deities, for they could be measured before their eyes. Guided by reason, they worshipped the one Creator and Lord of the world, not the things which he had made.

617. But when you wished that you had been more nobly created, you were surely not complaining because you were not born in the ranks of the angels. When the celebrated Lucifer was cast down from the height of heaven, and a third of the stars fell with him at his expulsion, in which category would you have been? Would you now remain as a bright image of God's goodness, or would you be following the army of hatred and the column of darkness? But where is your headlong course taking you? Do you wish to be good without any toil on your part? Do you believe that you could attain this if the stars under which you were born were different, and that it is their vacillation which makes you wicked? Why do you seek the empty refuge of Chaldean error in the stars? Though with anxious concern you consult the heavenly bodies, and deeply examine the exposed causes of things, you do not deny that God knows better the nature which he has implanted in each element, the law by which he

has commanded the movement of the sea, the force which he has allotted to the gentle breezes, the courses for which he has created the fiery stars. Though he is the pure source of what is right and good, he has imposed a harsh law with wicked commands if he has controlled men's behavior by means of the stars. For these are contrary positions, at war with each other, that he should demand actions without sin, punish wicked deeds, and summon all to the same promises, but then attach to us at birth a violent star which does not yield to man his will or discretion, but whose strength and error controls mankind in its ignorance from above. So either the stars of heaven exercise no rights over us, or if they keep any power over us they can lose it.

For I have been begotten for life, and the good Creator instills into my heart and ears the commandments of salvation. When I show eagerness he calls me with promise of reward, but when I am recalcitrant he summons me with fear. 'Revere God alone' he says 'and remember to serve him only; despise all foreign religions. Be careful to pursue good works and eschew evil ones. A blessed life is gained by the first, but death is begotten by the second. Within reach are both the water that saves and the fire that ravages. Extend your hand to that which you wish; both are equally available.' The warning of the Law, the writings of the holy prophets and God himself would proclaim this from his own mouth in vain, if an external power controlled our will.

But if there is any obstacle to virtue which hinders our minds, it is not the work of the stars above and it does not emanate from the sky but rises from our own heart. Freedom itself stirs up war; we are shattered by an internal conflict. Once effeminate pleasure has embraced torpid idleness, it refuses to embark on the hard road. Those who have attained a prize are too lazy to mount the heights for a hidden hope. When the crafty enemy observes that this is going on within you, he draws strength from your inclinations, and to divert you from worship of your true Parent he persuades you that your fate is implanted by the stars, and that men strive in vain against the gods. As a result men purchase lords over their lives by showing honor of different kinds.

670. Depart, error, depart afar off! The lies of that ancient guile have long been sufficiently unmasked. The Almighty warns us against them and delivers us from them, teaching us to avoid profane rites. We know at what cost some adored the star of Rephan, and worshipped the host of heaven, and dedicated ritual to the sun and moon. It is perfectly clear that these commands continued in the words of men, that they served him by delaying at his word, and that the daylight was extended by the appropriation of the hours of darkness; the light became a servant, and knew no end except when victory brought it. We know too that conditions were enjoined on heaven, and continued of old according to the will of the holy prophet; though the fields were parched, the heavens were not permitted to rain once they had been closed up at the allotted time. The prophet himself summoned fire to the holy altar from the regions above, and launched for profane use the fire which he had bestowed on the sacred rites. Its violence would have fallen even on the followers of Christ to exact punishment for lodging denied, if the long-suffering Lord had not forestalled his anger with pardon.

So no discretion has been entrusted to the elements against us; man has discretion over them. They cannot establish law; they are subject to it. The only God is the almighty King who apportions all the periods of our lives, and does not wish those whom he has set over the stars to be slaves to them. All those whom the Spirit has renewed with his sacred stream, who are born in Christ and cut away from their mortal root, already belong to the abode of heaven; no earthly lineage fetters them once they have been restored to the temple and the body of the Lord.

But if anyone maintains that the nature and the life of man is observed by marking the course and operation of the stars, I ask him what benefit he brings to fearful mortals by this art. This person, he claims, will be happy, and that one wretched; death will snatch one away in his youth, whereas another will exceed Nestor's tally of years in his old age. Is this false or true? If the forecasts of this prophet come true, no hope is in store for the wretched one, nor any fear for the one who is blessed. What reverence is to be accorded to the unchanging stars, if they cannot change the decrees which they can bring in their train? If all men devote themselves to continuous sinning, deceiving, plundering, slaying, confounding right and wrong, their stars will still continue unchanging. Once the hinge of the universe stands fast by the working of those stars, just as evils cannot be warded off by holy righteousness, so the blessings owed to us will not be free from debased conduct. But if the order of fate foretold can be changed, and the things which are to come can be diverted, the dubious power of fate is wholly subverted by uncertain chance. So the profession of scanning the movements of the stars has as its purpose the undermining of all religion, in persuading us that no God cares for mortal affairs, or when it teaches that the elements can be moved by prayers, its purpose is to penetrate countless people with the wretchedness imposed by the gods.

721. Now that we have exposed the snares of this hidden guile, and have ascertained how error seduced those who are charmed by such empty studies, it remains to answer the complaints which allege that God's care absents itself from the affairs of the world, while anxious toil often oppresses the good, and the lives of all evil men flow along untroubled. Tell me, you who think that human affairs proceed without the reins of the controlling Lord, what in creation forsakes the order imposed by nature? Which of the elements stir up wars? Which revolts and severs itelf from the ancient harmony of the world's parts? After the interval of the night the day is summoned back to the sun's rising, as before; the moon and stars journey on the same returning course; the seasons as they succeed each other cross once again the recognized boundaries. The winds blow as before, the rain descends from the clouds. The seeds as they each thrust forth their blossoms preserve their own species, and refuse to grow indiscriminately. The abiding order of the world does not abandon its original nature, but all things continue

according to the same causes. If the clever wisdom of the enduring King did not order these things and nurture the whole mass of nature with his breath, they would all fall and be reduced to nothing with sudden destruction.

Since these things are performed by the watchful care of the Almighty, proceeding on their sloping course to their fixed end, who would deny that the just God bestows his laws in a special way on the human race? He has granted us the hope of enduring life, bestowing on us the mark of his own image. As you who complain that punishment is not visited on the unjust, nor rewards on the holy, would you wish the avenging anger of the Judge to descend upon all blameworthy deeds? How then would the kindly patience of the great-souled King differ from the harsh savagery of a pitiless tyrant? What proportion of mankind being strangers to sin would inhabit the world, or what place would there be on earth for holy virtue? If the gifts of this world were available in abundance, virtue would prefer to be removed from them and to remain in heaven, so the end of the world would be hastened, and time brought to a close; future generations would not have been begotten, since the promised glory or punishment would have removed from the world just and unjust alike.

759. But as it is, the propagation of our race continues in depth; the young generation replaces the old from its double origin, born from the limbs of their fathers and reborn from the fount of Christ. As the kindly patience of the Lord spares mankind, we see many restored to the light from the foul darkness, radiant once they have laid aside the taint of sin. One man who at a thousand altars worshipped gods in countless shapes, bearded and smooth-skinned, young and old, as his ancestors did, now abandons the error of his elders and in submission adores the Only-begotten alone. Another who had followed the sophistries and empty doctrines of the Greeks now rejoices in Christ in his wisdom, and takes pleasure in his insensibility towards the world, for he is schooled in heavenly teachings in the academy of the apostles. How many had been driven far into the deep from the harbor of reason by the hurricane of vices! But now,

after they have been tossed over the whole sea, harshly harried by the errors that caused them to stray, it is the Lord's pleasure to welcome them back. Snug in their Father's embrace, they have no desire to abandon the anchorage of life.

If the severity of implacable anger had speedily struck them while they were enmeshed in the many sins of their former habits, they would have been cut off from the period of their reformed life. Having fallen, they could not have attained the strength to stand erect. 'I do not seek the sinner's death' says the Lord, 'and there is no gain from one who perishes; rather let him return, let him reform and be restored to the path which he quitted; let him enjoy true life.' Because he wishes those whom he has begotten to emulate his own virtues, he says: 'Leave vengeance to me; I shall apportion a penalty worthy of my judgment. A place must be accorded to anger.' Thus whilst the punishment of many wicked men is postponed, many of them are often recalled to goodly deeds, and each person becomes his own judge and harsh avenger, effacing what had gone before and transformed in his resurrection. But those who continue to wallow in their lengthy error may indeed grow old in many vices without penalty, but they will come to a harsh end. They will have no hope of pardon in the next world.

We ourselves seek a swift vengeance when we are angered by any cause, because when we are injured limited opportunity does not allow the chance to inflict harm to pass by. But nothing escapes the eternal God; everything is kept for his eye, and for him nothing is slow or swift. We should not consider that the times, which come and which change in relation to our affairs, are ever postponed or advanced. All that is being done everywhere, all that has been done and will be done exists at a single point of time in God's eyes. Our tomorrows and yesterdays are for him always the one day.

805. But though God preserves all things for that judgment at which all that now lies hidden will be exposed and revealed, he has given many proofs of the justice which rules the world through all the ages, when he shattered the great-

est kingdoms in wars, and often exhausted cities and proud peoples by disease, burned them with fire, submerged them in the waters; and when he enriched the poor, raised the downcast, reduced the prosperous, freed the enchained, and subdued the proud. But we must not consider it as without good reason that when the wicked experience his anger, the innocent also appear to incur the punishment of the guilty. In this world, many shared experiences await worthy and unworthy alike. The sun shines and the rain falls on all alike; cold and heat are endured equally. And just as water, light, air are shared by all, so the just must endure the evils of the unjust, so that whilst the innocent suffer many things in company with the wicked, there may be those whose merit ensures that wicked people are spared, and who by the witness of their virtue guide the others to conversion.

But whilst an unchangeable final fate oppresses those doomed to destruction, the same sentence does not oppress the holy. There are those whom the flood of the world does not submerge, who can escape Sodom before it burns. The angel who ravaged Egypt identified the doors marked with the sign of the cross, and refrained from smiting those marked with the sacred blood. The woman was not deceived by the ruddy fleece, and her house alone survived when that great city was destroyed. A path was made for the righteous through the swollen sea and over the river, and the devoted ones found a path through the desert. Food was provided by the ministering bird, and the greedy harvester was deprived of his banquet. So that God's servants should meet no obstacle, the order of nature is overturned, and the bonds slip and release the imprisoned. The prison falls open of its own accord; the bars do not keep the doors blocked. Water loses its wetness, fire its heat, lions their anger.

But there is no doubt that the young are sucked up in the whirlwind of great disaster, and though themselves innocent of sin they fall through the guilt of others, through the misconduct of their parents. We know that when the sea covered mankind, many thousands of girls and boys throughout the world were destroyed. Yet it does not seem unjust that the offspring who will increase the numbers of the wicked are removed from the earth. Great honor is conferred upon them at the time of their destruction because they fell through their fathers' sinning before they could themselves be guilty and die through their own fault.

But if the punishment of the wicked has embraced some just person as well, do not doubt that he was pleasing to God. For good men no death is evil, for after long and diverse toils any death is the avenue to rest. It is the hard road that bestows life; the crown is gained not on the field of contest but at its conclusion. But we are beguiled by seductive things and affronted by harsh trials, and we do not visualize with judgment what is good, nor what is evil by the truth, as we undertake to attend to business which is not ours, and we abandon our own interests through delight at those of others. We do not account an individual as wretched because he sins, or as blessed because he is virtuous; we inanely attach blame and honor to externals, and though our allegiance is to heaven we cherish the things of earth. The convention is to call happy those whom fawning power has raised to the topmost summit of windy distinctions, whom great wealth has enriched, on whom property scattered over the whole earth has bestowed massive revenues. Men praise costly garments, fine furniture, a large mansion, countless servants, dependants alert to our interests, all that is not ours, and all that a single day can remove from us as a single day bestowed it. We do not embrace what is man's special good and what fears no violence, but we account wretched those who do not have the possessions which destroy them and which perish in a thousand ways. As if grinding toil, pain of a sick body, the death of children, demeaning poverty oppress justice! We do not see what great victories enduring patience wins, nor the outcome of our short-lived battle here; instead we are afraid to sip the chalice of the cross and of life, and prefer to drink the serpent's poison smeared with honey. Indeed, those things which breed and nurture diseases and death in the soul, and like a cancer pluck out our weakened entrails, are sweet to taste and charming to look upon. When God deigns to send down from heaven his healing cure and utterly to excise diseased fibres, we feebly rebuke his aid, and prefer to waste away with disease rather than to steel ourselves to endure the force of the enemy.

884. So what we consider evils are not evils. When the right hand of the healing Physician does not spare the foul tumors, we should embrace that salvation rather than sharpen our complaints. The sinners whom God rebukes he at that moment loves and wishes to reform with a father's whip. He would rather set me with the ones he corrects than number me with those from whom he withdraws the whip and allows to proceed on the course of their own will, borne along by their whim. They are the ones who remain safe amid their sins, and are enriched by the reward of their crimes. Their old age unpunished prolongs their lives to the unsavory limits of extreme age. They have oppressed the just man with unjust hatred; through their agency, wars are unleashed against good people, and whips chastise the slow.

These same weapons harry all the faithful with a double effect. What tortures the wicked is the cause of growth for the holy; what brings punishment for guilt to evil men brings a crown for virtue to the good. In short, if you examine all the harsh happenings in worldly matters, you will find that God's servants have willingly anticipated them. One man grieves at the loss of gold and silver coins; another is pained because his household ornaments have been seized and his jewelry divided amongst the young matrons of the Goths. Yet another feels resentment because his flocks are driven off, his house burnt, his wine drunk, his children disagreeable, his servants unprepossessing. But the wise servant of Christ loses none of these things, for he has spurned them and earlier transferred them and set them in heaven. If any hardship befalls beneath the sky of this world, he fearlessly endures it, confident in the glory which has been promised, and eager to be released from the struggle which he has overcome.

913. When you lament your uncultivated fields and your abandoned hall and the fallen front of your burnt-out mansion, should you not rather shed tears for the losses which affect your person, if you looked instead at the ravaged

sanctuary of your heart, its beauty caked with a mass of dirt, and the enemy rampaging in the citadel of your captive mind? If our minds had not surrendered and been accessible through all their gates, and had not provided fuel for the torches to achieve their own destruction, the beautiful objects created by our hands would still remain, testifying to the merit of a devoted people. But since they now lie levelled in foul destruction, they thrust before our eyes both our own calamities and theirs.

So let us as a captive band lament these ashes of our temples, and these our princes' tombs which lie heaped together, within the abode of our plundered hearts. We were once the shining vessels of God, the devoted altars and shrines of Christ, in which the silver of eloquence, the gold of virtue, the sceptre of the cross, the tiara of honor have been captured. Let us not arouse justified anger by our wild complaints, by our blaming the judgment of God, which far transcends by a yawning gulf the working of our own minds and tongues. Unjust men in the short period of this fleeting life may wax proud and rejoice in the safe security of their crimes; their vines, their land may not disappoint them; they may inflict harm without redress and prosper in their sins. But all our property is in Christ; transient things should not preoccupy us, for we did not bring them with us when we were born, and we shall not take them out of this world when we depart.

941. But if any strength of mind remains to us, let us shake off the servile yoke of sin, and once we have broken asunder our chains let us return to the freedom and glory of our native land. The unholy pact with the savage tyrant, signed by our captive hands, will not impede us. That treaty can be revoked by Christ, for he can annul it with his just right, summoning back those who have turned away and honoring those who have turned back to him. Careless of the cost, he has purchased us with his own blood, provided only that our speedy desire anticipates the help of our Liberator, and wrings pity from the Lord with devoted tears. Just as none is saved against his will or when he is at rest in deep sleep, just as no-one who retires of his own accord is attacked by

violence, so the doors of life lie open to us if we return and hammer on them; the hall of heaven receives back the citizens who are saved.

Nurture with steadfast hearts the hope of this pardon, and make entreaty to God; abandon, my brothers, conflicts of words and disputes which arise from base thoughts. Merely because we have been routed and have fallen prostrate in the first engagement, we should not be afraid to stand fast and to begin a second battle. Though the foe fills the whole world with diverse fears, and blockades the closed gates with his alert forces, our war is against the conquered as long as we strip off our former bodies and are renewed in the body of Christ, and for ourselves demand from the Victor the entire power of victory. Whilst he joins our lot to his, he merges his own with ours; man does not therefore trust in human resource, but abandons himself to the One without whom men who seem to stand cannot stand, through whom the scattered unite, and the prostrate rise again.

These remarks composed in this short treatise will be enough for those without knowledge. Once they have tasted the pure water from the living spring, they themselves will spurt forth fountains from the river-bed of their hearts, and will provide for their brothers water-filled vessels."

HUMAN LOGIC AND THE WAYS OF PROVIDENCE

18. *John Chrysostom*

In spite of these sustained attempts to demonstrate God's loving care for men, many of the Fathers inevitably fall back on Paul's statement that God's judgments are incomprehensible and his ways unsearchable to men; our limited intellects cannot penetrate the mysterious motives of Providence, and we must rest content with the impaired vision which is ours. John Chrysostom and Augustine are both alive to the apparent inconsistencies in the fortunes of good and evil men, which affronted moral sensibilities. But John Chrysostom after acknowl-

edging that much must remain mysterious adduces a
powerful argument why evil is permitted to flourish in the
world; the heroic virtue of such figures as Archbishop
Romero in San Salvador can emerge only in a world in
which good and wicked men are free moral agents.

On Providence 12[18]

"If you do not have recourse to the inscrutability of God's
plans, and if you have always made it a practice to question
everything, there will be many things to trouble you in your
course. For example, why have heresies, and the devil, and
demons been given free rein? Why have the wicked been
allowed to outwit many? Above all, why does Antichrist
make his appearance with such powers of deceit to speak in
Christ's name that he causes even the elect to go astray, if
that is possible?

These are matters not to be investigated. We must attribute all of them to the incomprehensible nature of God's
wisdom. He who already shows noble commitment not only
remains unhurt but even becomes stronger though a thousand waves, a thousand storms buffet him. But the feeble,
weak, petty man often falls even if nothing troubles him. If
you seek to elicit a reason for this, hear the one which is
known to us. There are many others which are clear to God,
who orders our affairs outstandingly and wonderfully, but I
offer here and now the one which I know.

I say that scandals are permitted so that the rewards of the
just may not be diminished. God revealed this in his com-
ments to Job, when he said: 'Do you think that I have dealt
with you for any reason other than that your justice be made
plain?' (Job 40:8). And Paul says: 'There must be heresies so
that those proved worthy may be distinctive among you' (1
Cor 11:19). When you hear the words 'There must be heresies,' do not think that he says this to specify a command or
law; far from it. He announces beforehand what is to come,
and he foretells the benefit from it for those who remain
prudent. For then the virtue of those of you who are not

---

[18]Text: SC 79. 182, ed. Malingrey

deceived will be manifest more clearly.

Wicked people have been left unmolested for a second reason — so that they may not be deprived of the benefit which comes if they are converted; such deprivation would occur if they were taken early. Paul was saved in this way, and so were the good thief, the prostitute, the tax-collector, and many others. If they had been taken off before being converted, none of them would have been saved.

So far as Antichrist is concerned, Paul offers yet another reason, namely that it robs the Jews of their entire defence. What pardon could they have for having refused to receive Christ if they were going to believe in him? So Paul says: 'That all may be judged who have not believed in the truth,' that is, in Christ, 'but have consented to iniquity' (2 Thess 2:11), that is, to Antichrist.

They said that they did not believe in him because he said he was God; in the words of scripture, 'We stone you because, being a man, you make yourself God'(John 10:33). Yet on numerous occasions they heard him offering himself to the Father, and saying that he had come at the Father's bidding, and proving this in many ways. What will they say when they greet the Antichrist claiming to be God, yet making no mention of the Father and doing what is opposed to his will? This is what Christ foretold when he rebuked them with the words: 'I am come in the name of my Father, and you receive me not; if another shall come in his own name, him you will receive' (John 5:43). This is why the scandals have been allowed."

19. Augustine

Augustine takes up this problem, and points out that there is no consistency in human terms in the fortunes of good and evil men. It would be understandable if all good men prospered and wicked men suffered; it would be equally understandable if wicked men prospered and good men suffered in this world, with the prospect of retribution or reward in the next. But no such consistency is observable; our defective human reasoning can advance only so far as to assume that our fortunes in this life are of little import compared with what is to come.

City of God, 20.2[19]

"Nowadays we are learning to endure with equanimity the ills that we experience in the company of good men, and we are also learning to hold cheap the blessings which evil men also obtain. In this way God's teaching is salutary even in matters where his justice is not obvious.

We do not know why God's judgment makes a good man poor, and a wicked man rich. Nor why the man who in our eyes should be tortured with grief because his character is depraved makes merry, whilst he whose praiseworthy life is a convincing testimony for happiness is melancholy . Nor why the innocent man leaves court not only without recompense but even found guilty, either through the corrupt bullying of the judge or through being overthrown by false evidence. Nor why his guilty opponent not merely goes unpunished, but on acquittal waxes abusive. Nor why the wicked man enjoys the best of health, whilst the man of religion wastes away in illness. Nor why robbers live as fit as fiddles in their prime, whilst those who could not injure anyone even by words are oppressed in their early years by a variety of harsh diseases. Nor why the man who is a constructive force in society is removed by premature death, whilst the man who seems unworthy of human life continues for years and years. Nor why the man steeped in crimes is exalted by distinctions, whilst the man without reproach is buried in the darkness of anonymity. Who can assemble or count such numberless instances?

If such vicissitudes were consistent even in their absurdity, so that during this life (in which according to the sacred psalm, 'man is like to vanity, and his days pass like a shadow' [Ps 144:4]) only the wicked gained the transitory blessings of this world, this could be ascribed to the just or even the kindly judgment of God. For those who were not to obtain the eternal blessings which make men happy might be either

[19]Text: CSEL 40, Z.426

deceived by temporal goods through their own wickedness, or consoled by them through God's mercy. On the other hand, those who were not to suffer eternal tortures might be afflicted by temporal ills to atone for their sins, whatever or however trivial they were, or might be tried by evils to perfect their virtues. In fact, however, not only are good men found in evil fortunes and evil men in good fortunes, which seems unjust, but in many cases evil men experience evil fortunes and good men good fortunes, so that the judgments of God become even more inscrutable and his ways more unsearchable (cf. Rom 11:33).

So though we do not know by what judgment these things are carried out or permitted by God, in whom is the highest virtue and the highest wisdom and the highest justice, and in whom there is no weakness nor rashness nor unfairness, it is none the less salutary for us to learn not to regard as important the good or evil fortunes which we see shared by good and evil persons alike. Rather we must seek out the good things peculiar to the good, and give the widest berth to the evils peculiar to evil men. When we come to God's judgment, the moment of which is called Judgment Day or the Day of the Lord, not only will the judgments passed there be seen to be most just, but all judgments made from the beginning, and those which are still to be made until the time of the Judgment, will likewise be clearly fair. Then too it will also become clear how just the judgment of God is in causing so many — in fact, almost all — of his judgments to evade men's grasp and understanding. However in this matter religious people who have faith do not fail to realize that such hidden judgments are just."

20. Jerome

In this respect an important lesson is taught by St. Jerome (331-420). Though the human condition in its subjection to suffering is the result of the corporate sinning of the race, we must not attribute an individual's privations to his personal faults. In 397 when Jerome was in Palestine, an eager Pannonian Christian in spite of his blindness set out on a pilgrimage to Bethlehem. Jerome writes to reassure him that his blindness is not a visitation by God, and that such physical constraints are of little importance for one with spiritual vision.

Letter 68 to the blind Castricianus[20]

"I beg you not to believe that the physical weakness that you bear is the outcome of your sinning. When the apostles suspected this in the case of the man blind from birth, and asked the Lord Saviour if he or his parents had sinned and thus caused him to be born blind, they were told: 'Neither he nor his parents sinned. It was to allow the works of God to be made manifest in him' (John 9:2f.). Many are the pagans, Jews, heretics, freethinkers whom we see rolling in the filth of lusts, reeking with blood, outdoing wolves in savagery and kites in greed, yet 'the whip does not draw near their tents' (Ps 90:10), and they are not beaten like other men. So they wax arrogant against God, and their mouths widen as far as from here to heaven. By contrast, we know that holy men are afflicted with illnesses, wretchedness and need, and perhaps they say: 'In vain, then, have I kept my own heart pure, and washed my hands in innocence' (Ps 72:13). In blaming themselves they at once say: 'If I speak thus I have rebuked the generation of your sons' (Ps 13:15).

If you think that sinning is the cause of blindness, and that God's anger inflicts what doctors often cure, you will be falsely charging Isaac, who was so unacquainted with this light of ours that he even gave his blessing to the unintended son because he was misled by error (cf. Gen 27). You will be reproaching Jacob with sin: with his inner eye and prophetic spirit he foresaw the distant future, and saw that Christ would come from royal stock, but his sight was clouded, and he could not see Ephraim and Manasses (cf. Gen 48-9). What king was more saintly than Hosea? Yet he was killed by an Egyptian sword (4 Kings 23). What finer men could

---

[20]Text: CSEL 54. 675, ed. Hilberg

there be than Peter and Paul? Yet their blood stained Nero's sword. I need not, however, speak of mortal men. The Son of God endured the shame of the cross. And do you still think that those who enjoy the happiness and pleasures of this world are blessed?

It is when God shows no anger to sinners that his anger is great. So in the case of Ezekiel he said to Jerusalem, 'Now I shall not be angry with you, my jealousy has quitted you' (Ez 16:42). For 'God chastises those he loves' (Prov 3:12), and 'disciplines every son whom he accepts' (Heb 12:6). The Father schools only him whom he loves. The master rebukes only the pupil who he sees has a more zealous talent. Once the doctor stops trying to cure, he gives up hope. Your response may well be: 'As Lazarus endured evils in his life, so I shall gladly endure torments now, so that glory may be stored up for me in the future; for the Lord will not punish the same sin twice' (Nahum 1). The reason why Job, a holy and spotless man, a man just in his own day, suffered so grievously, is described in his book.

So that I may not go too far and overrun the length of a letter by piling up instances from the Old Testament, I shall tell you a brief story which happened in the days of my childhood. When the blessed Antony was summoned by St. Athanasius, bishop of Alexandria, to the city of Alexandria to confute heretics, and Didymus, a most learned and blessed man had a meeting with him, they had a discussion about the holy scriptures. Antony admired the other's brain, and praised his mental sharpness. Then he asked: 'I imagine that your blindness does not depress you?' Didymus in his shame said nothing. But when Antony asked a second and third time, he finally succeeded in eliciting from Didymus a simple expression of grief. Antony said to him: 'I am surprised at a wise man grieving at the loss of what ants, flies and gnats have, rather than rejoicing at having what only the saints and apostles have deserved to get.' From this you can realize that it is much better to see with the spirit than with the flesh, and to possess the eyes which the mote of sin cannot enter."

21. Fastidius

Fastidius, who was a bishop in Britain about 430 and has Pelagian connexions, offers his solution to the problem why evil men prosper, along lines proposed by earlier Fathers: that God's patience and longanimity allows them time to repent.

On the Christian Life[21]

"It is the merciful Lord's longanimity and patience which makes many unbelieving, shameless and treacherous people sin without fear. Because of it they think that God is not the avenger of their sins, since he does not seek to punish sinners straight off. These wretched and ungrateful persons lack any forethought for their salvation. They even impute to God the postponement of their destruction. They do not know that by divine providence they are preserved for two reasons: first, that through the exercise of his long-suffering, regard may be shown for the interests of the human race, and second, so that he may not be judged to be impatient if he should condemn forthwith those who sin. For if he were not so patient, the birth of the human race would long ago have ceased. Nor would we have sinners becoming just men if God were straightway to punish those who commit sin. We know and have read of many who, in the blindness of ignorance, or because of unbelief, or deceived by the vanity of youth have been held fast in many different varieties of sinfulness; and yet through the most merciful patience of the God who sustains them they have been subsequently converted from the error of their ways, and have performed greater works of justice than the sins they had previously committed.

For God does not condone sins; he delays things. Nor does he free the contumacious sinner from death; he waits patiently until sooner or later the sinner is converted and lives. As the blessed apostle Peter says, 'the Lord does not delay what he has promised; he works patiently for your sakes, unwilling that any should perish, but that all should

[21]Text: PL 50. 385-86

be turned to penitence' (2 Peter 3:9). So in his fatherly love, his kindness and his clemency, he does not punish immediately so that you may recognize the extent of his loving regard for you, and of his compassion. He would rather wait for you than punish you in your sin. So it is that the Lord speaks through the prophet, and by the loving kindness of his words he bestows upon man all the merciful and fatherly love he desires when he says: 'And if the wicked be converted from all the iniquities they have perpetrated, and keep all my commandments, and do right judgment and justice and mercy, living they shall live; they shall not die. All the sins that they have done will not be in my mind, and in the justice which they have wrought they will live' (Ez 18:21-22). And he adds: 'Is it my will that a sinner should die, says the Lord Adonai, rather than that he be converted from his evil ways, and I should make him live?' (Ez 18:23). Elsewhere he says: 'In whatsoever day he shall turn from his wickedness, the iniquity of the wicked man shall cease to hurt him' (Ez 33:12). And again he says: 'Return my children, be converted, and I will heal you in your contrition' (Jer 3:22).

See, then, how God instructs and incites you, so that you may be converted from your sins, late though it is, and come to salvation. See how he exhorts you, doomed to death as you are, so that you may live; and with what sweetness and gentle compassion he cajoles you, so that he does not deny a father's love even to the sinner. So he still addresses as his children those who have lost God their Father because they have sinned. And he himself is witness that he has lost the sinners, when in another passage he cries out with tears and agonizing lamentations: 'I am become without sons, I have lost my people because of their sins' (Jer 15:7). From this you can recognize how much God loves you, and how desirous he is that you should live and not perish. Yet you continue to condemn and despise him, though he loves you more completely than you love yourself, and though he wants you to live when you yourself want to die. 'I desire not the death of the sinner, says the Lord God, but that he be converted and live' (Ez 18:32). By your sinning you wished to die, but he wants you by your conversion to live. What a

fool, what an irreverent ingrate you are, when you will have
nothing to do with this God who wishes to bestow on you his
compassion, and would rather save you by his fatherly love
than that you should perish by your sins!"

22. Boethius

As we should expect, Boethius (no. 16 above) makes a
spirited attempt at rational explanation of the diverse
fortunes encountered within the ranks of good men, and
likewise of those within the ranks of evil men. But he too
concludes that we cannot hope with our limited intellects
to elucidate the motives of the divine Intelligence.

The Consolation of Philosophy 4.6[22]

"Often Providence invests good men with the supreme
direction of affairs, so that proliferating wickedness may be
beaten back. To some she furnishes mixed fortunes in accordance with their mental calibre. Some she incommodes so
that they do not become degenerate through continued
prosperity, or they are afflicted with hardships to strengthen
their mental virtues by the employment and practice of
patience. Some are more fearful than they should be of what
they can endure, whilst others are more contemptuous than
they should be of what they cannot bear; Providence puts
both to self-trial by afflictions. Some win the revered esteem
of the world at the cost of a splendid death; others are
unbowed by severe punishment, and show the rest of the
world that virtue is unconquered by evils. There can be no
doubt how rightly and appropriately these events occur;
they are in the interest of those to whom they are seen to
happen.

Likewise wicked people sometimes experience affliction
and sometimes obtain their desires, and for the same reasons. No-one is surprised that they suffer hardship, because
everyone believes that they have deserved ill treatment; and
the punishment they suffer deters the rest of the world from
wicked deeds, and improves those it visits. But the happi-

[22]Text: CCL 94, ed. Bieler, p. 82.

ness wicked people attain inculcates an important lesson about how good men ought to assess the kind of success which they see often attending the wicked.

I believe that provision is made for the man whose nature is perhaps so headstrong and impatient that lack of possessions could launch his resentment into crime; Providence heals this sickness by the remedy of bestowing money on him. Another man looks into his heart which is fouled with wickedness, and comparing himself with the fortune which he enjoys, he may fear the grim loss of what he delightedly exploits; so he will change his ways and abandon wickedness through fear of losing his fortune. There are others who have exploited their prosperity unworthily, and it has consigned them to deserved disaster. Some of them are granted the right to punish, so that good men can be schooled and evil men tormented, for just as no compact exists between honourable and dishonourable people, so dishonourable men cannot agree between themselves — inevitably, for each is at odds with himself as his vices prise apart his conscience, and often he performs deeds which he decides are regrettable once he has done them.

The result is that the highest Providence often brings forth a striking phenomenon: evil men make other evil men good. Some think that they suffer unjust treatment from the scum of the earth, and as they blaze with hatred at those who inflict harm, they return to the honesty of virtue in their eagerness to be disassociated from those they hate. It is only God's power which accounts evils as goods, for it uses them appropriately and achieves some good outcome.

A kind of order embraces all things. . .so that in the realm of Providence chance can achieve nothing. But 'it is disgraceful for me to say all this as if I were a god' (Homer, *Iliad* 12.176). A man cannot mentally comprehend or verbally explain all the workings of divine activity. It must be enough merely to realize that God is the begetter of all natures, and orders everything by guiding it to the good. Whilst he hastens to preserve what he has brought forth in his own likeness, he outlaws every evil from the boundaries of his state by the chain of predestined necessity."

Chapter Two

SUFFERING AND CHRISTIAN GROWTH

The previous chapter presented the negative aspects of Christian teaching on suffering. It was not God's plan or desire that his creatures should suffer. The physical and moral frailties which are a necessary part of the human condition are an inheritance from the sinning of our first parents. We compound that sinning through our own faults and thus share a corporate guilt with them.

But the traditional Christian teaching stresses also the positive aspects of suffering. The first of these is one which scripture repeatedly emphasizes, that suffering can have a corrective and improving function. "Yahweh reproves the man he loves as a father checks a well-loved son" (Prov 3:11f.); "The Lord punishes the one he loves" (Heb 12:6); "When the Lord punishes us, it is to correct us" (1 Cor 11:37). Suffering therefore can be a test of the virtue of patience, productive of spiritual strength. The supreme exemplar in the Old Testament is Job, but the prophets generally from Jeremiah to John the Baptist attest the importance of this teaching. In the testing times of the early Church, martyrdom was the supreme manifestation of such patience. In all this we are to believe that God gives us sufficient strength to endure. "You can trust God not to let you be tried beyond your strength" (1 Cor 10:13).

23. Hermas

The need for a positive attitude towards grief and disappointment is stressed in an interesting passage from *The Shepherd* of Hermas, who ranks amongst the Apostolic Fathers of the second century. He himself suffered the loss of his property, and condemnation by his own family; he clearly preaches to himself. He sees grief as a destructive force because it afflicts the holy Spirit dwelling within us; he proclaims that to be cheerful is a mark of the true Christian.

The Shepherd, Mand. 10.3[23]

"Now hear how melancholy afflicts the holy Spirit and also preserves it. When the perplexed person embarks upon some business and fails because of his perplexity, melancholy enters him, and afflicts and distresses the holy Spirit. Again, when anger attaches itself to a person because of some matter, and he is greatly embittered and does an evil thing, melancholy again enters the heart of the angered person, and he is grieved at his action, repenting of having done wrong. So the grief brings salvation because the one who has performed a wicked deed repents.

But both things grieve the person. Melancholy, because he failed in his attempt, and anger, because he did a wicked thing. So both afflict the holy Spirit. So abandon your melancholy, and do not afflict the holy Spirit which dwells within you, in case it petitions God and abandons you. For the Spirit of God which is assigned to the flesh does not bear with melancholy of the flesh nor with distress. So be cheerful, for this is always acceptable and welcome to the Lord, and take delight in it. Every cheerful person performs good deeds, and thinks straight, and despises idle grief. But the melancholy man is always ill-tempered and acts unlawfully, having no contact with, or forgiveness from, God; for the melancholy man's request has not the power to reach up to the altar of God... So purify yourself of all evil melancholy,

[23]Text: PG 2. 941; SC 53.190

and you will live for God. All will live for God if they dispel melancholy and espouse cheerfulness."

24. Clement of Alexandria

> Clement of Alexandria (c.150-215) offers similar pastoral advice; he radiates a spirit of Christian optimism, urging that prayer and whole-hearted trust in God is the sure remedy for anxiety and grief.

To those just baptised[24]

"Renounce your numerous anxieties about the body by taking heart from your hopes in God. He will provide sufficient necessities — food for life, covering for your body, and protection against the winter's cold. The whole earth and all that grows from it belongs to your King. God has scrupulous care for the bodies of his servants as for his own limbs, for they are his temples and holy places. For that reason do not go in fear of serious illnesses or of the onset of old age which we must expect in due course; illness too will abate when we carry out his commands with whole-hearted attention.

In knowledge of this keep your soul strong even in the face of sickness. Be of good heart, like the athlete in the stadium who shows himself outstanding at enduring his ordeals with strength unimpaired. Do not be wholly crushed at heart by grief, whether it is illness which weighs you down or whether some other harsh experience comes your way. Confront your hardships with nobility of understanding, giving thanks to God even in the midst of your painful difficulties. His purposes are wiser than men's, and it is not possible or easy for men to divine them. Show compassion to those who are having a trying time, and pray that the help which comes from God may visit men. God will grant a favour if one dear to him asks for it, and he will give help to the distressed, for he wishes to make his power known to men. So when they become aware of it they may come back

[24]Text: LCL, ed. Butterworth, 370

to God, and enjoy happiness without end when the Son of God appears to bestow blessings on his own."

SUFFERING AS A TEST OF VIRTUE

25. Cyprian

> These preliminary passages serve as an appropriate introduction to later disquisitions on the theme of patience. This was particularly germane to the era of savage persecution in third-century Africa, and Cyprian (above, no. 8) devotes a special treatise to it.

On the good of patience, 5ff.[25]

"Patience, dearest brothers, is a divine attribute. When in his gospel the Lord was offering precepts for salvation, and offering advice from heaven to school his disciples to perfection, he emphasised this so that we can realise it more fully, and observe that whoever is gentle, patient and mild is imitating God the Father. This is what he said: 'You have heard it said, Love your neighbour and hate your enemy; but I say to you, Love your enemies and pray for those who persecute you, so that you may be the children of your Father who is in heaven, who makes his sun to rise on the good and the evil, and who rains on the just and the unjust. If you love only those who love you, what reward will you have? Why, even the tax-collectors do this. If you greet your brothers only, what more are you doing? Even the gentiles do this. Be you therefore perfect, as your Father in heaven is perfect' (Matt 5:43ff.). He said that we become the perfect sons of God, he showed that we are fulfilled, he taught that we are reborn in heavenly birth if the patience of God the Father remains in us, if the divine likeness which Adam had lost by sin becomes clear and bright in our actions. . .

Jesus Christ our God and Lord did not merely teach us this by words; he fulfilled it also by deeds. He said that he came down to do the will of the Father; and among the other

[25]Text: CCL 111A. 120, ed. Moreschini

wondrous virtues by which he revealed the proofs of his divine majesty, he maintained also the patience of his father by his continuing endurance. All his deeds from his earliest coming are stamped with the association of patience. When he first came down to earth from the height of heaven, the Son of God did not despise the clothing of human flesh and the burden of others' sins, though he was not a sinner. He temporarily laid aside his immortality and allowed himself to become mortal, so that though innocent he might be slain for the salvation of the guilty. The Lord was baptised by the servant; he who was to grant remission of sins did not disdain to wash his body in the cleansing water of rebirth. He through whom others get their fill fasted for forty days; he went unfed, and experienced hunger so that those starved of the word and of grace might be filled with the bread of heaven. He joined issue with the tempting devil, and content merely to have overcome him, he confined his efforts to words. He did not rule over his disciples with a lordly power as though they were slaves, but in kindness and gentleness loved them with a brother's affection; he even deigned to wash the apostles' feet, so that by demonstrating this kind of lordship over his servants, he might teach us by his example how a fellow-slave ought to treat his fellows and equals.

We should not be surprised at this behaviour towards his followers, for he was able to show protracted patience towards Judas to the very end. He took food with his enemy, he knew the foe within his house but did not expose him, he did not refuse the traitor's kiss. What boundless even-temperedness and patience he showed in his indulgence towards the Jews! He turned unbelievers to belief by persuasion, warmed the ungrateful by serving them, answered gently those who contradicted him, endured the arrogant with kindliness, yielded humbly to persecutors, seeking to the very hour of his cross and passion to gather to the fold the killers of prophets and obstinate rebels against God.

Just before the passion and cross, before they proceeded to the cruel execution and the shedding of blood, what taunting rebukes he patiently listened to, what sneering insults he endured! Why, he who had restored the sight of the blind man with his spittle was now the recipient of the spittle of revilers. He in whose name the devil and his angels are now scourged by his agents, himself suffered scourging. He who crowns the martyrs with eternal blossoms was crowned with thorns. He who bestows true palms on those who prevail was slapped on the face with palms. He who clothes the rest of mankind with the garb of immortality was stripped of his earthly garments. He who bestowed the food of heaven was fed on gall. He who served the cup of salvation was given vinegar to drink. That innocent and just Man, the personification of innocence and justice, was counted amongst criminals. Truth was oppressed with false testimonies. The Judge to come was judged. God's Word was led unspeaking to the cross. Though at the Lord's crucifixion the stars were in chaos, the elements awry, the earth quaking, the day shut out by darkness, and the sun restrained even from gazing at the crime of the Jews so that it withdrew its rays and eyes, he said nothing, was not stirred to action, did not proclaim his majesty even in his passion. He bore everything to the very end with constancy and endurance, so that a full and perfect patience might be attained in Christ.

After all this he nonetheless welcomed his murderers, if they turned to him; with the patience that bestows salvation, he showed kindly concern to save all, and excluded none from his church. If those foes, those blasphemers, those ever hostile to his name showed repentance for wickedness and acknowledged the wrong they had done, he not merely pardoned their sin but also granted them the reward of the kingdom of heaven. What greater patience or kindness can be adduced? Even the man who shed Christ's blood is given life through Christ's blood. This is the nature and extent of Christ's patience; if it had not existed in such quality and measure, the Church would not possess Paul as its apostle.

Now if, dearest brothers, we are in Christ, if Christ is our garment, if he is the path of our salvation, let us as we follow in Christ's saving footsteps progress by following his example. The apostle John gives us this instruction: 'He who says he abides in Christ ought himself to walk as Christ walked'

(1 John 2:6). Again, Peter, upon whom by the Lord's graciousness the Church was founded, lays this down in his epistle: 'Christ suffered for you, leaving you an example so that you should follow his steps. He did no sin; no deceit was found in his mouth. When he was reviled he did not revile in return; when he suffered, he threatened not; he delivered himself to him that unjustly judged him' (1 Pet 2:21f.).

Finally we discover that the patriarchs, prophets and all just men who in anticipation exhibited the form of Christ paid attention to nothing in the glory of their virtues more than to maintaining patience with brave and constant serenity. Abel, the first to encompass and dedicate martyrdom and the suffering of the just man, did not resist or fight back, but was slain in humility, gentleness and patience. When Abraham, who trusted in God and planted the root and foundation of our faith, was tried through his son, he did not hesitate or delay, but obeyed the Lord's commands with the totality of devoted patience. Isaac, too, who, when offered up by his father to be sacrificed, prefigures the Lord as victim, was found to be patient. When Jacob was driven from his land by his brother, he left patiently, and with greater patience by his pleas and gifts of reconciliation he later won back to harmony that brother when he was still more wicked and persecuting. Joseph was sold and banished by his brothers; he did not merely pardon them with patience, but also generously and indulgently bestowed corn on them without payment on their arrival in Egypt. Moses was often scorned and almost stoned by an ungrateful and treacherous people, yet with gentleness and patience he prayed to the Lord on their behalf. In the case of David, from whom sprang Christ's birth in the flesh, what great, wonderful, Christian patience it was to have repeatedly had the chance of killing King Saul, who pursued and sought to slay him, and yet to have preferred to save him when Saul was made subject and delivered to him! Not merely did he forego revenge on him as an enemy, but he also avenged him when Saul was slain. In short all murdered prophets, all the martyrs distinguished by glorious deaths, attained their heavenly crowns by the merit of their patience. The crown for pains and sufferings cannot be won unless patience in pain and suffering comes first.

So that we may know more fully and clearly, dearest brothers, how useful and necessary patience is, we must ponder God's judgment imposed at the beginning of the world and of the human race upon Adam, when he neglected the command and transgressed the law which had been given him. Then we shall realise how patient we must be in this world; our birth imposes the necessary toil of pressures and struggles. God said: 'Because you listened to the words of your wife, and ate of the tree from which alone I had forbidden you to eat, the earth will be accursed in all your works. In sadness and groaning you will eat from it all the days of your life. It shall yield you thorns and thistles, and you shall eat wild plants. With the sweat of your brow will you eat your bread, until you return to the earth from which you were taken. For you are earth, and to earth you will return' (Gen 3:17ff.). We are all bound and fettered by the bond of this judgment until we leave this world, and death is abolished. We must live in sadness and groaning all the days of our life, and eat our bread with sweat and toil.

So when each of us is born and is received in the lodging of the world, his beginning is tearful; though still unaware and ignorant of everything, our only experience at birth is of crying. By the providence of nature we grieve for the worries and toils of mortal life, and our uninitiated souls bear witness to the storms of the world which we enter by our laments and groaning. There is sweat and toil here all life long. The only consolations to help us as we sweat and toil are those of patience. They are appropriate and necessary for all in this world, but still more for us, since we are shaken more by the onset of the devil. Every day we stand in the battleline, wearied by our conflicts with that ancient and practised foe. In addition to our various and continual struggles against temptations, there is the warfare of persecution; we have to abandon our family-possessions, submit to imprisonment, wear chains, lose our lives. We must endure the sword, wild beasts, fire, the cross — in short, all kinds of torture and punishment — by faith and the virtue of patience. The Lord instructed us with the words: 'These things I have spoken to you that you may have peace in me but affliction in this life. But have confidence, for I have overcome the world' (John 16:33). Now if we who have renounced the devil and the world, endure the afflictions and the attacks of the devil more frequently and more violently, how much more we should hold fast to patience, so that by its help and companionship we may endure all these hostilities.

Patience is necessary also to endure the maladies of the flesh and the frequent harsh pains of the body, by which the human race is wearied and shaken every day. When God's command was first transgressed, bodily strength departed with immortality, and weakness entered with death. We cannot recover that strength until we recover also our immortality; so we must always wrestle and struggle with this frailty and weakness of the body. This wrestling and struggling can be endured only by the power of patience. In the testings and probings which we endure, various pains are imposed, and the nature of our trials is manifold: we lose our faculties, suffer the heat of fever, the torture of wounds, the loss of dear ones. Nothing so much distinguishes the unrighteous from the righteous as the fact that the unrighteous man complains and blasphemes in adversity through lack of patience, but the righteous man is proved by patience. As scripture says: 'In pain endure, and in your lowliness have patience, for gold and silver are tried in the fire' (Eccl 2:5f.)."

26. Augustine

> Augustine in his *Commentary on the Psalms* stresses that such endurance of sufferings is vital if we are to attain to everlasting life.

Commentary on the Psalms 37.23[26]

"*For I am ready for scourges.* These words are uttered most solemnly, as though their message is: 'For this I was

[26]Text: CCL 38. 397, ed. Dekkers-Fraipont

born, to suffer scourges. All who are Adam's sons inevitably merit scourging. But sometimes sinners are not in this life punished wholly or commensurately with their deserts, because their behavior is already beyond hope of improvement. But those for whom life everlasting is being prepared must of necessity be afflicted in this world, according to the truth of these words: 'My son, reject not the correction of the Lord, and do not faint when you are chastised by him' (Prov 3:11f.). 'For the one whom the Lord loves he chastises, and he scourges every son whom he receives' (Heb 12:5f.). So my enemies need not cast insults, nor boast in triumph. Even if my Father chastises me, I am ready for scourges, because my inheritance awaits me. If you will not bear correction, you will not receive the inheritance, for chastisement is the lot of every son. So true is this that the Father did not spare even him who had no sin."

27. Augustine

Augustine further stresses the role of suffering as a testing-ground and correction when in *The City of God* he reflects on the privations suffered in the sack of Rome in 410.

The City of God 1.1ff.[27]

"...Many have emerged unscathed who now speak calumny against these Christian times. They saddled Christ with the evils which Rome suffered, but do not credit him with the blessings which enabled them to live as a testament to his glory. These they ascribe to their own fate. But if they were right-thinking, they should rather have attributed to divine Providence the harsh and grim treatment which they experienced from the enemy. Providence is in the habit of using wars to correct and to afflict the debased manners of men, and likewise by such oppression to test righteous and praiseworthy lives; and when they have been tested, to transport them to a better life, or to keep them for other purposes longer on this earth.

[27]Text: CCL 47.2

Someone will ask: 'Why then did God's mercy extend even to the wicked and ungrateful?' The only evidence we have is that he who dispensed it 'makes his sun rise on good and bad, and rains on just and unjust' (Matt 5:45). Some of them ponder on this, repent, and amend their wickedness; but some, as Paul says, 'despise the riches of God's goodness and long-suffering, because of the hardness of their hearts and their unrepentant souls,' and they lay up for themselves 'wrath on the day of anger, on the day of the revelation of the righteous judgment of God, who will render to every man according to his works' (Rom 2:4-6). God's patience entices the wicked to repent, and God's scourge schools good men to have patience. Likewise God's mercy embraces the good, and they will be cherished; and his harshness arraigns the wicked for future punishment. For divine Providence has ordained for the just the future provision of blessings which the unjust will not enjoy, and for the wicked, sufferings which will not torture the good; but the good and evil things of this transient world he has decided should be shared by both. In this way we may not seek too eagerly the good things which we see are possessed also by the wicked, and we may not shamefully avoid the evils which good men often have to endure.

Now give some thought to this. Do faithful and holy people suffer any evil which does not redound to their good? Surely not, unless we are to regard as idle the thought of Paul when he says: 'We know that to them that love God all things work together for good' (Rom 8:28).

So those critics lost everything they had. Did they lose, then, their faith and their religious feeling, those blessings of the inner man who is rich in God's eyes? That is the wealth which Christians have, the source of Paul's wealth when he said: 'Godliness with sufficiency is great wealth. For we brought nothing into this world, and certainly we can carry nothing out. But having food and wherewith to be covered, with these we are content. For they that will become rich fall into temptation and a snare, and into many foolish and hurtful desires which drown men into destruction and perdition. For greed is the root of all evils, which some coveting have erred from the faith, and have entangled themselves in many sorrows' (1 Tim 6:6-10).

So those whose worldly wealth was lost in the sack of Rome, if only they had possessed it as recommended by Paul, who was outwardly poor but rich within — in other words, if they could have regarded the world as if they did not regard it — could have uttered the words of Job, sorely tested but wholly unconquered: 'Naked came I out of my mother's womb, naked shall I return to the earth. The Lord gave, and the Lord hath taken away. As it hath pleased the Lord, so it is done. Blessed be the name of the Lord' (Job 1:21). . .

You say that some good men, even Christians, were tortured to make them reveal their goods to the enemy. But they could not betray or lose the Good by which they were themselves good. If they preferred torture to betraying the mammon of iniquity, they were not good; they ought to have been advised when they endured as much for gold as they should have borne for Christ, to learn to love him who could enrich with eternal blessedness those who have suffered on his account, rather than to love gold and silver. To suffer on behalf of these things is indeed wretchedness, whether lies kept their riches successfully hidden or whether telling the truth surrendered them. During this torture no person lost Christ by confessing him, and no one kept his gold except by denying that he had any. So perhaps the tortures which taught them that they should love the imperishable good were more efficacious than the goods which inflicted tortures on their owners without beneficial reward for loving them.

True, there were some with nothing to reveal who were disbelieved and tortured. Perhaps they were keen to have wealth and were not poor by a holy act of will, and so had to be shown that it is not wealth itself but the desire for it which is worthy of such torture. But if they had no gold or silver hidden away because they had planned a better life (I am not sure whether any such people were tortured because they were thought to have wealth), at any rate, anyone who during such torture confessed a holy poverty, thereby confessed Christ. So even if he did not win belief from the enemy, such a confessor of holy poverty could not have been tortured without winning a heavenly reward.

They also say that the long period of hunger ravaged many Christians. The good and faithful turned this to their advantage by enduring it with devotion. Those whom the famine killed were taken from the evils of this life as if by a physical illness, and those whom it did not kill it taught to live more economically, and to fast more extensively.

But, you say, many Christians were also killed, and many were destroyed in a foul assortment of numerous deaths. If we are to resent this, we do at any rate accept it as the common lot of all born into this life. Of this I am sure, that no person ever died who would not have died in any case some time in the future. The end of life brings the same result in the case of a long life as in that of a short one."

28. Ps-Augustine

There is a further treatise by Ps-Augustine on patience in which similar points are made:

On Patience 7-8[28]

"People put up with many extraordinary sufferings for the sake of their illicit pleasures or even crimes, as well as for this temporal life and its security. This is enough to remind us what we should suffer on behalf of a virtuous life, so that it may last for ever without its ever ending, and be secure in true happiness without loss of its usefulness.

The Lord says, 'In your patience you shall possess your souls' (Luke 21:19). He does not say 'your villas, your honours, your luxurious living'; he says 'your souls'. If then the soul suffers so much to possess the means of its own demise, how much should it suffer for survival? Further (to speak of something which is blameless), if it suffers so much for the salvation of the flesh at the hands of doctors who cut

[28]Text: PL 40.614-618

and cauterise, how much more should it suffer for its salvation from the furies of certain enemies? Doctors prescribe pain for the body to prevent its dying, but enemies threaten pain and death to the body to force soul and body to be killed in hell.

Yet greater care is observed for the body too if its temporal safety be set at nought for justice's sake, and pain and death are endured with the greatest patience for justice's sake. Paul speaks of the redemption of the body which will come at the end of time when he says: 'And we groan within ourselves, awaiting the adoption of sons, the redemption of our body.' And he adds: 'For we have been saved by hope. But the hope that is seen is not hope; for why should a man hope for what he sees? But if we hope for what we do not see, we await it through patience' (Rom 8:23-25).

When certain evils bring torment but evil works do not, it is not simply the soul that is kept in patience; when the body itself is in patience afflicted for a time or even lost, it is taken up into eternal permanence and salvation, and an inviolable health and blessed immortality is prepared for it through pain and death. So the Lord Jesus exhorts his witnesses to patience when he promises them the future integrity even of the body without the loss of a single member or even a hair of their heads: 'Amen, I say to you, not a hair of your head shall perish' (Luke 21:28). And since, as Paul remarks, 'no man ever hated his own flesh' (Eph 5:29), he who is faithful watches over the condition of his flesh with patience rather than impatience, and pays the price of momentary harm, whatever it may be, for the inestimable reward of future incorruption....

We are supported by this patience even when our bodies are healthy, because our blessedness is delayed by the hindrances of this world. So it was said above, 'If we hope for what we do not see, we wait for it with patience.' With this patience the holy David bore the rebukes of the one who taunted him. Though he could easily have taken vengeance, he not only refrained from it but restrained another who was pained and moved on his behalf (cf. 2 Kings 16:5-12). He manifested his royal dignity more by withholding his vengeance than by exercising it. On that occasion his body was not afflicted by any wound or sickness, but he acknowledged the moment of humility and bore the will of God, for whose sake the bitterness of the insult was absorbed with a most patient spirit. The Lord taught this patience on the occasion when he spoke of the servants who were upset by the sowing of the cockle among the wheat, and wanted to go and gather it up. He told us that the master of the household replied 'Let both of them grow until the harvest' (Matt 13:30). It is necessary to bear patiently what cannot be removed in a hurry. He himself set forth and gave us an example of his patience when before his bodily passion, and before he had revealed that his disciple Judas was the traitor, he put up with his thieving (cf. John 12:6, 13:29); and before he experienced chains, cross and death, he did not deny the kiss of peace to his lying lips (cf. Matt 26:29)...

So let the devoted people listen now to the sacred precepts of patience from sacred scripture. 'My son, when you come to the service of God, stand in justice and fear, and prepare your soul for trial. Humble your heart and endure, that your life may grow for the end-time. Bear all that shall come upon you, and stand firm in your sorrow, and show patience in your humiliation. For gold and silver are tested in the furnace, but those who are acceptable in the fire of humiliation' (Eccl 2:5). We read in another place: 'My son, do not reject the correction of the Lord, and do not chafe when you are chastised by him. For the Lord loves those whom he chastises, and punishes every son whom he accepts' (Prov 3:11-12). The phrase 'the son whom he accepts' matches 'those who are acceptable' in the first testimony. It is just, then, that we who were expelled from Paradise and its pristine happiness because of our wanton lusting should be taken back because we accept vexations with humility and patience. We became fugitives by the evil we did; we are taken back by the evils we suffer. There we acted against justice; here we are patient for the sake of justice.

What, then, is the source of that true patience which is worthy of the name of virtue? Some would say that it comes from the resources of the human will, from free will and not from divine aid. This error comes from the pride of those who have plenty. As the psalm has it, 'We are a reproach to the rich, and contempt to the proud' (Ps 122:4). Such patience is not 'the patience of the poor, which does not perish for ever' (Ps 9:19). The poor receive this patience from him who is rich, to whom it is said: 'You are my God, you have no need of my goods, (Ps 15:2), 'from whom is every best gift and every perfect gift' (James 1:17). The poor and needy cry out to him, they praise his name; they ask, seek and knock, saying: 'Deliver me, my God, from the hands of sinners, and out of the hands of those who transgress the law, the unjust. For you are my patience, O Lord, my hope from my youth' (Ps 70:4-5).

Those who possess an abundance disdain to show their needs before God, lest they receive true patience from him. They glory in their falsehood, and wish to confound the counsels of the needy for whom God is the hope. They do not notice that as mere humans attributing everything to themselves and their own will they incur the judgment of scripture: 'Cursed be every man who puts his trust in man' (Jer 17:5). So though through their own proud will they endure something harsh and difficult, because they do not wish to displease men, or to put up with something even more difficult, or because they wish to gratify themselves or their own presumption, we must say the same thing about this kind of patience as the blessed James says with regard to wisdom: 'This is not the wisdom which descends from above; it is earthly, sensual, devilish' (James 3:15). The patience of the proud is false, as is their wisdom. True patience comes from him who dispenses true wisdom; to him the poor in spirit sings: 'My soul is subject to God, for my patience is from him' (Ps 61:6)."

29. *John of Damascus*

John of Damascus (c. 675-749), one of the most celebrated of the Greek theologians, is famed chiefly for his composite work called *The Fountain of Wisdom*, the third part of which bears the sub-title *The Orthodox Faith*. In reflecting on the role of Providence, John first insists that we must accept what befalls us without complaint, accepting it as the higher judgment of God. But he then offers a series of explanations why the just man may be permitted to suffer: the virtue which is evinced in such suffering may be beneficial in various ways both to the sufferer himself and to the onlookers who witness it.

The Orthodox Faith, 2.29[29]

"Providence is God's care for things that exist; again, Providence is God's will, through which all existing things obtain their appropriate guidance. If Providence is God's will, it is inevitable that everything that happens through Providence must logically happen in the most beautiful and divinely appropriate way, and could not come to pass in a better manner. For the Creator of things must be identical with him who makes provision for them; it is neither fitting nor logical that there should be a creator and a different provider, for in that case both would be utterly defective, one in creating and the other in making provision. So God is both Creator and Provider; his power of creating, maintaining, providing is his good will. 'All that the Lord pleased, he hath done, in heaven and on earth' (Ps 134:6), and none has resisted his will (cf. Rom 9:19). He willed that all things be made, and they were made. He wills the world to abide, and it does abide. All that he wills comes to pass.

We can most correctly assess that he makes provision, noble provision, in this way. God alone is by nature good and wise. So being good, he makes provision; one who does not make provision is not good. Even men and creatures without reason naturally provide for their own offspring; he who does not is reproached. And being wise, God looks after things in the best possible way.

So bearing these facts in mind, we must admire and praise and accept without demur all the works of Providence, even

[29]Text: PG 94.964

if they seem unjust to many because God's providence cannot be known and understood; our thoughts and deeds, and what is to come, are known to him alone. But when I say we must admire 'all,' I mean what is not in our control; for what is at our discretion lies not within Providence but within our own free will.

Some things happen with God's approval, some by his permission. All that is incontrovertibly good is by his approval. The things which are permitted are of several kinds. The just man is often permitted to meet with disasters, so that he may show to other men the virtue hidden within him; this happened in the case of Job. On occasion he permits something outrageous to be done, so that through the apparently outrageous act some great and wonderful success can be achieved, like the salvation of men through the cross. In yet another variation he allows a holy man to suffer harshly, so that he may not forsake his right conscience, or become proud as the result of the power and grace allotted to him, as in the case of Paul (cf. 2 Cor 12:7).

A man is deserted for a time to put another to rights, so that when others consider his position they may gain instruction. Lazarus and the rich man are a case in point (cf. Luke 16:19ff.); when we see people suffer, our nature makes us humble. A person may be ignored also for another's glory, rather than because of his or his parents' sins; for example, the man blind from birth, for the glory of the Son of man (cf. John 9:3). Again, a man is permitted to suffer to arouse the emulation of another, so that when the victim's glory is hymned, the rest may embrace suffering in the hope of glory to come and in eager anticipation of future blessings, as the martyrs did. A man is permitted to fall into evil ways sometimes to straighten out some worse vice; for example, a man may put on airs because of his virtues and achievements, and God allows him to fall into fornication, so that by his stumbling he may attain awareness of his weakness, and after being humbled he may draw close and make confession to the Lord."

THE EXEMPLAR OF JOB

30. *John Chrysostom*

The classic example in scripture of tribulation visited on the just man and endured with edifying patience is found in the Book of Job. If any of the Fathers seeks to fortify or comfort any individual or flock in time of bereavement or oppression, Job is the example to which he instinctively turns. For Job was 'a perfect and upright man, one that feared God and eschewed evil', and the essential merit of the drama enacted around him is that it faces the problem squarely: by human calculation the vicissitudes which he suffers are wholly unjust and inappropriate. The Book of Job does not offer any easy solution, but it depicts the saintly fortitude which the man of God exhibits in the bewilderment and humiliation of his lot.

John Chrysostom (see above, no. 12) has left behind him in his body of writings not only a meditation on Providence but also in the present passage a reflection on false and true assessments of what constitutes real harm and real deprivation. With Boethius he argues that worldly losses constitute no real loss, and adduces Job as the living example of this.

No-one is harmed 1ff.[30]

"Many of the more wretched and foolish among us observe the just man being hauled about, lacerated, throttled, while the man who is a desperado, dishonorable, dishonestly rich, powerful is feared by the common folk and inflicts on just people savageries beyond counting. This happens indifferently in cities, countryside and desert; it happens on land and sea. Those who observe this are gripped by a curious madness, and they inveigh against God's providence. So this letter of mine must take issue with this attitude, and fight a new and unusual engagement

[30]Text: PG 52.459

which will be useful, true and profitable for those willing to listen and be persuaded. It claims to show that none of those who suffer wrong do so at the hands of another, but at their own hands.

To make my words clearer, let us first examine what injustice is, and in what kinds of things its stuff consists. What is a person's proper quality, and what injures it? What seems to injure it, but in fact does not? Every object has something that injures it; iron suffers rust, wool suffers moths, flocks of sheep suffer wolves... Our bodies suffer fever, paralysis and swarms of other sicknesses. So everything has something which harms its excellence. Let us examine what afflicts the human race, and what afflicts man's true quality. Most people have erroneous ideas and propose different causes for what detracts from our excellence. Some suggest poverty, other physical sickness, others loss of money, others slander, others death. They never stop lamenting and bewailing these things, nor pitying those who suffer them. They weep and are aghast, and say to each other: 'What sufferings so-and-so has to put up with. He has been stripped of all he has!' A friend speaks of someone else: 'What's-his-name has been struck down by a terrible illness; he is given up by the doctors attending him.' One man grieves and is sorry for people in prison, another for those expelled from their native land and forced to live abroad, another for those who have lost their freedom, another for those imprisoned in the hands of enemies, another for one who has been drowned or burnt, another for a man who has been buried under the debris of his house. But nobody grieves for those who live wicked lives; what is more tragic, they often regard such men as happy. This attitude is the cause of all our problems.

So let us demonstrate that none of the experiences mentioned harms the man of wisdom, and could not affect his virtue. When a man has lost all his property or has been robbed of it by informers, robbers or dishonest slaves, how has this loss affected his human quality?... In what does this human excellence consist? Not in riches, which cause one to fear poverty; and not health, making you tremble at illness; not in the opinion of the crowd, causing you to fear a bad reputation; not in life pure and simple, entailing apprehension of death; not in freedom, causing you to shun slavery. It lies in the keen awareness of true beliefs, and in right living. The devil himself will not be able to pillage these possessions if the person who has acquired them guards them with appropriate care.

The devil who is most wicked and fierce is aware of this. It caused him to pillage the possessions of Job — not to make Job poor, but to force him to utter some blasphemous word. He afflicted Job's body, not to invest him with sickness but to lay low the excellence of his soul. He put into action all his devices. He made him poor from being rich. What seems to everyone the most horrific fate, he made him childless after he had had many children. He lacerated Job's whole body more savagely than the public officials at the court-house do — their nails do not tear the flesh of those who fall into their hands as much as the worms nibbled and wasted Job's body. The devil caused him to incur an evil reputation; Job's friends came up to him and said: 'You have not been afflicted as much as your faults deserved.' He not only had Job expelled from his city and his house, and transferred to another city; he gave him a dungheap as his home and city. Yet in spite of all this he did not do him any harm, but made him even more splendid through the plots which he laid against him. He did not merely fail to deprive him of any of his goods, in spite of the fact that he robbed him of all these; he actually made his wealth of virtue greater, for subsequently Job enjoyed greater trust because he had fought a more taxing fight.

If, then, one who endured such pains suffered no wrong, if he suffered at the hands not of a man but of the devil who is more wicked than all men, who can still find support for people who say: 'Such-and-such wronged and harmed me'? If the devil, embodying such wickedness, set in motion all his instruments, hurled all his weapons, and all that men account as evils, with such great force, emptying them upon the just man's house and person, yet did not do him any wrong, but rather as I said helped him, how will people be able to accuse particular individuals on the grounds that they suffered wrong at their hands?"

31. Gregory

> The most famous of the patristic discussions of Job is that of Gregory the Great (c. 540-604). Like so many of the Fathers who discuss the problems of suffering, Gregory had direct pastoral experience of it. The Italy in which he became pope in 590 was molested by flood, famine, disease, and the Lombard invasions. His *Commentary on the Book of Job* offers the threefold literal, allegorical and moral interpretation inherited from earlier Greek exegesis; these extracts exemplify his moral reflections.

Moral Reflections on Job 11:47, 14:36, 14:40, 14:67[31]

"*Even if he kill me I shall hope in him* (Job 13:15). The virtue of patience is never to the fore in times of happiness. The truly patient person is he who is exhausted by adversity, yet is not deflected from the rightness of his hope. It is the false man's thoughts of which scripture says: 'He will praise you when you bring him benefits' (Matt 5:16). The difference between the just and the unjust heart is seen in this, that the just utters praise of almighty God even in adversity. He is not shattered with his possessions, he does not tumble with the fall of his external reputation, but shows by his greater strength without possessions what he was like when he had them.

There follows: *And I shall rise from the earth on the last day.* In other words, God will at some time manifest in us the resurrection which he revealed in himself. For he has promised us the resurrection which he revealed in himself, since his limbs follow the glory of the Head. So our Redeemer accepted death so that we should not fear to die. He revealed the resurrection so that we may be sure that we can rise again. That is why he decided that his death should last for

---

[31]Text: SC 212, ed. Bocognano, 108, 372, 378, 422

no more than three days, so that we should not succumb wholly to despair if his own resurrection were postponed. Of him the prophet's words are well said: 'He shall drink of the torrent on his way, and he shall therefore raise his head high' (Ps 109:7). He has deigned to drink of the river of our suffering, so to say, not by halting but by continuing on his way; for he met death 'on his way', that is for three days, and he did not continue in the death which he experienced as we shall until the end of the world...

14:36 *At least now understand that God has afflicted me with an unfair judgment* (Job 19:6). How harsh are the words of the just man smitten by blows! They are forced out of him not by pride but by grief. But the just man does not abandon justice at the hour of pain. Because the blessed Job had a gentle heart, he did not sin even when speaking harshly. If we say that he sinned in using these words, we acknowledge that the devil achieved his design when he said: 'Touch his bone and his flesh, and see if he will curse thee to thy face' (Job 2:6). So a serious problem arises, for if Job did not sin when he said 'At least now understand that God has afflicted me with an unfair judgment', we agree that God did something unjustly, which it is sacrilegious to claim. But if Job did sin, the devil fulfilled his promise.

We must accordingly demonstrate that God treated the blessed Job rightly, yet that Job did not lie when he said that he was afflicted by God's unfair judgment, but that the enemy lied when he predicted the guilt of the blessed man. Sometimes the statements of good men are considered base because they are not pondered in their inner meaning. The blessed Job had considered his life, and weighed the stripes which he suffered, and he saw that it was unjust that he should receive such punishment for such a life. When he said that he was afflicted with an unfair judgment, he was saying openly what the Lord had said about him in his secret heart to his enemy: 'You have moved me against him that I should afflict him without cause' (Job 2:3). So how did Job sin when he said nothing which was at odds with the statement of the Creator?...

14:40 *Behold I shall cry, suffering violence, and none shall hear, I shall cry aloud, and there is none to judge* (Job 19:7).

Almighty God knows what can be of benefit to us, and he pretends not to hear the cries of those in pain, so that he may increase what is in our interest. He seeks to purify our lives by punishment, so that we may seek elsewhere that peaceful repose which cannot be found in this world. But there are some even of the faithful who are unaware of this grace which lies in his ordering of events. Job speaks in their person when he says here: 'Behold I shall cry, suffering violence, and none shall hear: I shall cry aloud, and there is none to judge.' What is being suggested is that there is none to judge when he who is present pretends not to judge, for there is none to judge our cause against the foe save him who does so judge. But postponement of judgment does not mean absence of judgment, for when the blessed Job said this, both the merits of that holy man and the punishment of the foe were increasing. So it is at the discretion of the Judge to postpone the judgment. But the economy which God justly ordains in secret is one thing, and what the human heart bruised with scourging openly requests is another. So Job further says about the infliction of these blows:

'He has hedged my path round about, and I cannot pass: and in my way he has set darkness.' He saw his path hedged about with blows when he sought to pass to an untroubled state, but he could not escape the whips. Because he saw that he was being beaten when he did not regard his manner of life as deserving it; he experienced the darkness of ignorance in the way of his heart, for he could not penetrate the reason for his being scourged. This can quite appropriately be applied also to weak members of holy Church...

14:67 *For I know that my Redeemer liveth* (Job 19:25). Job says not 'Creator' but 'Redeemer', so he openly proclaims him who after he created all things appeared among us in the flesh to redeem us from captivity, and by his passion freed us from enduring death. We must observe the depth of faith with which Job commits himself to the strength of that Godhead of whom Paul says: 'Though he

was crucified in his weakness, he lives by the power of God'
(2 Cor 13:4). Job says: 'I know that my Redeemer liveth', as
if he were clearly saying: 'The man without faith can know
that he was scourged, mocked, beaten with palms, crowned
with a crown of thorns, smeared with spittle, crucified,
dead; but I believe with unwavering faith that he lives after
death, I confess with free utterance that my Redeemer who
perished at the hands of the ungodly lives on.' Blessed Job,
announce in clear tones, please, your sure belief in the
resurrection of your own flesh, which arises through his
resurrection."

MARTYRDOM: SUFFERING AS WITNESS

32. Cyprian

The supreme example of suffering as the test of virtue is
martyrdom. From the age of Nero in the first century AD
(Tacitus in his *Annals* vividly portrays the sufferings of
Christians in the Roman amphitheatre following upon
the fire of Rome) until the age of Diocletian (the Great
Persecution of 303 took place in his reign), those who had
undergone suffering and in many cases death were visual-
ised as heroic successors to those Old Testament figures
who had likewise though in a different sense witnessed to
Christ. As representative examples of the glorification of
such martyrdom, we offer a letter of Cyprian written in
the Latin west in third-century Africa, and an extract
from John Chrysostom's *On Providence* which hails
martyrs in the Greek-speaking east a century later.

Letter 8[32]
"*Cyprian to the martyrs and confessors: perpetual salva-
tion in Christ our Lord and in God the Father.* .
I rejoice and exult, my brothers so strong and blessed of
God, and I give thanks for your proven faith and virtue in

[32]Text: CSEL 111,2.485, ed.

which mother Church takes pride. She makes her boast especially in the steadfast witness given by Christ's confessors and the punishment recently embraced which has made them exiles. Your present witness is the more splendid and brings you greater honor because it became more assured in suffering. For when the battle grew fiercer, so the feats of the warriors increased in glory. Nor did the fear of torments turn you from the battle-line; rather they urged you further into the fray, and with prompt fidelity you returned to the fiercest fighting of the engagement with courage and steadfastness. I have ascertained that some of you have already been crowned, and others are on the point of receiving the crown of victory. But all of you in this glorious band whom the dungeons have embraced were animated with the same high degree of virtue in your forward advance in the struggle, as is fitting for Christ's soldiers in God's army, so that no blandishments could beguile the incorruptible quality of your faith, no threats could make you fearful, no torture nor torment conquer you, for he who is in us is greater than anyone that is in the world (1 John 4:4), and earthly punishments are less powerful to cast you down than the divine protection to set you upright.

We have had proof of this in the glorious combat of the brethren, who became leaders of the rest in order to win victory over torture. They showed the example of virtue and faith in joining battle until the defeated line acknowledged surrender. How then shall I praise you, mighty brothers? How shall I publicly commend your hearts of oak, your enduring faith? You survived the harshest of inquisitions to the glorious consummation. You never yielded to torture; torture instead bowed its head before you. The crown of martyrdom not the torture made an end of your pains. The stiffer examination by torture was protracted not to throw down your upright faith but to dispatch the men of God to their Lord more quickly. The crowd of bystanders watched the heavenly contest with wonderment; it was God's affray, a spiritual struggle, Christ's battle. There stood his servants, speaking out spontaneously with pure hearts, divinely inspired though defenceless, unarmed with this world's weapons but as believers accoutred with the arms of faith. There they stood, victims of torture yet stronger than their tormentors. Their battered and lacerated limbs overcame the 'claws' which tore and ripped at them. The savage, oft-repeated lashes could not defeat their inextinguishable faith, though once their entrails were prised apart it was not the organs of God's servants but their open wounds that were racked. It was as though their blood flowed to extinguish the fires of the persecution, to damp down the flames and burning coals of hell with its glorious streams. O what a marvellous sight it was before the Lord, how sublime, how precious! How welcome a sight to God's eyes is the allegiance and self-offering of his legionaries! So it is written in the Psalms, when the holy Spirit speaks likewise reminding us 'How precious in the sight of the Lord is the death of his just' (Ps 115:15).

Precious indeed is this death which purchases immortality at the price of its blood and which has received the crown at the finishing-line of virtue! How joyous Christ was then! How willingly did the Protector of the faith fight and conquer in such servants as these! On those who believe he bestows all that the recipient believes he obtains. Christ was present at his own contest. He raised up, strengthened, enlivened those who fought for and defended his name. He who once conquered death on our behalf is always the conqueror in us. 'When they shall deliver you up,' he said, 'take no thought what you shall say, for it will be given you in that hour what to speak. For it is not you that speak, but the Spirit of your Father that speaks in you' (Matt 10:19-20). We had an example of this in the present struggle. A voice alive with the holy Spirit came forth from the lips of a martyr when the most blessed Mappalicus in the midst of his tortures spoke to the Proconsul: 'Tomorrow you will witness the contest.' What he said in witness of faith and power the Lord brought to pass. The heavenly contest was staged, and the servant of God received his crown in the struggle of the promised contest.

It is this same contest which the prophet Isaiah foretold when he said: 'Is not your struggle with men a small thing, when God puts a contest before you?' (Isa 7:13). In order to show what this contest would be, he went on to say: 'Behold a virgin shall conceive in her womb and bear a son, and you shall call his name Emmanuel' (7:14). This is the contest of our faith in which we join battle, conquer, and receive the crown. This is the contest which the blessed apostle Paul reveals to us, the one in which we must run and attain the wreath of glory: 'Do you not know,' he said, 'that all who run in the race do indeed run, but only one takes the palm? So run to win. Others run to receive a wreath that fades, but we for one that does not' (1 Cor 9:24-25). Again, he talks of his own contest. He promises that he will soon become the Lord's victim: 'Even now I am ready to be sacrificed, and the time of my adoption is at hand. I have fought a good contest, I have finished the race, I have kept faith. What now remains for me is the crown of justice, which the Lord, the just arbiter, will present to me on that day, and not only to me but to all who love his coming' (2 Tim 4:6-8). It was this contest, foretold by the prophets, commissioned by the Lord, fought by the apostles, that Mappalicus in his own name and that of his comrades promised to the proconsul. Nor did this faithful witness cheat on his promise. He fought the fight to which he had pledged himself, and received the prize he deserved.

So now I desire and exhort the rest of you to follow hard after this most blessed martyr and the rest of his company, his fellow-soldiers and steadfast comrades in the faith, patient in suffering, victors in the inquisition. In this way those whom the bonds of confession of faith and the lodging of the gaol have joined together may be linked also by perfection of virtue and a heavenly crown. So too the tears of mother Church, who mourns the ruin and deaths of so many, may be dried by your joy, and you may ensure steadfast endurance among the others by the challenge of your example. If the battle calls you to action and the day of your own struggle comes, fight courageously and war with constancy, knowing that you fight in the sight of the Lord who is with you, and that you attain his glory by confessing his name. He is not one simply to watch his servants; he fights in us, takes on the opposition, both bestows and receives the crown in the heat of our contest. And if before the day of your battle dawns peace supervenes by the mercy of the Lord, let your purpose remain heart-whole and your conscience unsullied.

None should grieve as being inferior to those who suffered tortures ahead of you, and who, having overcome and trodden the world underfoot, have made the blessed journey to the Lord. It is the Lord who searches the heart and reins, who probes what is secret and sees what is hidden. The witness of our future Judge is enough to decide who merits a crown. So the roles of both martyr and confessor, beloved brothers, are equally lofty and glorious. The one is more certain, hastening to the Lord at the attainment of victory; the other is happier, obtaining a furlough after winning glory and basking in the praise of the Church. How happy is our blessed Church, for the Lord has deigned to illumine her by this honor; she is made famous in our times by the glorious blood of the martyrs. Before she was lily-white through the brethren's works of charity; now she has become red with the blood of martyrs. Her bouquet lacks neither lilies nor roses. Now each one must strive for the splendid dignity of either distinction. Let them receive white wreaths for their good works, or red for their suffering. In heaven's army both peace and war have their own flowers with which Christ's soldiers are crowned for glory.

I wish you, most blessed and steadfast brothers, good and abiding health in the Lord, and ask for a remembrance. Farewell."

33. *John Chrysostom*

On Providence, 19[33]

"Give some thought to all those who have crowned themselves with martyrdom. Some were scourged, or thrown into prison, or chained up as criminals, or exiled from their state; some lost all they had, or were expelled outside their

---

[33]Text: SC 79.234, ed. Malingrey

borders, or were slain. Some experienced these sufferings; others anticipated them. Whilst swords were unsheathed, daggers sharpened, menaces uttered daily, while those in authority exhaled rage and threatened murder and countless forms of punishment and vengeance, they did not yield or surrender. Men and women alike stood unmoved on the rock, choosing to do and suffer everything rather than participate in the lawlessness of those who had demonstrated such effrontery. Women in fact showed themselves in many cases more courageous than men in stripping for the fight; and young persons and children likewise.

Tell me, is this a slight matter that the Church gained such a great crowd of martyrs? For all these were martyrs. It is not only the people dragged into court, those who refused when ordered to make sacrifice, and those who endured suffering who were martyrs, but also those who consented to endure pain for any of God's purposes. These in fact are more precisely martyrs than the first group. Consenting to endure some suffering to avoid losing your soul when such destruction and loss overhangs you is not the same as undergoing the same punishment for some slighter gain. I shall try to show you by Paul's words that it is not only those who were slain, but also those who were prepared and ready for death, and those mentioned previously who were slain for lesser reasons who have achieved martyrdom. The blessed Paul begins to enumerate those ancestors whose light shone bright. He begins with Abel, advances to Noah, Abraham, Isaac, Jacob, and then he added: 'Similarly we too have around us a huge crowd of witnesses' (Heb 12:1). Yet not all of these were slain — in fact none of them except two, Abel and John. The others all ended their lives by natural death. John himself was not executed for refusing to sacrifice when ordered; he was not brought before an altar, or dragged to an idol. He was punished for a single statement. He said to Herod: 'You cannot have the wife of your brother Philip' (Matt 14:4), and this was why he was imprisoned and executed."

CONSOLATION IN BEREAVEMENT

34. *Paulinus of Nola*

Just as the martyrs were called upon to demonstrate patience and courage in their personal suffering, so those who survived the deaths of close relatives were exhorted to show virtue in bearing their sorrow at the departure from this life of their dear ones; further, they were urged to manifest joy in Christian hope that their departed ones were united with Christ. These are the salient themes in the Christian development of the genre of the *consolatio*, which had earlier been practised by such Classical writers as Cicero and Seneca. Of the numerous extant examples of the Christian consolation (cf. Ch. Favez, *La consolation latine chrétienne*, Paris, 1937) we select two contributions characteristic of the genre.

Paulinus of Nola (c. 354-431), a native of Aquitania, established a monastery at Nola near Naples. From there he wrote this letter of consolation to the leading Christian senator of the day, Pammachius, in 396. Pammachius had in the previous year lost his wife Paulina, daughter of the celebrated Paula and sister of Eustochium.

Letter 13[34]

"I have just heard in a letter from my holy brother Olympius, our mutual dear friend, the news of your unexpected and unanticipated sorrow. Even if my personal feelings of affection remained mute, the charity of Christ our Lord and God (in whom and through whom we are joined as the limbs of a single body) would not allow me to grudge a share in your grief, or to withold my duty to speak. The Lord God, who guides us not only in our way of life but also in our devoted love, has taught us through his chosen heavenly vessel 'to rejoice with them that rejoice, to weep with them that weep' (Rom 12:15), to show sympathy to each other and to 'bear each other's burdens' (Gal 6:2), so that by offering each other consolation, we may strengthen our common faith and warm our weary hearts. God has so

[34]Text: CSEL 29.84, ed. von Hartel.

generously endowed this service of consolation that he has promised that the one who performs it will be exalted as a great city. He announced through his prophet that 'A brother that is helped by a brother will be raised like a great city' (Prov 18:19). This is because the sympathy of a brother lends strength to a struggling soul, and resists like a wall the buffets endured by the oppressed heart...

I confess that I have been doubtful whether to write words of sadness which expressed my love for you, or words congratulating you on your faith. For I have heard not only that my holy sister has been called to God, but also of your devoted piety in Christ. The father of the household who prompted this letter has told me of your wise, holy and true love for your dead wife. Like most men you accompanied her to burial with her proper tribute of tears, but unlike those deprived of Christian hope without empty pomp and honor. Indeed, you first fittingly performed the proper rites for the body of your dear one when you sprinkled and bedewed it with affectionate and copious tears of love, and then in more religious fashion you honored her burial by attending her with remedies that bring salvation, and with works that live — in other words with almsgiving.

I shall first praise the devotion which you manifested. Holy scripture shows that this too is pleasing to God with the words: 'My son, shed tears over the dead, and begin to lament as if you had suffered some great harm, and neglect not his burial.' (Eccl 38:16). In short, our patriarchs provide a precedent for this religious behavior. The father of faith mourned his wife Sara, the mother of our calling, not because he doubted that she would be reunited to him, but because he missed her when she went before him. How could the father of faith, the first to hear the blessed promise, doubt the resurrection? But mindful of his human nature, he did not neglect the care of the body because her soul was safe, but he bought a field for the burial, and laid his dead wife in a costly grave. By so doing he taught us what provision we should make on this earth. After leaving his country and kindred at God's command, he bought none of the vast territories traversed by different tribes, and he was a stranger in every land; but he bought one field for a grave, land not for acquisition but for peace, an eternal and not transient possession...

So scrupulous burial is good, and so are the loving tears with which father Abraham buried the mother of our pledge. Good too are the tears of affection which Joseph duly bestowed on his father. Good are the tears in prayer with which David watered his bed night after night. But why should I proclaim the tears of holy men, when Jesus too wept for a friend? He shed tears over a dead man, and with human weakness mourned the person whom with divine power he intended to revive. But in that one man the merciful and pitying Lord bewailed the universal condition of the human race, and washed us with the tears with which he wept for our sins.

My brother, your tears were holy and dutiful like theirs, because they flowed with the same love. You lamented a wife worthy of your chaste bed, not because you have any doubts about the resurrection, but because of your longings of love. 'The grace of a wife charms her husband' (Eccl 26:16) whilst he has her, and arouses his longing when she is taken before him. As she always was, so shall she be 'a crown for her husband for ever, and her lamp shall not be put out' (Prov 31:18); for, as scripture says, 'she has applied her hands to useful works, she has opened her mouth wisely, she has rendered her husband good' (Prov 31:26). She has crowned you with fame and distinction so that she might share your joy in your final days. So she is more worthy of tears than grief. It is better for you to long for her unceasingly rather than to mourn her. The thought of her merits enjoins bitter sadness on her surviving husband, for when a just person dies he will leave regret behind; yet it also offers abundant solace to the believer, for 'the memory of the just one is immortal' (Wis 4:1). Do not, holy brother, let the stab of pain feel sharper because she died at an early age. God's word offers consolation for this eventuality; 'If death comes early to the just man, he will live at rest' (Wis 4:7).

The same Wisdom in the words that follow proves to you that she was also old, so that she may not seem to you to have died before her time: 'Venerable old age is not that of long time, nor counted by the number of years. For the understanding of men is their gray hair, and a spotless life their old age' (Wis 4:8f.). So let us be thankful for her rightful summons, and her death at a ripe age. Though she was young in the bloom of years, she had grown gray in the purity of her manners, and she adorned a girl's youth with the meritorious service of age. So the very causes which inflame your heart's wound can bring a greater consolation, for though so holy a woman is not now with you, she has been with you in the past. The loss of a mortal woman you share with all, but few share with you the former possession of so excellent a wife. So I am not surprised that she did not linger in this world, but was summoned more quickly to Christ. For her soul pleased God, and so as scripture says, 'He hastened to bring her out of the midst of iniquities' (Wis 4:14). . . .

David in the loss of his two sons exemplified the mystery of this truth. He had wept for the son he loved when the boy was ill, but not when he was dead, for he was sure that the child had passed to the happiness of eternal peace. But he grieved for the dead Absalom, whom he had treated as an enemy, because as prophet he was aware of divine justice. He despaired of rest for the impious son, and he knew that the blessing of resurrection was not owed to one who killed his brother. As I have said, he wept for the first child during his illness, and changed his royal garb for black clothes, and prayed to God with the support of fasting, goathair and ashes. But when death brought an end to his son's sickness, he made the end of the boy's life the end of his own grief. So the father was delivered from sorrow as the son was delivered from his body. David laid aside his sad heart with his garments, took food, put on again his royal apparel, and cleansed his dust-begrimed hair with perfume. When his servants in astonishment queried his strange dispensation of paternal love, which grieved before bereavement and rejoiced after it, David answered: 'I shall go to him, but he shall not return to me' (2 Kings 12:23).

I think that the king-prophet has provided sufficient

instruction on the anxiety which we should feel when our
dear ones are gone. We are to concern ourselves with the
journey by which we follow, rather than with the arrival of
those who have preceded us. It is a loving act to be sad when
dear ones are torn from us, but a holy act to be joyful
through hope and trust in the promises of God, and to say to
our anxious soul: 'Why are you sad, my soul, and why do
you trouble me? Shall he that sleeps rise again no more?'(Ps
40:9).

The joy of gratitude is more acceptable to God than
prolonged and complaining grief. By this example of David
we learn not to shed superfluous tears. Tears bestowed on
the dead are especially vain; they do nothing for the one
whom God has taken, and they oppress the one left behind.
So David wept while his son lived, but was glad for him
when he was dead. While the boy breathed, the father could
by prayers and tears still obtain a respite from death, but
once the child had been summoned by God, it was David's
duty to be thankful, as indeed he was. We must not doubt
that God's will is better than our own wishes.

So let us discharge the duties of love without breaching
our faith, and exhibit the joys of faith without forsaking our
love. Doubtless our love may weep for a time, but our faith
must continue to rejoice. Let us long for our dear ones who
have gone before us, but let us not despair of getting them
back. For 'ours is the God of the living, and not of the dead'
(Matt 22:32). Paul says that the dead are sleeping in Christ;
you are to grasp from the word 'sleeping' that death is not
permanent. One who sleeps is later roused, and gets up. So
in our love for our dear ones, we should show the longing of
close attachment, but we should console ourselves by the
confidence in the resurrection which springs from our faith.

You must observe, then, dearest brother, the authority of
these heavenly words and examples, both in shedding tears
of love and in restraining them. Scripture says 'there is a
time for everything' (Eccl 3:1). The time for lamenting is
past, and now is the time for thankfulness. The Lord is at
hand. Divine scripture, which allows us to prolong our tears
to disperse our grief, also enjoins limits to them at the

prescribed time, when it says that 'bitterness of grief is to be borne for a single day' (Eccl 38:17). What riches God's goodness affords! With what loving care for us he makes this stipulation! He does not begrudge our headlong love, but he is aware of our weakness, and restrains any excesses. He bids us prolong our tears over the dead, but restricts our bitter weeping to a single day. He allows us to indulge the tears which relax our grief and renew the spirit; but he cuts short the sorrow which overcomes our minds with uncontrolled and irrational torture, and which our frailty cannot longer endure.

All this God in his love explains more fully in words of his own. To the last passage quoted, he adds: 'Comfort yourself at the proper time in your sadness, for out of sadness hastens death, and it will overwhelm your strength. Only the sorrow that God approves wins salvation'(Eccl 38:19). On the other hand, as Paul states, 'the sorrow of the flesh', which is of human dimensions and springs from weakness, 'brings death' (2 Cor 7:10). Though the two authors are different, the message of scripture speaks harmoniously through both holy men with the one spirit and word of God. True death lies in the overshadowing of our powers. Now Christ is 'the power of God' (1 Cor 1:24) and our life; you see the truth of the statement that death is hastened by the grief with which this power is overwhelmed. The whole man is, as Paul says, 'swallowed up with a sorrow too oppressive' (2 Cor 2:7) as if by a whirlpool of hell...

I shall turn now to proclaim your good works and devoted deeds, which were inspired by your holy tears. You performed what was due to both parts of your dear wife; you shed tears over her body, and lavished alms on her soul. As a son of light truly aware of the truth, you wept where you apprehended death, and you performed good works where you believe there is life. So upon the empty you bestow empty things, but on the living living things.

So it was that you, a rich man, gathered together a crowd of the poor, the patrons of our souls, those deserving of alms from the mass of Rome's impoverished. I feast on this splendid scene of your good works. I seem to see all those

devoted swarms of wretched folk, the wards of God's affection, pouring in great lines deep into the huge basilica of the
renowned Peter, through the venerable colonnade smiling
from afar with azure front, so that all the precincts are
thronged — inside the basilica, before the gates of the
entrance-hall, and the level area before the steps. I see the
gathering divided among the separate tables, and all filled
with abundance of good; before my eyes appears the plenty
bestowed by the blessing in the gospel, the picture of the
crowd which Christ, the true Bread and the Fish of living
water, filled with five loaves and two fishes."

35. Jerome

Jerome's correspondence contains many letters of consolation which are more uncompromising in tone than
that of the gentler Paulinus. Here Jerome writes to a
Dalmatian compatriot Julian, who has lost his family
and his property, presumably in the Gothic invasion
under Radagaesus in 406. Jerome deliberately evokes the
sufferings of Job throughout.

Letter 118[35]

"I hear that within a brief period you have lost two young
daughters, who have been buried one after the other; and
that Faustina, your most chaste and faithful wife, or rather
your sister in the ardor of her faith, your only solace after
the loss of your children, has been taken from you by sudden
death. Your experience is like that of the man who after
shipwreck encounters brigands on the shore; or as the
prophets put it, it is as if a man were fleeing from a bear and
met a lion, or if a man put his hand on the wall, only for the
snake to bite him (Amos 5:19). The loss of your property
followed the devastation of your whole province by the
barbarian enemy. In the general depredation, you suffered
the personal destruction of your possessions, the removal of
your cattle and sheep, the imprisonment and slaughter of

---

[35]Text: CSEL 55.434, ed. Hilberg

your poor slaves. Your remaining daughter, so much dearer to you through your numerous other bereavements, married a man of the highest nobility, but the choice has — I spare you the details — brought you more grief than joy. This is the list of your trials, these battles in which the ancient enemy wars on Julian, Christ's new soldier.

For you these are titanic struggles, but for a really courageous warrior they are mere sport and shadow-boxing. The blessed Job first endured his evil trials, and then found his most wicked wife kept in reserve to teach him how to blaspheme (Job 2:9). In your case the best of wives has been taken from you, so that you have lost your consolation in your wretchedness. It is one thing to bear with a wife unwillingly, another to miss the one you love. Job lost those children, and had his fallen house as his sole tomb; he tore his garments to show a father's feelings, and sank to the ground in adoration, saying: 'Naked I came from my mother's womb, and naked I will return. The Lord gave, and the Lord hath taken away. This has happened according to God's will. May the Lord's name be blessed.' But you (to put it succinctly) have buried your dear ones with the support of many relatives and the consolation of friends. Job lost all his wealth at one blow; as successive evil tidings struck him one by one, he remained unmoved, the embodiment of the sage's praise: 'If the world should break up and collapse, the debris will strike him unafraid' (Horace, *Odes* 3.3.7f.). But the greater part of your property has been preserved for you, so that you are able to endure the trials you bear. You have not yet reached the stage of encountering the foe with all his armed forces.

Job, who was previously a rich lord and a richer father, was suddenly left isolated and naked. But in all that befell him he had not sinned, or said anything stupid before God, so that God rejoiced in the victory of his servant, and accounted Job's patience as his own triumph. He said to the devil: 'Have you observed my servant Job? There is none like him on the earth. He is innocent, a true worshipper of God; he does no evil, and continues to abide in innocence.' (These last words are splendid, for it is hard for innocence when oppressed by evils not to show resentment, not to feel our faith threatened when we see ourselves suffering unjustly.) The devil replied to the Lord's words, and said: 'Skin for skin; all that a man has he will give for his life. Stretch out your hand, touch his bones and flesh, and then see if he will bless you to your face.' That craftiest of adversaries, that veteran of evil days knows that there are things which are 'externals', things which the secular philosophers call 'indifferent', loss of or contempt for which does not constitute perfect virtue. But there are other things, 'internal' things which come from within, and force him who loses them to grieve. This was why the devil boldly denied God's proclamation about Job, and said that Job was being vainly praised, since he had given nothing of himself but merely external things. In place of his own skin he offered that of his sons; he surrendered his purse, but retained his bodily wealth.

In your wisdom you realise that your trials are bounded by this same line, that you have given skin for skin and hide for hide; that you are ready to give everything for your life, and that God's hand has not yet been extended over you, that your flesh has not been touched nor your bones broken; these are pains at which it is hard not to groan or to 'bless' God to his face ('bless' here means 'curse', which is why in the Book of Kings [1 Kings 9] Naboth is said to have 'blessed' God and the king and to have been stoned for it by the people.) But God knew that the enemy could not overcome his athlete, his most courageous hero, in this supreme and decisive combat, so he said: 'See, I give him to you, but you must guard his life.' The flesh of the holy man was consigned to the devil's power, but the health of his soul was maintained. Indeed, if the devil had smitten the region of his feeling and mental judgment, any fault would have been not the transgressor's but his who had upset the balance of his mind.

Others must praise you and hymn your victories over the devil, because you have borne your daughters' death with serenity, because forty days after their passing you exchanged your mourning garments for white ones, in order

to dedicate the martyr's bones. You did not feel the grief of
bereavement which the entire city felt. Instead you celebrated the triumph of the martyr, for you escorted your
most holy wife regarding her not as a corpse but as one
setting out on a journey. I shall not beguile you with flattery,
nor trick you with deceitful praise; instead I will tell you
what it is right for you to hear: 'My son, when you enter
God's service, prepare your soul for a trial' (Eccl 2:1); and
'When you have done all your tasks, say "I am a useless
servant; I have done no more than I should have done (Luke
17:10); you have removed the children which you gave me.
You have taken back the handmaid whom you lent me as a
short-lived consolation. I am not resentful that you have
taken her back, but thankful that you gave her to me.'"

THE ADVANTAGES OF SUFFERING

36. *Peter of Blois*

It is striking that nowhere in the Fathers do we find any
lengthy or systematic theology of suffering. Their attitude is clear-cut: the pains of this world are to be borne in
serene anticipation of future joys. The first extended
treatment of suffering appears amongst the writings of
the twelfth-century scholastic Peter of Blois. Peter, a
former pupil of John of Salisbury, became successively
archdeacon of Bath and secretary to Queen Eleanor. He
composed a partial commentary on *The Book of Job* as
well as this somewhat scholastic treatise.

Twelve Advantages of Tribulation[36]

"The first advantage which tribulation brings lies in the
fact that it is *the Lord's faithful assistance to deliver the soul
from the hands of all its enemies.* These enemies are false
joys and deceitful prosperity in this world; they seduce the
unschooled heart the more hazardously as they fawn on it

[36]Text: PL 207.989

ingratiatingly. These are the enemies of whom the common proverb says: 'The fool does not fear them'. The more seductive their enticements and ultimate deceits, the more they are to be feared. They are the foes who kill with kindness, and fawn on us as they kill. Joab is a type of them; he held Amasa by the chin as if to kiss him, and then killed him (cf. 2 Kings 20). So Gregory says: 'All fortune is to be feared, but good fortune more than ill-fortune.' This becomes clear because the foe who wars on us secretly is more to be feared than he who attacks us openly.

Note that God does not merely dispatch the succour of this tribulation; he is the leader and marshal of the array, ordering it for the liberation of his friends. So God promises through the prophet David: 'I am with him in tribulation', that is, he is sorely tried and tested. Next comes: 'I shall deliver and glorify him' (Ps 90:15). So since God is with us in our tribulation, we must endure it patiently and gladly, for God draws nearer to the oppressed according as the tribulation grows heavier. So the Psalmist says: 'The Lord is close to those who are troubled at heart' (Ps 33:19). So whilst the presence of tribulation oppresses you, the presence of the Saviour who stands with you in tribulation affords you inner consolation.

Your reply may be: 'I feel my immediate tribulations, but not the companionship of God in my suffering. If he showed the sweetness of his presence as clearly as the bitterness of the tribulation, I would endure my trials patiently and cheerfully.' Perhaps you add that you experienced the sweetness of God more before your tribulation than when you were plunged into it. One can answer this by saying that the presence of God in tribulation can be marked or understood in two ways, as is clear: first, in the bestowal of virtue and grace, for God multiplies virtue and grace proportionately to the increase in tribulation. As Paul says: 'God is faithful. He will not allow you to be tried beyond your strength, but with the temptation will also provide the way of escape, that you may be able to endure it' (1 Cor 10:13). In other words he will give you increase of grace and virtue to enable you to endure your tribulation patiently. Just as lords are wont to send provisions and reinforcements into castles under siege, so God's practice is to pour increase of grace into the oppressed soul. Secondly, the presence of God in tribulation can be marked or understood by the bestowal of inner consolation which he pours into the afflicted one. So Paul says: 'As Christ's sufferings abound in us, so consolations abound through Christ' (2 Cor 1:5).... From all this we can conclude that the afflicted soul must not consider itself under attack when it suffers tribulations, but as freed and delivered from the deceit of worldly prosperity and the desolation of the flesh's comforts. So since tribulations deliver the soul from its enemies, they must though sometimes burdensome be endured gladly and without grumbling for the Lord's sake. If a person inveighs against his tribulations by grumbling, he is attacking his supporters and aiding his enemies.

The second advantage of tribulation is that *it shuts the devil's mouth*, preventing him from daring to address and tempt the soul which is afflicted. He fears to be rejected and overcome. This is foreshadowed in the Book of Job, where we read: 'None spoke a word to him, for they saw that his grief was fierce.' Scripture speaks there of the feigning friends of Job (they represent the demons warring on the soul) who dare not approach the oppressed soul when they behold its grace in tribulation, for they fear to be overcome by such a soul. Note that the devil's temptation is not dangerous or harmful to a man unless there is a positive response of pleasure and assent.

The third advantage of tribulation is that *it purges the afflicted soul*. In this connection we must realise that there are five categories of material purging: first, purging of the human body by the twin methods of potions and bleeding; second, of metals, for example gold is cleansed by fire and iron by filing; third, of trees by breaking off branches or digging out suckers; fourth, of grain by means of the threshing-flail; fifth, of grapes or wine by the wine-press. Tribulation purges in all these ways. First, the purging of the body by potions; when tribulation lays hold of you, think of it as a medicine sent to you by the Lord to cleanse you of excessive humors and uncontrolled emotions. Just as bad humors are purged by a bitter potion, so the soul's evil ways are purged by tribulations. As Gregory says, 'Evil manners are bad humors'. So humbly take the medicine sent to you by the Lord, for he is the supreme Physician who knows the innermost condition of your heart; he is aware how much you can endure, and will give you nothing except what is useful to you. The son of God imbibed the tribulation of death for your salvation and purgation rather than for his own. So scripture says: 'Drink, my friends, and become inebriated, dearest ones' (Cant 5:1). The sons of Zebedee were asked: 'Can you drink the cup which I shall drink?' (Matt 20:22); this is the cup of salvation which the Lord took as he gave thanks, saying: 'I shall take the cup of salvation' (Ps 115:13). If it seems difficult for you to swallow because of its bitterness, summon the Lord to help you, as David says in the verse that follows: 'And I shall call upon the name of the Lord.' Note too that just as bodily medicine should not be tasted or held for long on the tongue but quickly swallowed, so tribulation ought not to be held back rebelliously. Just as the effect of a medicine is sometimes hindered not by its inadequacy but by the perverse attitude of the recipient, so the effect of tribulation is hindered by the wrong disposition of a hard heart and a spirit rebellious in its obstinacy. The Pharaoh is a clear example, for the more afflicted he was the harder his heart became (cf. Exod 10); likewise Solomon says 'It will go hard with an obstinate heart in the final days' (Eccl 3:27).

Secondly the human body is purged by bleeding, either by opening a vein or by blood-letting. Opening a vein is like confession; blood-letting is like tribulation. Observe that just as superfluous blood harms the veins and blood-vessels, so sin (which scripture calls 'blood') corrupts and stains the soul. The 'vein' through which the blood which is sin is extracted is the mouth; we read in *Proverbs*: 'The just man's mouth is the life's vein' (10:31), for the just man is first and foremost his own accuser in confession. Observe that just as in bleeding a man must expel his bad blood and keep the good to nurture his heart, so in confession a man must tell his sins so that they may be cast out, and leave unsaid the good things which he has done so that they may not be lost; for when good deeds are mentioned in confession they are lost through boasting and vainglory. The Pharisee who in boasting recited his good deeds makes this clear: 'I fast twice a week, I give tithes of all that I possess. But the tax-collector did not dare raise his eyes to heaven but beat his breast, saying 'O God, be merciful to me a sinner' (Luke 18:12f.). What follows is that the tax-collector went down to his house justified by his humble confession, as distinct from the Pharisee, who because of his boasting remained fast in his sins; for sins revealed in true and humble confession are expunged. So the Psalmist says: 'I have stated: I will confess my injustice before the Lord to my own despite, and you have forgiven the impiety of my sin' (Ps 31:5).

Blood-letting is like tribulation. All the tribulations which God imposes on the heart are so many blood-lettings to purge it. Observe that just as before the purging by blood-letting it is necessary to warm the flesh so that the blows may be endured more easily, so the human heart must be inflamed by the fire of charity so that it can bear tribulations easily. So Augustine says: 'Love makes all harsh and monstrous things easy and virtually non-existent.' The holy Spirit descended on the apostles in tongues of fire to foreshadow this. As a result they were strengthened by God, and after receiving him 'they passed rejoicing from the sight of the council, since they were accounted worthy to endure insult for Christ's name' (Acts 5:41), though before receiving him they were exceedingly fearful. Peter was a clear case of this. He denied the Lord when a single maid servant challenged him, but after receiving the Spirit he gladly bore the suffering of the holy cross for the Lord's sake.

The second type of purgation is that which purifies metals, like gold with fire and iron with the file. So first tribulation purges the soul and purifies it as fire does gold. So Augustine says: 'As the flail acts on grain and fire on gold, so tribulation acts on the just man.' In other words, as fire separates gold from other metals and cleanses it of dross, so tribulation purifies the soul. Hence *Wisdom* describes martyrs: 'He tried them like gold in the furnace' (Wis 3:6). Job was tested with this fire of tribulation when he said: 'He has put me to the test, like gold which passes through fire' (Job 23:10). Observe that there is no metal more precious than gold, and none cheaper than lead, but gold is not tested without lead, for in the furnace the lead draws dregs of gold along with it. Good men, signified by the gold, are often cleansed by means of the wicked, denoted by the lead. So if one asks in what way the wicked serve the good, the reply can be: as lead serves gold. So Solomon says: 'The fool will serve the wise' (Prov 11:29), namely by purifying him. This was how Esau served Jacob, by victimising him. Scripture says of him: 'The greater will serve the lesser' (Gen 25:23).

Secondly, tribulation purges the soul as the file cleans iron, by scraping and polishing it. A sword which never leaves the scabbard and a knife which never cuts gather rust, and in the same way the human heart without being exercised by tribulation gathers spiritual rust. Jeremiah says: 'Moab has been at ease from his youth, and has settled on his lees' (Jer 48:11). So do not complain if God scrapes your heart with the file so that it may gleam and shine and be splendid, for otherwise you will not be able to behold God. In Matthew's words, 'Blessed are the pure of heart for they shall see God' (5:8).

The third mode of purging appropriate to tribulation is the pruning of trees; for example, the vine is pruned of its superfluous branches. Christ says of this: 'Every branch of mine that bears no fruit he will prune, and every branch that does bear fruit he prunes that it may bear more fruit' (John 15:2). By the vine we understand the human heart, and the sap which makes it fruitful is love. The degree of love determines the amount of sap; the more sap is diverted along superfluous branches of the vine or any other tree, the less the vine bears fruit. In the same way the more the heart's love is dispersed among companions of the flesh and temporal things, the less fitted is the heart to bear spiritual fruit. If a wise gardener prunes and cuts back the superfluous branches of a vine or another tree so that it may bear more fruit, it is not surprising that God, the cultivator of the human heart — as John has it, 'My Father is the vinedresser' (John 15:1) — cuts back from your heart the superfluous love for parents and boon-companions with the hoe of death which he holds in his hand, and the love of temporal goods, so that the love and longing of your heart may not go beyond due bounds. The Lord himself says: 'Those whom I love, I reprove and chasten' (Rev 3:19). And the apostle says: 'He chastises every son whom he receives' (Heb 12:6). God does all this so that the love of your heart may not be separated from him and be squandered on temporal things, where you stand to lose a great deal, obtaining no good but an evil end. As Gregory says, 'If you lean on the unsteady, you inevitably collapse with it.'

The fourth kind of purging appropriate to tribulation is the purging of grain by the flail so that the grain emerges separated from the chaff. So Augustine says, 'As the flail purifies grain...' as we quoted earlier. Just as the flail forces the grain from the chaff, so tribulation forces the human heart to be separated from merely human love, for the world is displeasing to a troubled heart. So David, aware of the profitability of the flail of tribulation, said, 'See how I was schooled by the flail to endure, that my heart be cleansed' (Ps 37:18). So Augustine says: 'Do not complain of the flail of tribulation if you wish to have bread fit for adults, and you are desirous of a place in heaven where only unsullied grain will be stored.' But sometimes it happens that the grain is unripe and not dried out, and it is not dislodged from the chaff by the blow of the flail, but clings to it; and in the same way the heart which is damp with affection for the flesh is not separated from the world by the flail of tribulation, but instead clings fast to it in love and delight, but from it obtains only torture and toil. 'Man is born for toil, and birds for flying' (Job 5:7). As scripture says, 'Do not love the world or the things in it. If anyone loves the world, the love of the Father is not in him' (1 John 2:15).

The fifth type of purging appropriate to tribulation is the cleansing of wine in the press. Just as the press squeezes the grapes so that the precious juice can be separated from the sediment, so God puts the soul in the press of tribulation to cleanse it of the dregs of evil affections and sins by bodily sickness, or persecution, or grief at the death of friends, or loss of temporal possessions. So do not reject the press of tribulation if you wish to be stored in Christ's cellar; in the words of scripture, 'The king has set me in his wine-cellar' (Cant 1:4). So Augustine says that martyrs in this life are squeezed in such a way that the gross matter of their bodies remained in the press, while their precious souls like the precious wine were stored in the cellar of eternal life. So do not complain if God sets you in the press of tribulation, for he himself earlier trod the press underfoot; as scripture has it, 'I alone have ground the press with my heel, and from the peoples no man was with me' (Isa 63:3). He says 'no man' here and not 'no woman', because at his passion all the apostles abandoned him and fled, but the blessed virgin Mary did not forsake him unfaithfully, but shared his suffering with compassion. This was why Simeon had made that promise to her: 'And your own soul a sword shall pierce' (Luke 2:35).

The fourth advantage of tribulation is that *it enlightens a person's heart with self-knowledge*, in which the perfection of the human condition consists. So Augustine, who had read and listened to so much, sought nothing further. He says in his *Book of Soliloquies*: 'Let me know thee.' In Wisdom we read: 'To know yourself is perfect understanding' (6:15). We observe that a blow of the cane forces a pupil to put his head down, to scrutinise the book afresh, and to repeat what he has read. In the same way, tribulation is sent to you by the Lord that through its intervention you may learn to acknowledge your Creator. So the blessed Bernard says: 'God made himself known by caning the one who had forgotten him; as long as he spared him, he remained unknown to him.' We have an example of this in the proud king Nebuchadnezzar, whom God expelled from his kingdom and made to dwell with wild animals and beasts so that 'he ate grass like an ox, but at the end of his days'(that is, of his tribulation and repentance) he 'lifted his eyes to heaven, and his understanding was restored to him' (Dan 4:33-34).

The one who raises his eyes to heaven is he who guides his understanding towards the Creator. By this raising of his eyes understanding was restored to him who had lost it by his descent to lower things. So Nebuchadnezzar before his tribulation had closed his eyes to the Creator by training his gaze on earthly things; but after it he raised his eyes to heaven, where he who had caned him was, for God wishes those in tribulation to turn their faces to him.

So realise, O soul, that it is the custom of lovers to send letters to each other, and to remind each other of the welcome and reciprocated kindnesses shown to each other, and to fear that these may be forgotten. This is why your lover Jesus Christ has visited tribulation on you; perhaps he had been wholly forgotten whilst you lived in prosperity, just as the steward of the Pharaoh when he prospered forgot about Joseph who had interpreted his dream (cf. Gen 40:23). Realise, then, that Jesus has kept the scars of his wounds which he endured for you as keepsakes, just as a knot is put in a shoelace as a reminder of something. So Christ himself says: 'I shall not forget you; I have graven you on the palms of my hands' (Isa 49:16), that is, 'when I was stretched on the cross for love of you'. So if Christ has kept the scars of his wounds as keepsakes, do not be angry if he sends tribulations on you to make you mindful of him. The more tribulations you have, the more messages he is sending you to call you back to remembrance of him. So do not reject these good counsellors, for the proverb has it that a good counsellor wields great power in the state.

But you could say that tribulations are unnecessary to induce this remembrance of him, for God by conferring benefits gives us sufficient warning, as Augustine says, that God's kindnesses are nothing other than reminders that we should proceed to him. So it should be enough for God to convey warnings by conferring kindnesses, for such warnings befit God more than those delivered with canings. To this a possible reply is that though kindnesses recall you to acknowledge him, on occasion an uncontrolled love for those very kindnesses holds us fast, and the Creator, the highest unchangeable God who bestows eternal blessings, is then forgotten. So God complains about such people with the words 'I stretched out my hands' (he means in granting kindnesses) 'and there was none to behold me' (Prov 1:24). He does not say that there was none to accept, because many gladly accept, but few look back in gratitude; from greater to lesser all love the gifts, and retributions follow.

But you might say that though it is appropriate that God should by tribulations recall hard and undisciplined hearts which do not turn to him because of his kindnesses, it is not fitting that God should call back in this way good men who acknowledge their Creator through his kindnesses. To this one can say that though the good heart acknowledges its Provider through natural pleasure at his kindnesses, it will not attain perfect knowledge of God without tribulation to test it. As scripture says, 'What things does a man untried know? But he who is tried in many things understands many things' (Eccl 34:9f.). But note that God called Solomon back to knowledge of him by bestowing gifts, whereas Job he called back by bestowing his kindnesses and then imposing misfortunes. But those tribulations led him to perfection, whereas the gifts led Solomon to stupidity and destruction. So if Solomon who was endowed with such knowledge lost his awareness of God in time of prosperity through the things that enticed him, do not be sure that you can keep God in mind for long in such prosperity. So endure tribulation patiently and gladly so that you can attain knowledge of God. And if you are disheartened by great tribulation, seek consolation in the fact that greater tribulation causes you to win a greater crown.

Now that I have explained how tribulations call the heart back to the knowledge of the Creator, we must now explain how they call it back to knowledge of itself. The heart which has been distanced from itself by worldly joys cannot identify itself. So David as the spokesman of such people says: 'And the light of my eyes, it also has gone from me' (Ps 37:10). Woe to him who has expended the lamp of his knowledge on outward things, and keeps none of it for knowledge of himself! How could he recognise himself when he does not keep himself company? Worldly prosperity removes the soul from his company, insofar as he pursues and loves that prosperity. But when besieged or smitten by the violence of enemies he is forced to return to himself, and the more hardships he bears the better the avenues affording a return. So the adversity which restores you and makes you return to your own lodging is a happy adversity. So we read in Exodus: 'Let each man remain in his own company' (16:29). In other words, let each man know himself and not abandon himself through uncontrolled love. The house in which no-one dwells is soon destroyed, and similarly the heart which ceases to be a virtuous residence is plundered and levelled. Woe to the heart which like a jester gulps down random and despicable scraps, and the more it sings in another's lodging, the more it finds to lament in its own! So the more the heart takes pleasure in worldly things, the less consolation it finds in itself.

So tribulation is imposed on the heart to force it back upon itself from worldly joys, just as the jester is finally compelled to return to his own house and remain there, and like the dove which could find nowhere to rest its foot and returned to Noah in the ark. Noah is a type of Christ; his ark signifies repose of the mind. When the human heart finds no external place where its love can take rest, it returns to itself. The dove's foot signifies the heart's love. The dove cannot find a place to rest its foot when the human heart ceases to place its love in any earthly thing and returns to itself, saying with the Psalmist: 'Turn, my soul, to your rest' (Ps 114:7). Then too in the *Song of Songs* the Lord says to the sinning soul which allowed its heart to wander amongst worldly things: 'Return, return, O Shulammite, that we may look on you' (Cant 6:13), that is, 'both you and I, that you may behold yourself with the eye of conscience, and I may behold you with the eye of mercy'. Christian soul, through your tribulations endure so that you may return to yourself and to God, for worldly prosperity has distanced you from both; especially as tribulations bind and draw you close to your Creator after the depraved license of the world had detached you and made you fly away in arrogance.

So Job, who had experienced such misfortunes, said, 'If I

am armed with the goad of poverty, it will reveal their works to them' (36:8). Observe that by poverty here he means not lack of temporal things but the absence of temporal consolation consisting of temporal riches. So his situation is that described in Ecclesiasticus: he is poor since he is without resources amongst many. All tribulations are called goads of poverty; they are sent by God to detach the heart from the consolations of the world. These are the goads or cords of our first parent Adam, which are ours by right of inheritance, and by which God draws many to him as if by force. We read in Hosea on this: 'By the cords of Adam'(that is, by tribulations) 'I shall draw you with the bonds of love'(11:4). In other words, they have been sent out of love. So Bernard says: 'We are drawn to God when we are schooled by tribulations.' So do not think, you soul drawn tight by bonds, that you are a prisoner, and that those not enmeshed are truly free when they are allowed all that they seek. You would not regard a sick person as in good health or as having good hopes of recovery, if the doctor allowed him everything that he asked for because he despaired of his condition and said 'Let him eat whatever he wants'. That is the most clear-cut sign of impending death.

So it is clear that freedom in the world is nothing but a proof and mark of dying. So the greater the freedom with which wretched men attain what they wish without tribulation, the more quickly they go down to hell. So if you want God to be merciful to you, endure constriction by the bonds of tribulation, for they come from God and they draw you to God. This is why the Lord says to Ezechiel: 'See, I have placed my cords on you' (Ez 3:25). This allows us to realise that the bonds of tribulation are gifts of God. Our discussion makes it clear that tribulations are bonds which bind the soul to Christ, and the harsher the tribulation, the more closely it binds the soul to God.

The fifth advantage of tribulation is that *it hastens your journey to God.* Each of the tribulations you bear is a message sent you by God bidding you hasten to him and not linger on the way. Observe how debased are the considerations which make the degenerate soul reluctant to hasten to

God. Tribulation removes the delight and pleasure in transient things which prevent men hastening to God; so Gregory says: 'The evils which oppress us here force us to go to God.' So do not underestimate the benefit of tribulation, which frees you from an oppressive prison and hastens your journey to the kingdom of heaven; as Ecclesiastes has it, 'A man is brought into the kingdom from prison and chains' (4:14). By 'prison' is signified whatever the heart loves without due measure in the world, and the chains with which he is fastened are debased affections. The greater the love, the deeper the prison. God leads you out of this prison by tribulation when he deprives you of something you love or will come to love beyond due measure, or he makes that thing your enemy. This was revealed in scripture. Peter was being guarded in Herod's prison, and then the angel of the Lord stood by him and smote Peter on the side, and roused him with the words 'Rise up quickly' (Acts 12:7). 'Side' here means your brother, who came out of the same side as you did, or in general all those joined to you by blood or by marriage. So when the person who ought by natural right to be your friend is opposed to you or removed by death, realise that you are being smitten on the side to leave prison and to set your heart on God alone, who cannot fail you.

Observe that Peter does not complain about the blow on his side by which he was freed from prison, and in the same way you must not complain about tribulation, which heals and frees you from an evil or false love of the world. If the blow of tribulation is difficult for you to endure, think of Christ who was wounded in the side for you, and then you will bear it more easily. In the same way a good soldier who observes his lord's wounds no longer feels his own. So do not reject the Lord's messages which recall you and make you hasten to him, for the one who rejects the messages rejects the Lord. The message is rejected when the heart through lack of patience opposes the tribulation. Observe that tribulation does two things: it afflicts the soul by purging, and it purges it by affliction. But when the heart rebels under tribulation, it is not purged by the affliction of that tribulation. Such a person sustains the bitterness of tribulation and squanders its usefulness; yet like it or not he must endure it.

The sixth advantage of tribulation is that *it is imposed to pay the debts which you owe to God*, which you cannot escape and which you cannot reduce or conceal. These debts are the punishment owed for the sins which you have committed. Though eternal punishment is due for mortal sins, that eternal punishment is by contrition and confession commuted to temporal punishment; and this temporal punishment is lessened by fasting and by tribulations. Sometimes it is wholly removed, especially by tribulations. So whatever you endure for God is counted by him as payment of your debts. A king's steward when rendering account of his lord's receipts calculates those receipts with lead or copper pence, and sometimes at the end of his reckoning one copper or lead coin, in itself of little value, stands for a hundred gold or silver marks. Similarly the tribulation of a single hour when endured with patience at the present time frees us from the tribulation of hell which is most oppressive and eternal. We have an example in the thief who was strung up on Christ's right hand. When he was enduring the torment of the cross for his wicked deeds and was liable to the further punishment of hell, he showed contrition for his misdemeanours at that hour, and turned to the Lord with the words 'Remember me when you pass into your kingdom'. At once he was forgiven every sin and freed from every debt, for he deserved to hear the sweetest of utterances: 'Amen I say to you, this day you will be with me in Paradise' (Luke 23:43).

Woe to him who pays none of his debt in this life, but heaps sin on sin; as the psalm says of him: 'The sinner will borrow, but will not discharge his debt' (Ps 36:21). Woe to him who is compelled to make the justest reckoning for his abundant and wasteful outlay! Such a person has always lived without a reckoning, and he deserves to pay the penalty perpetually in hell without remission of any of his debt. Then will many traders weep who now laugh and rejoice at the range of their temporal consolations; and this is indicated in the Apocalypse with the words 'The merchants of the earth will weep' (18:11). 'Merchants of the earth' signify those who have set their thoughts and affections on earthly things. They will lament those affections because God reveals their wicked merchandise to all. But the heavenly merchants will smile when they see that they have gained the glory of Paradise in return for modest tribulation. This is revealed by the words of scripture, 'A man gains much in return for a modest price' (Eccl 20:12). This modest price is the endurance of the tribulation of this life, which God accepts as payment for a great debt. As the common proverb has it, 'One gets hay or oats from the bad debtor'. If it happens that you owe no debt for mortal or venial sins from which tribulation could free you, it still guards you against incurring or committing any sin; as Gregory has it, 'Many are the innocent ones who would quickly have lost their innocence if tribulations had not saved them'. So if a soul feels that it is in debt, or fears having to make future payment, it must endure patiently the tribulation of this world while it has time to pay the debts owed to God. All the tribulations of this life are as nothing compared with the tribulation of a single hour in the next world. Likewise if all the tribulations of the world were placed together, they would not be sufficient to win the glory of Paradise. As Paul says, 'The sufferings of this time do not suffice for the future glory which will be revealed to us' (Rom 8:18).

The seventh advantage of tribulation is that *it enlarges the human heart to obtain glory and the grace of God*. Just as the mallet of the goldsmith by repeated blows flattens gold or silver to make a precious vessel, so God the Maker of the whole creation dispenses tribulation to enlarge the heart, to store there the gifts of grace. The Psalmist says of the tribulation: 'By tribulation you have enlarged my heart' (Ps 4:2). So endure the blows of this tribulation, for the more your heart is enlarged by greater endurance, the more numerous will be the spiritual gifts which the Lord will store in you. Reflect that the more precious a metal is, the more malleable and obedient to the hammer's blows; likewise the heart that is precious and meek shows greater patience in tribulation. Though the blows of the hammer, which is tribulation, sorely afflict you, console youself with the thought that it is God the Goldsmith who wields the hammer of tribulation, and he is well-skilled at controlling his blows according to the capacity of the metal to endure them. So do not be like shapeless metal unflattened; such are the hard and unschooled hearts, in which tribulation or discipline finds no place. Again, do not be like an old cauldron which is so ancient that it cracks under a blow, and in place of one long-standing crack sustains many new ones; this is how the hard, impatient heart sustains further loss in tribulation. So endure cheerfully the tribulation that enlarges your heart. The Sage urges you to do this with the words 'Endure the trials which God sends by joining yourself to God; endure, that your life at the end may be enhanced' (Eccl 2:3). In other words, endure patiently and gladly the tribulations of this world for God, who has endured many things for you; reciprocate this service. 'Be joined to God, and endure,' that is, ally yourself to God, endure whatever he lays upon you, and know that he will not burden you beyond your capacity. So Paul says: 'God is faithful. He does not allow you to be tried beyond your capacity to bear' (1 Cor 10:13). So cheerfully endure in the ways I have outlined, so that your life at the end may be enhanced, for by this means you will live forever in glory.

The eighth advantage of tribulation is that *God by depriving us of the earthly consolations below forces us to seek the heavenly consolations above*. Just as a lord on earth who wishes to sell his wine forbids anyone to open an inn until he has sold his wine, so God sometimes debars earthly consolations to bestow the heavenly ones which are his. This is indicated in Joel in these words: 'The beasts of the field looked up to thee like a parched enclosure, because the streams of water had run dry' (1:20). He calls the affections and desires of the flesh 'beasts of the field', and worldly consolations 'streams of water'. So when the streams of water run dry — in other words, when in times of adversity worldly consolations fail — the heart is then compelled to look heavenward and to seek the Dispenser of heavenly rewards and consolations. Then the Lord shows greater kindness of heart corresponding with the degree of bitterness which the heart experiences in externals. But you may say: 'I am not resentful because the inn of worldly consolations is not open to me, but because the inn of heavenly consolations is closed to me, for I find consolation neither below nor above.' The answer to this is that you will not obtain heavenly consolations merely because earthly consolations are forbidden you; you must first return to your own heart by longing for and seeking God and the things above. This is what God wants, for greater merit consists in longing for and seeking the Lord than in taking one's whole delight in him and for his sake. Likewise the more eagerly you long for and seek him, the greater will be the consolation bestowed on you, and the greater the sweetness you will find in it, just as a hungry person finds something tastes better than does one who is not hungry. And you will know that if earthly consolations are denied to you by tribulation, heavenly consolations will not be long postponed if you beg and seek them eagerly, even if they appear to be postponed. As Solomon has it, 'He will give the just man his desire' (Prov 10:19).

The ninth advantage of tribulation is that *it makes God remember you*, for through tribulation he recalls you to mind. The greater the tribulation the more you are impressed on his memory. This is not because God, who sees all things, forgets anyone, but because scripture says that God forgets the man to whom he does not lend succour by showing him spiritual consolation when he is in tribulation, and by increase of grace. So if a soul wishes to make God remember it (and this is the means of its salvation, whereas if he forgets it, it is damned) it must learn to bear adversity patiently, and by this endurance ponder inwardly on God. Then God in his turn will think about you, as a friend thinks more frequently about a troubled friend than about an untroubled one. So if, O soul, you feel that you are abandoned in tribulation, console yourself that this very tribulation makes God remember you, and God's remembrance is worth more to you than all that tribulation could take from

you. The Lord foreshadowed this when he said: 'I saw the
affliction of my people in Egypt, and came down to free
them from the hands of the Egyptians' (Exod 3:7-8). Two
points are to be considered in these words. First, that God
looks on his afflicted people with a merciful eye; and second,
that by affliction God restores his covenant which he made
with his afflicted people. The gaze of the Lord brings a
special gift by which God himself condescends to take pity
on his afflicted friend. So though the persecuting Egyptians
afflict you, take consolation in the fact that God's eyes upon
you have great power in your affliction. So scripture tells us
that David fled from the presence of his son Absalom, and
when Shimei saw this he cursed him with the words:
'Depart, man of blood and man of Belial. . .'. Abishai upon
seeing this said to the king: 'Why does this dog curse the lord
my king? I will go and cut off his head.' David replied: 'Let
him go that he may curse me, fulfilling the word of the Lord:
If perchance he may gaze on my affliction, and render good
to me for this curse of today' (2 Sam 16:5ff.).

In this matter reflect that David wished to bear the male-
diction of his foe so that he could have the blessing of God.
So the more you long for God's blessing, the more patiently
you should endure the curse of your enemy, for the enduring
of the cursing of evil men provokes God's blessing and
brings forth freedom out of evil. This was indicated in
Daniel, where it says that the angel of the Lord descended
with Meshach and his companions into the furnace, and he
made the centre of the furnace like the breath of a moist
wind, and the flame was blown out upon the king's servants
who were tending the fire (3:19ff.). Note that not only did he
dislodge the unrighteous flames of the furnace; he also
provided a cool place for the boys. From this we realise that
God attends the afflicted person. So if you wish to be
granted refreshment in tribulation, and if you wish to have
your enemies burnt when they are causing you tribulations,
then endure those sufferings patiently, for God is with you in
your privations and will deliver you from them, and will
bestow great merit on you because of them. These three
aspects are mentioned in a psalm: 'I am with him in his

tribulation' (the comradeship of God), 'I will rescue him' (the deliverance), 'And I will glorify him' (the reward) (Ps 90:33ff.). So tribulation makes God remember you, and this bestows on you more than tribulation can remove.

The tenth advantage of tribulation is that *it causes your prayers to be heard and offered before God.* He does not make a habit of rejecting the prayer which an afflicted person makes before him, but he listens to it. So Solomon says: 'The Lord will listen to the entreaty of the wounded' (Eccl 35:16). God whips men, and inflicts tribulations on them repeatedly to force them to ask for mercy, to open their lips to entreat him in tribulation because they kept them closed in time of good fortune. So Augustine says: 'God visits certain people with tribulations so that they may be roused by them to seek from God what he wishes to bestow on them.' The psalmist acts as the spokesman of such persons. 'When I was in tribulation, I cried to the Lord, and he heard me, (Ps 119:1). If it chances that you call on God when in good fortune, so that prosperity does not put you entirely to sleep, it none the less sometimes makes you sleepy, and your cry in time of good fortune is not so effective as that in misfortune. If your ill-fortune so lays hold of your heart that it does not concentrate on prayer as much in adversity as it did in prosperity, your evil plight will still make your prayer more precious. But if tribulation so affects you that you cannot open your mouth to cry out to the Lord, your affliction still does the praying for you as long as you have patience. Master Peter Lombard says of Lazarus that he had as many mouths beseeching the Lord as he had wounds, for when Lazarus was silent his wounds cried out for him. It was in this sense that the Lord spoke to Cain about his brother Abel whom he slew: 'The voice of your brother's blood cries out to me from the earth' (Gen 4:10).

So clearly tribulation makes prayer more precious and acceptable, for tribulations are so to say the payment for liberation instead of papers of freedom. So Job says: 'Who will grant that my request may come, and that God may give me what I look for? And that he that hath begun may destroy me, that he may loose his hand and cut me off? And that this may be my comfort, that afflicting me with sorrow he spare not?' (Job 6:8-10). Observe that Job, who had lost his possessions and his sons and daughters, was smitten with the worst of wounds extending from the soles of his feet to his head; he was also oppressed by friends and reviled by his wife. Yet he thought that God did not afflict him enough, and he sought consolation only in the fact that God did not spare him. If you ask how this is germane to being freed of his affliction, the reply can be that his affliction is his official discharge, as when a poor man who drinks wine in a tavern and has no money to pay his bill asks to be whipped and put out. But if you ask wherein lay Job's consolation when he begged to be afflicted, one answer is that God refrains from sparing some people in this life so that he can spare them in the next. Job's consolation lay in his knowledge that through his immediate tribulation he would escape future affliction. So have the consolation of knowing that if you are afflicted here and endure it patiently, God will spare you in the future. Scripture says that God will not pass judgment on the same sin twice (Nahum 1:12). So Job, who entreated that God should not spare him in this life, asks in another place that God spare him in the future; 'Spare me, for my days are nothing' (Job 7:16). So endure tribulation in this life that God may spare you in the next, for tribulation cleanses the soul. In Job's words, 'He wounds and heals' (Job 5:18); he wounds the body by unleashing tribulation, but heals the soul.

The eleventh advantage of tribulation is that *it guards and nourishes the heart*. As a fire is guarded and nourished in its ashes, so the heart of the friend of God is guarded in tribulation. This was why God commanded that the tabernacle be shrouded with covers of haircloth (cf. Exod 26:7). Haircloth covers were used to protect precious cups and gold and silver vessels against wind and rain; and the meaning of this is that in the hardships of tribulation the previous virtues of holy men, and especially humility, are preserved. Tribulation forces a man to be humbled when perhaps human success gives him too much fortune beyond the limits of his weakness. Tribulation feeds the heart as a

wetnurse feeds a child. Just as a mother chews the food
which the child cannot digest, and swallows it so that in her
belly the food may become milk to nurture the child, so in
scripture Christ is called our mother because of the intense
love which he shows us, and because of the bitterness which
he endured on the cross. There he chewed for us the punishment of cruel scourging and insults, to nourish us and to
build us up spiritually to endure by his example the tribulations of this world. Just as wine is filtered through a spice-
filled bag, so the person who endures tribulations must filter
them through the Lord's body by meditating on the affliction and suffering which he endured for us. In this way the
tribulations will be sweetened and become bearable, whereas they seemed unbearable before.

The twelfth advantage of tribulation is that *it affords a
person certain evidence that God loves him*; in the words of
the Apostle, 'Those whom I love I rebuke and discipline'
(Apoc 3:19). Ecclesiasticus says 'He who loves his son often
canes him' (30:1), that is, he punishes him time after time.
Jesus Christ our highest Father always keeps his children
beneath a whip or cane, so that when they are delivered from
one they are subject to another. He does not subject them to
all simultaneously, but to one after another, as an archer
shoots one arrow after another. As for the wicked — who
live their present lives without enduring God's whip or
castigation, and who are not dragged from the error of their
ways by the correction of all those tribulations which God
directs one after another at good people particularly for
their cleansing in this life — they will endure all the arrows
simultaneously in the next life. All the torments apportioned throughout the whole world in this life will come to
rest in their due place in the next world. As the Lord says: 'I
will gather evils upon them, and discharge all my arrows
against them' (Deut 32:23).

So if you wish to be loved by God, dear soul, do not reject
the tribulations which reveal to you the proof of divine love.
But if you react by saying that God's sons receive good and
evil things at his hands, so why is the experience of evil
things a stronger indication of the love of God than expe-

riencing good things, the reply is this: it is certain that God bestows superior blessings on his spiritual friends and on those whom he loves more. Now he loved Christ incomparably more than he loved the whole world, yet in this world he bestowed on him many evils and few temporal goods. As Bernard puts it, from entering the virginal womb until he mounted the gibbet of the cross he endured nothing but poverty and tribulations. So the consolation of affliction and hardship is a greater indication of God's love than the consolation of temporal prosperity. Moreover, Jesus Christ the Son of God who lived in this world was like a merchant at market choosing good commodities and rejecting the bad; he chose tribulations and avoided good fortune, as the gospel makes clear. He fled into the desert when the Jews wanted to force him to be their king, but he did not flee when they sought to destroy him and kill him. On the contrary, he said to them: 'I am' (John 18:37). So since Christ was most wise in his choice, it is clear that those who spurn tribulations and hardships and opt for worldly prosperity are fools. That prosperity will not avail to free them from the hands of their enemies, the demons in the life to come.

So endure your tribulation here and now with Christ, so that you may in the end win a crown in the kingdom of heaven. Otherwise you will not enter into the kingdom of heaven. As the Apostle says, 'We must enter the kingdom of heaven only by many tribulations' (Acts 14:21). May this be granted us by almighty God who lives and reigns for ever. Amen."

Chapter Three

VICARIOUS SUFFERING: JESUS THE SUFFERING SERVANT

For Christians the heart of the mystery of suffering is to be found in the passion, crucifixion and resurrection of Jesus. In his apostolic letter *Salvifici doloris*, John Paul II has clearly delineated the interconnection between the sufferings of Christ and our own experiences of pain and grief; in the mysterious dispensation of Providence, our own sufferings can complement or fill out the sufferings of Christ which have effected the salvation of mankind. Christ suffers not only for us but also with us; our sufferings in turn are aligned with his.

The Fathers lay great stress on Christ's shouldering of the burden of our guilt. The supreme scriptural passage in which this notion of vicarious suffering is explored is the Song of the Suffering Servant, the type of Christ, in the Book of Isaiah: "On him lies a punishment that brings us peace; through his wounds we are healed" (53:5). The Fathers repeatedly draw attention to the implications of this passage; in addition to those cited below we may note Justin's *Dialog with Tryphon the Jew* (*P.G.* 6.500ff), Hippolytus, *On Christ and Antichrist* 44 (*P.G.*, 10.761ff.), Origen's *Homily on Jeremiah* (*P.G.* 13, 360f.), and many others.

163

37. Clement of Rome

> Clement of Rome, who was bishop there in the final
> years of the reign of Domitian (c. 96 A.D.), in writing to
> the sister church of Corinth exploits this chapter of Isaiah
> and also verses of Psalm 21 to inculcate the message of
> reconciliation by depicting Christ the suffering servant as
> the model for all of us.

First Letter to the Corinthians, 16[37]

16. "Christ is one of those who humble themselves, not
one of those who exalt themselves above his flock. Our Lord
Jesus Christ who is the Sceptre of God's majesty did not
come in arrogant and haughty pomp as he might have done.
He came in lowly guise, as his Spirit remarked of him in
these words: 'Lord, who could believe what we have heard?
And to whom has the power of the Lord been revealed? We
have announced him as a child in his presence, like a root in
arid ground. He has no beauty nor glory; we looked on him,
and he had no looks nor beauty. His appearance was despised, deficient by comparison with men. He was a man
subject to blows and toil, and schooled in enduring weakness; for his face was turned away, despised and disregarded. He bore our sufferings and grieved for us, and we
thought of him as one in the toils, browbeaten and afflicted.
Yet he was wounded for our faults, weakened through our
transgressions. On him lies the discipline that brings us
peace; we have been healed through his bruises. We had all
wandered like sheep; mankind had roamed from its path.
The Lord surrendered him for our transgressions, and he
did not open his mouth at his afflictions. Like a sheep he was
led to the slaughter, like a lamb dumb before his shearers,
never opening his mouth. He was judged in humiliation, and
who will tell of his lineage? His life was torn away from the
earth; the faults of his people drove him to death. For his
burial I shall consign the wicked, and for his death the
wealthy, for he did no wrong, nor was guile found in his
mouth. The Lord seeks to deliver him of his affliction. If he

[37]Text: SC 167.124

is surrendered for sin, yours will be a long life. The Lord seeks to free his soul from affliction, to show him light, to endow him with understanding, to justify him who by his justice has served many; he will carry their sins. Hence he will claim many as his own, and will gain a share in the spoils of the strong, because his soul was consigned to death, and was reckoned with the wicked. He bore the sins of many, and through their sins he was betrayed' (Isa 53:1).

Again, Christ himself says: 'I am a worm and no man, scorn of mankind and outcast from the people. All who see me jeer at me, they sneer and shake their heads: "He hoped in the Lord, let the Lord save him. Let the Lord deliver him because he wants him"' (Ps 21:7-9). Do you see, dear people, the example which is given us? If the Lord humbled himself in this way, what shall we do, for through him we have passed beneath the yoke of his grace?"

38. *Eusebius of Caesarea*

Eusebius of Caesarea (c. 260-340), celebrated chiefly as the author of *The Ecclesiastical History*, wrote a *Commentary on Isaiah* greatly influenced in its allegorical approach by Origen.

On Isaiah, 53:1-7[38]

"*Lord, who believed what we had heard? And to whom was the arm of the Lord revealed?* God's prophets asked this in amazement when they observed the disbelief of the Jewish race, and the conversion and obedience of the Gentiles. We have frequently pointed out that God's arm is his only-begotten Son, who became known to all the nations who believed in him following the words of the prophets.

We reported it: he was like a child in his sight, like a root in a parched land. He had no looks nor fame; we beheld him, and he had no looks or beauty. The enigma of the untrodden land indicates the Virgin untouched by any man; the root denotes her of whom it was said: 'A rod shall come forth

---

[38]Text: GCS, Eusebius Werke, IX. 334

from the root of Jesse, and a bloom shall come forth from the root' (Isa 11:1). In that passage too it was revealed that he would ascend, but from the rod of Jesse; here it is from the untrodden land which is mentioned.

But his appearance was dishonoured and deficient by comparison with the sons of men. He was a man afflicted, one acquainted with weakness, for he turned away his face, was despised and accounted as nothing. He bears our sins and grieves on our behalf; and we regarded him as a man of sorrows, oppressed and afflicted. The prophet speaks in general terms, associating himself in fellow-feeling with those who did not esteem the Saviour; we did not value him or espouse him or consider who he was. But he was the Saviour of our souls, ministering to them and cleansing them all of sin. But such was the opinion we had of him in our foolishness. He suffered all this for us to free us from all sin.

He was wounded for our sins and weakened because of our transgressions. The chastisement that brought us peace was upon him, and by his stripes we were healed. So he was afflicted and scorned, and endured the foulest suffering, not for any sin of his own but for our sins. And the chastisement that brought our peace was on him; what we ought to have suffered as schooling for our sins befell him, that we might win peace with God. In just measure he bore stripes and wounds over his body through beating, whipping, blows on the face and assaults on the head with a reed; but these stripes were our salvation, for 'by his wounds we were healed.' 'We' are those who have long strayed and given no thought to him, not recognising who he was.

All of us like sheep have gone astray; each has wandered on his own road. The Lord has laid our sins on him, and in his affliction he did not open his mouth. Like a sheep he was led to the slaughter, like a lamb dumb before the shearer he does not open his mouth. People went on their diverse paths of error, with varied and opposing views about him, but his fate was not without divine purpose. He surrendered himself for our sins to be a scapegoat and a ransom; so he became the Lamb of God who takes away and purges the sin of the world."

39. Hilary of Poitiers

Hilary of Poitiers (see no. 14 above) deploys the words of Psalm 68 to teach the lesson that Christ's sufferings were voluntarily undertaken. The importance of Paul's vision of the interrelationship between his own sufferings and those of Christ, which is underlined in this passage, is strikingly taken up in the apostolic letter of Pope John Paul (below, p. 218ff., 243ff.)

Commentary on Psalm 68[39]

17. "*You know my reproach, my confusion and my shame; all those who afflict me are in your sight. My heart has expected a reproach and misery* (Ps 68:20-21). This confession is no different from the one above, where it says: 'O God, you know my foolishness, and my offences are not hidden from you' (Verse 6). Lest there be any mistake in interpretation, it was known only to God that this weakness was assumed by him, and was not his by nature. He had to suffer these things because of enmity, for the sake of the salvation and eternity of humankind. And he bears witness to these predetermined dispositions when he says, 'My heart has expected reproach and misery'; indicating that he had been longing for the sufferings of this time, according to the sacrament of divine communion, 'With desire I have desired to eat this pasch' (Luke 22:15). For it was in these desires of his suffering that the effect of this blessed time was achieved.

However, in this expectation of suffering in order to achieve our salvation, he was held by a further desire, another hope. The words follow: 'And I looked for one who would grieve along with me, and there was no one; and for one that would comfort me and I found none.' What he looks for is not so much the solace of a fellow-sympathiser or comforter, but faith: for someone who leaves the law behind and comes to understand the prophecy of all these sufferings, and stands with him in the fulfillment so to speak of the Law itself. This is what Paul did afterwards when he

[39]Text: CSEL 22. 327

completed the sufferings of Jesus Christ (Col 1:24), was buried with him in baptism, and recognised that Christ was the end of the Law. For he who was to be the finish of all that was done for the consummation of his human sufferings and of the prophetic sayings, he it was who uttered the complaints. What follows reads (Verse 22): 'and they gave me gall for my food, and in my thirst they offered me vinegar to drink.' As is read in the scriptures, all this was fulfilled; the gospels testify that gall was forced upon him, and his drink was vinegar. According to Matthew, when we was offered the gall, he refused it (27:34); but according to John, he was thirsty for the vinegar. For there it is written: 'Afterwards, Jesus, knowing that all things were now accomplished, that the scripture might be fulfilled, said: I thirst. Now there was a vessel set there full of vinegar. And they, mingling a sponge full of vinegar with hyssop, put it to his mouth. And when Jesus had taken the vinegar, he said, It is finished' (Jn 19:28-30). He had come to the lost house of Israel, and his expectations, that someone would console him and grieve with him, were disappointed. It was not that he needed consolation in his wish to suffer and to die; but he looked for one who would grieve over the impiety of the whole people; who would console himself with the salvation of the one who grieved with him; so that when everything to do with such enormous wickedness was finished, he might at least find solace in those who would be saved, according to the saying, 'he shall be consoled in his servants' (Deut 32:36). For though Israel was unbelieving, the gentiles would find faith in him. The prophetic word does not say that he was thirsty, but that he said he was thirsty, that all might be fulfilled. For all our infirmities which were in him were not his by nature; they were assumed...

So the Lord was stricken, taking upon himself our sins, and suffering for us. He was beaten down to the weakness of the cross and of death, so that we might receive health through his resurrection from the dead. He himself gave witness to his stricken state when he reminded his apostles of the prophecy, 'I will strike the shepherd, and the sheep of the flock shall be scattered' (Mt 26:31; Zach 13:7). But the

Apostle equally confirmed its meaning when he wrote, 'He (the Father) did not spare his beloved Son' (Rom 8:32). Indeed he did not spare his beloved Son. He handed him over to the vinedressers when he knew that they would kill him (cf. Mt 21:37). He had not spared the first Adam, fashioned from the slime of the earth. After his sin he cast him out of Paradise, lest he should touch the tree of Paradise and remain in an eternity of pain. So the second Adam from heaven assumed the nature of his body, and was smitten with the same death, so that he might call that nature back into eternal life, but without an eternity of pain. So it was that they persecuted the One smitten by God, adding the suffering of persecution to the pain of his wounds. For according to the prophet he suffered on our behalf (Isa 53:4), and we have thought of him as one afflicted by suffering."

40. Cyril of Jerusalem

Cyril of Jerusalem (c. 313-386) is chiefly known for his five mystagogical catecheses on the sacraments, which are of unique value for the light which they cast on the liturgical practice of his day. But in one of his earlier lectures or sermons he too stresses the vicarious nature of Christ's sufferings.

On the Crucified and Buried Christ, 4[40]
"So Jesus did indeed suffer for all men. The cross is no fantasy, for otherwise the redemption would be fantasy. His death is no fiction, for if it were, salvation would be fiction. If his death was mere illusion, those were true words of the men who said: 'We remember that deceiver saying whilst he was still alive, "In three days I shall rise again."' So his passion was genuine; he really was crucified, and we are not ashamed. He was crucified, and we do not deny it; indeed I boast to declare it. If I should deny it, Golgotha here refutes me as we all stand near it. The wood of the cross refutes me,

[40]Text: PG 33. 776

now distributed in particles throughout the whole world. I acknowledge the cross, for I experience the resurrection. If he had remained here after being crucified, I would perhaps not have acknowledged him, but would have retired into hiding with my Master. But since the resurrection followed the cross, I am not ashamed to recount it."

41. Ambrose

St. Ambrose (339-397), one of the three outstanding and formative figures of Christian humanism in the fourth-century West, claims attention not only as a bastion of orthodoxy at Milan (his splendid hymns were composed in part to counter the Arian threat) but also as the bridge between Greek scriptural learning and liturgical practice on the one hand and the churches of the West on the other. The following passage of scriptural commentary, which well demonstrates that fondness for allegorical interpretation inherited from Origen which helped to influence the conversion of Augustine, emphasises the role of Christ as the Levite who cleanses men's sins and the Lamb who is sacrificed for our salvation.

On Cain and Abel, II, 3[41]

"Let us take an example from the Law. When the Egyptians oppressed the Jewish people with various hard works in clay and brick, the children of Israel were groaning, and they moved the Lord to have mercy upon them. He said to Moses: 'I have heard the groaning of the children of Israel, how the Egyptians are oppressing them with servitude, and I am mindful of my covenant with them. Go and tell the children of Israel that I am the Lord, and I will bring you from out of the power of the Egyptians, and I will take you from your servitude, and I will deliver you with a strong right arm and with a mighty judgment, and I will take you to me to be my people, and I will be your God, and you will know that I am the Lord your God who brings you out of

[41]Text: CSEL 32. 386, ed. Schenkl

the power of the Egyptians and into a land over which I will stretch my hand' (cf. Exod 3:7ff.). See how the fruitless work of the people of the Hebrews became fruitful, so that they who once labored in clay, now worked in the hope of the eternal kingdom. So it was that the Lord in the gospel had mercy on the vain works of the Gentile people, who were building with clay the walls of superstition, held fast by the pleasures of the body. And so he says: 'Come to me all you that labor and are burdened, and I will refresh you. Take my yoke upon you and learn of me, because I am meek and humble of heart, and you will find rest for your souls' (Matt 11:28). It is in this call, I believe, that the fuller meaning of the words and mystery of the Law are acknowledged; because he taught that the ass's foal be redeemed with a sheep, or else with money (Exod 34:20)...Let us then buy off our evil works with good, with the price of faith, and by showing mercy.

Our price is the blood of Christ. So the apostle Peter says: 'You are bought not with gold and silver, but with his precious blood' (1 Pet 1:18). And Paul says: 'You have been bought at a price, so do not become men's slaves' (1 Cor 7:23). We have a right to be surprised that the Lord Jesus in the gospel rode on the foal of an ass (Mk 11:7); so the Gentile people began to be the sacrifice of Christ, because according to the Law they were reckoned as unclean. So it is written of the Levites that they are the people's redemption, in that they cleanse the people's sins with their prayers and their holiness of life. In these mysteries the true Levite appeared in the figure of a lamb; it was he who would take away the sins of the world by his bodily suffering. Levite means 'lifted up on my behalf', or 'he is easy to me'; for he who has perfect virtue gives the promise of healing to his people. He was the one who came as the longed for salvation of all the people; and he was also born of a virgin for me, offered for me. He tasted death for me and rose again on my behalf. In him we have the redemption of all mankind, in him the resurrection is realised. He is the true Levite, so that he might make us Levites cling to God, pour out continual prayers to him, hope for salvation from him, flee earthly cares, and be counted as God's possession. As it is written, 'Lord, possess us' (Exod 34:9). He alone is the possession which is never subject to storms, and bears the fruit of perpetual grace. The Levite is a redeemer, because the wise man is the redemption of the foolish. Like a doctor he heals the sick and foolish spirit, and distributes more trustworthy medicines with well-founded skill. He is like that Doctor who came from heaven to show humankind the ways of prudence and to reveal the paths of wisdom to little ones. He saw that those who labor could not be saved without a remedy, and so he gave medicine to the sick."

42. John Chrysostom

John Chrysostom's treatise *On Providence* has already been cited earlier (see nos. 12, 18, 33); this passage is an appropriate meditation on Christ's altruistic suffering.

On Providence, 17[42]

"Though we hymn our common Lord for all sorts of reasons, we hymn him particularly to give him glory, since we stand astonished because of the cross and his death attended by curses. Does not Paul depict that death as a sign of his love for us? Christ dies for men like us. Paul refrains from speaking of sky, earth, sea and all that Christ committed to our use and recreation; he repeatedly returns to the cross with the words: 'God has demonstrated his love for us, because when we were still sinners Christ died for us' (Rom 5:8). So Paul extends to us goodly hope when he says: 'For if when we were enemies we were reconciled to God by the death of his Son, much more, being reconciled, shall we be saved by his life' (Rom 5:10). Is it not because of this in particular that Paul himself rejoices and glories and jumps and flutters for joy, telling the Galatians: 'God forbid that I should glory, save in the cross of our Lord Jesus Christ' (Gal 6:14)? Why should you be surprised that he jumps and leaps and exults? He who endures these sufferings calls them his

[42]Text: SC 79.224, ed. Malingrey

glory: 'Father' he says 'the hour is come. Glorify thy Son' (John 17:1).

The disciple who wrote this said: 'For as yet the holy Spirit was not in them, because Jesus was not yet glorified' (John 7:39). He calls the cross a glory. When he wanted to demonstrate Christ's love, of what did he speak? His signs and wonders and marvels? No, he gives prominence to the cross, with the words: 'God so loved the world that he gave his only begotten Son, that all who believe in him may not perish, but may have eternal life' (John 3:16). Paul too says: 'He spared not even his own Son, but delivered him up for us all; so how will he not also in company with him give us all things?' (Rom 8:32). When he exhorts us to humility, it is from the cross that he derives his advice with the words: 'If there be any comfort in Christ, if any comfort of charity, if any communion of the Spirit, if any bowels of compassion, fulfill my joy, that you be of one mind, having the same charity, being of one accord, agreeing in sentiment. Let there be no contention or vainglory, but in humility let each esteem others as better than himself' (Phil 2:1-3). Then he commences his advice with the words 'Let this mind be in you which was also in Christ Jesus, who being in the form of God thought it not robbery to be equal with God; but emptied himself, taking the form of a servant, being made in the likeness of man, and in habit found as a man. He humbled himself, becoming obedient unto death, the death of the cross' (Phil 2:5-8).

On another occasion, when he is counselling on love, he announces: 'Love each other as Christ loved us, and has delivered himself for us, an oblation and a sacrifice to God for an odor of sweetness' (Eph 5:2). When he joins wives to husbands in harmony, he says: 'Husbands, love your wives as Christ loved the Church, and delivered himself up for it' (Eph 5:25). Christ himself shows how the cross was his chief concern, and how great was his love of suffering. Hear how he addressed the first of the apostles, the foundation-stone of the Church, the leader of the apostles' chorus, when Peter said to him in ignorance 'Heaven preserve you, Lord; this must not happen to you'. He said to Peter, 'Get behind me,

Satan; you are a stumbling-block to me'(Matt 16:22-23). By this exaggerated insult and rebuke he showed the great importance which he attached to the cross.

He achieved the resurrection in secret, in a remote corner, leaving the proof of it to subsequent generations. But he endured the cross in the middle of the city, during the festival, amidst a crowd of Jews, when both Roman and Jewish tribunals were in session, when the festival was attracting all the crowds, at midday, before a gathering of the whole world. Since only those present witnessed the event, he commanded the sun to be eclipsed, and to announce that deed of daring throughout the world. Yet, as I have been quick to emphasise, the event was a scandal for many. But we must concentrate not on them, but on those who were saved, those who won through."

43. Augustine

In his commentary on Psalm 62, Augustine visualises the problem of suffering within the framework of the doctrine of Christ's mystical body. All the members of the Church, past, present and future, in a mystical sense shared in his passion and death, since they are his limbs; and equally since he is our Head he shares in our sufferings though he is in heaven.

Commentary on Psalm 62:2[43]

"The psalm is spoken in the person of our Lord Jesus Christ, both head and members. He alone who was born of Mary, suffered, was buried, rose again, ascended to heaven and is now seated at the right hand of the Father interceding for us, is our Head. If he is the Head, we are the members. The whole of his Church wherever she is scattered constitutes his body, of which he is the Head. We mean not only the faithful now living but also those who existed before us and those who will succeed us till the end of the world; all these do indeed form part of his body. He who is ascended into heaven is the Head of this body (Col 1:18). Since we now identify head and body (him as head, us as body), when we hear his voice we must hear it as coming from both head and body. For whatever he has suffered we too have suffered with him, and what we suffer he too suffers with us. If the head suffers in any way, how can the hand assert that it does not suffer? If the hand suffers, how can the head say that it does not suffer? If the foot feels something, how can the head say that it does not feel it too? When one part of our body is in any pain, all the rest rush together to help the suffering member.

It follows then that if he has suffered and we have suffered with him, and he is now ascended into heaven and is seated at the right hand of the Father, whatever his Church suffers by way of this life's tribulations, temptations, constrictions and deprivations (for she must be schooled to be purified like gold in the fire), this he also suffers. That we have suffered with him we demonstrate from what Paul says: 'If you are dead with Christ, why do you continue to judge things as though you were living in this world?' (Col 2:20). Again, he says: 'Our old self has been crucified together with him so that the body of sin may be destroyed' (Rom 6:6). If therefore we are dead with him, we are also risen with him. As Paul himself has said; 'If you are risen with Christ, then relish the things that are above, seek the things that are above, where Christ is sitting at the right hand of God' (Col 3:1). If then we have died with him and are risen with him, and he is also dead with us and risen with us (for he is the unity of head and members), then most certainly his voice is also ours, and our voice is his too. Let us listen to the psalm then, and realise that it is Christ who speaks in it."

44. *Fulgentius*

A similar meditation on our fellow-suffering with Christ is offered by Fulgentius, bishop of Ruspe in North Africa (468-533), in a letter to a friend.

To Trasimund, 3.29-31[44]

"The Son of God, Word and Wisdom of the Father, is himself the Salvation of which the prophet says 'My salvation shall not tarry' (Isa 46:13). He is the Power and the Wisdom: 'For Christ is the Power of God and the Wisdom of God' (1 Cor 1:24). He is the One that satisfies, for 'He is the Bread that came down from heaven' (John 6:58), the One who is the Way, the Truth, and the Life. He is our Joy and Gladness of whom the prophet says 'Your word was to me the joy and gladness of my heart' (Jer 15:16). He is the true Light which 'enlightens everyone that comes into the world' (John 1:9).

Along with all these names he is also designated unalterable and impassible. Salvation cannot fall ill. Power has no experience of weakness. That which satisfies knows no hunger. The Way never deviates. Wisdom never alters. Life never dies. Light is never extinguished. Truth is never corrupted. Gladness has no truck with sadness. The Godhead cannot be outreached. So the humanity of Christ remained without sin because his divinity took it up into the unity of the Person who of his nature never knew sin. The man Christ deigned to carry the sins of others since he had none of his own. He had natural ties with those whose sins he wished to carry; as the Apostle tells us, 'For both he who sanctifies and they who are sanctified are all of one origin. For which cause he is not ashamed to call them brethren when he says: "I will declare your name to my brethren"' (Heb 2:11-12). And Isaiah the prophet foretells the effect of these brotherly feelings so as to declare openly that Christ carries the name of human being when he says: 'Lord, who has believed our report, and to whom is revealed the arm of the Lord?' (Isa 53:1). When he says 'the arm of the Lord' he means the divinity of the Son of God.

From then on Isaiah begins to tell forth the mystery of the Incarnation and the Passion. 'We have made him known as one growing up like a root in a thirsty land. There is no beauty in him nor comeliness. We beheld him, and he had no

[44]Text: PL 65.293.

splendor or beauty. His appearance was unsightly, and most abject beyond compare of all men; one covered with bruises, well-experienced in enduring feebleness, one shunned, of despicable appearance, reckoned as nothing. He bears our sins, and grieves on our behalf. We reckoned him as full of pain, overborne with wounds and molestation. He has been wounded for our iniquities; he has lost his strength because of our sins. The discipline which brings our peace was imposed on him, and by his bruising we have been healed. Like sheep we have all gone astray, and man has wandered from the right path; so the Lord has handed him over on account of our sins. Whilst he was handled sorely he never opened his mouth. He was led like a sheep to the slaughter, and like a lamb in the hands of the shearer he did not open his mouth. Judgment was laid on him in humiliation. And who shall speak of his lineage? For he shall be cut off from the land of the living. He was led to his death for the iniquities of my people' (Isa 53:2ff.). The prophet intended to show Christ's full humanity when he added a little later: 'He will carry their sins. So he will have many for his inheritance, and will divide the spoils of the strong, because his soul was consigned to death and he was counted among the wicked. He himself has borne the sins of many, and was betrayed for their iniquities' (53:12). From these words of the prophet, it is evident that the spirit and the flesh of the Saviour were delivered up, for on our behalf the whole man was led to the cross. So then the record of our sins had to be deleted, so that while our old man was being nailed to the cross, the victory of the triumphing Christ should be exposed as by a trophy...

It is Christ as man who became both our Priest in submitting himself to his suffering and Victim when he accepted it. Of him it is said, 'You are a priest for ever in the order of Melchisedech' (Ps 109:4). Yet both Priest and Victim bear not only the titles of humankind but also its functions. Since this Priest has accepted and possessed our weaknesses, the Apostle says of him: 'The priest we have is not one who could not feel for us in our weakness' (Heb 4:15). And to inform us that he is speaking of human nature, he adds 'One

tempted like us in all things, but without sin.' He goes on:
'Every high priest is chosen out and ordained on men's
behalf in the things which belong to God, that he may offer
up gifts and sacrifices for sins, and can have compassion on
those who are ignorant and go astray, for he himself is also
compassed about with weakness' (Heb 5:1-2). Insofar as he
was surrounded with weakness, he had compassion on our
ignorance and our deviations, and thus showed fellow-
feeling with our weakness. The compassion that unites lies
where there is identity of nature. Our high priest suffered
with us according as we suffer with him; as the blessed
Apostle says: 'For the Spirit himself gives testimony to our
spirit, that we are the children of God. And if children, then
heirs as well, heirs of God and fellow-heirs with Christ; if we
suffer with him, so we may also be glorified with him' (Rom
8:16-17). So too the blessed Peter exhorts us to the grace of
this compassion when he says: 'Dearly beloved, do not
tremble at the burning heat which is sent to try you. Do not
be afraid, as if something new were happening to you.
Rather rejoice in sharing the sufferings of Christ, so that
when his glory is revealed you may rejoice and exult' (1 Pet
4:12-13). So it was that the high priest in his human nature
embraced his passion truly, and in that nature knew how to
have compassion with his members. So blessed Paul spoke
of 'fulfilling in my flesh those things that are lacking in the
sufferings of Christ, for the sake of his body which is the
Church' (Col 1:24).

No wonder then that we share the suffering of our high
priest in our unity of nature with him, when the blessed
Apostle testifies that we have died with him. 'If you have
died with Christ, why do you still judge things as though you
were still living in the world?' (Col 2:20). And he says to
Timothy: 'Be mindful that Jesus Christ has risen from the
dead, he who is of the seed of David. This is according to my
gospel, for which I labour to the point of being in chains, as
though I were a malefactor. Yet the word of God is not in
chains. I endure all things, then, for the sake of the chosen,
so that they also may obtain the salvation which is in Christ
Jesus with heavenly glory' (2 Tim 2:8-10). Paul therefore

knows that Jesus Christ of the stock of David is risen from the dead, and that his sharing of our human nature is made manifest. The apostle states that we have died with Christ in the death which he knew Christ endured: 'A saying worthy of credence: if we have died with him, then we shall live with him. If we endure with him, we shall also reign with him' (2 Tim 2:11). Therefore the High Priest 'who offered himself for us' as the Apostle says as an oblation and a sacrifice to God in the odour of sweetness' (Eph 5:2), even as he died for us made all of us die with him."

Chapter Four

DEATH,
THE GATEWAY TO LIFE

Death, and our attitude towards it, lies at the heart of the problem of suffering; it issues the supreme challenge to the virtue of hope. It is a fundamentally human trait to resent the prospect of death, and it is for this reason that so many of the Fathers counsel their flocks not to stand in fear and reluctance at its advent, but to adopt an attitude which is literally other-worldly. God did not intend us to die; sin ushered death into the world. But since the penalty of that sinning is that all must endure the punishment of death, our attitude towards it should be positive and accepting. Patience in the act of dying will stand to our credit.

In order to encourage us to look on death with equanimity, the Fathers lay stress on two aspects: first, the sorrows and struggles which are an inevitable concomitant of this earthly life, and from which death and the ensuing resurrection will deliver us; and secondly the abiding joys of our future life with Christ, in which all sadness and tears will be wiped away.

Some of the Fathers envisage a world which is already drawing to its close. The physical afflictions which became so widespread in the death-throes of the Roman empire in the west seemed to represent the fulfillment of Christ's prophecy of the forthcoming dissolution of the world and the advent of the kingdom. This is presented as an additional reason for welcoming the prospect of death in some of the passages which follow.

45. Cyprian

> St. Cyprian (see above, no. 7) preached untiringly to his third-century African flock in this strain; his *On Mortality* is a meditation on death which contrasts the wretchedness of this life with the joys in the next extended by Christian hope.

On Mortality, 2ff.[45]
"Dearest brethren, the person who fights for God, who is stationed in heaven's camp and aspires to things divine, ought to acknowledge his identity, so that we have no fear or trembling in the face of the storms and tempests of this world. The Lord foretold that these events would come; with prophetic exhortation he instructed, taught, prepared, strengthened the people of the Church to endure wholly all that is to come. He foretold and prophesied the outbreak of wars, famine, earthquakes and plagues in every place. So that no unexpected and unprecedented fear of hostile events should shake us, he forewarned us that in the final days afflictions would become more and more common. His words have come to pass; since what was foretold earlier is now happening, all that has been promised will ensue. The Lord's own promise was this: 'When you see all this come to pass, know that the kingdom of God is at hand' (Lk 21:31). Dearest brothers, the kingdom of God has begun to be at hand. Our reward of life, the joy of eternal salvation, perennial joy, the possession of Paradise lately lost are approaching as the world passes away. Heavenly things are supplanting earthly, great things succeed to small, and eternal things to transient. What place is there here for anxiety and worry? Only the person without hope and faith is fearful and sad. It is the person who is unwilling to go to Christ who

---

[45]Text: CCL 111A. 17, ed. Simonetti

fears death; it is the one who does not believe that he has begun to reign with Christ who is unwilling to go to him.

Scripture says: 'The righteous man lives by faith' (Rom 1:17). If you are righteous and live by faith, if you truly believe as one who will be with Christ and who accepts the Lord's promise, why do you not embrace the call to Christ, and feel gratitude at being free of the devil? The righteous Simeon, who was truly righteous in his observance of God's commands with fullness of faith, was told by a divine voice that he would not die before he had seen Christ. When the infant Christ came to the temple with his mother, he acknowledged in spirit that the Christ foretold to him had now been born; after looking upon him, he knew that he would shortly die. So he rejoiced at imminent death and was untroubled at the impending summons. He took the Child in his arms, cried out a blessing to God with these words: 'Now you discharge your servant in peace according to your word, O Lord; for my eyes have seen your saving one' (Lk 2:29f.). What he proved and attested was that servants of God attain peace and a free and calm rest when we are delivered from the storms of this world and make for the harbor of our untroubled and eternal resting-place, when the present death is shaken off and we come to immortality. That is our peace, our tranquility of faith, our secure, strong, enduring certainty.

Life in this world is nothing but a daily battle against the devil, a continual engagement against his darts and weapons. We struggle with greed, with impurity, with anger, with ambition; our unending and burdensome fight is with the sins of the flesh and the enticements of the world. Man's mind is under siege, and encompassed on all sides with the hostility of the devil, and can scarcely confront and resist its foes one by one. If greed is dispatched, lust looms; if lust is prostrated, ambition takes its place; if ambition is spurned, anger embitters, pride inflates, drunkenness entices, envy brings disharmony, jealousy destroys friendship. One is impelled to utter the curse which the law of God forbids, one is driven to swear the oath which is not permitted.

All these persecutions the mind endures every day, and with all these perils is the heart oppressed; is it still your pleasure to linger long among the devil's swords? You should rather long and desire to hasten to Christ with death's more speedy help. As Christ himself instructs us: 'Amen, amen, I say to you: you will lament and mourn as the world rejoices; you will be sad, but your sadness will be turned into joy' (John 16:20). Who would not choose to forego sadness, who would not hasten to attain to joy? The Lord himself makes clear on another occasion when our sadness will turn into joy: 'I shall see you again, and your heart will rejoice, and no man will take your joy from you' (John 16:22). So since beholding Christ is joy, and there can be no joy for us unless we behold Christ, what mental blindness is it to love the hardships, pains and tears of the world, and not to hasten instead to the joy which cannot be taken from us?"

46. Hilary

Hilary of Poitiers (see no. 14 above) in his commentary on Psalm 118 specifically counsels his readers to console themselves in their various trials and indignities with the prospect of the future life which is offered by Christian hope.

Commentary on Psalm 118, 7:1-2[46]

"The entire word of God contained in the holy scriptures summons us to hope for the blessings of heaven. Because of this the prophet, certain that he has abided by all God's precepts, says unceasingly: 'Remember your word to your servant.' God surely does not forget his promise? Heaven forbid that we should believe that forms of human weakness should creep into the eternal and unwearied Power. But the prophet, who trusted the promises of God, who was preoccupied by a longing for heavenly things, who spurned the

[46]Text: CSEL 22. 418

present in his hope for the future, does not recall God to the recollection of his word, but begs him to be mindful of his word as it affects his servant. In other words he prays that he may be accounted worthy that God may deign to be mindful of his word in regard to his servant, for in that word he has placed his hope. That hope must not be empty or proclaimed only in words, but shown by actions. So if ever sickness, persecution, loss, bereavement, insult befall us, we are to console ourselves in the threats and oppression of the present age with the hope of the eternal promises.

We are instructed in all this, but the prophet has already experienced it. He says: 'This hope has consoled me in my humility, for your word has given me life' (Ps 118:50). The hope is the hope which God has implanted in him. It has consoled him 'in his humility', that is when he is spurned, mocked, vexed by injustices, dishonored by insults, for he knows that he is soldiering through his present trials. But the hope instilled by the Lord consoles him in these wars endured in his weakness, and he is lent life by the utterances of God. By these he knows that the glory of his weakness is outstanding in heaven. He knows that his soul, renewed by the utterances of God, contains within it, so to say, the nourishment of eternal life. He lives by God's utterances, and is untroubled by the empty fame of the proud, for he knows that his need is richer than their wealth. He knows that his fasting is abundantly fed by the blessing of heaven and the gospel, that his humility will be rewarded by the glorious prize of honor. So he added: 'The proud behaved wickedly without cease, but I did not decline from your law' (Ps 118:51)."

47. Jerome

St. Jerome (see no. 20 above) presents the negative aspects of this certainty of a future life when he rebukes the hedonists who argue that there is no life and no judgment after death. There will be a judgment, and the nature of our future life will depend upon the quality of our life here.

Commentary on Ecclesiastes[47]

"The fool declares after the fashion of rhetoricians and poets: 'Man, after death you are nothing, and death itself is nothing. Listen then to my counsel. Whilst you are living this brief life enjoy its pleasures, go to the banquets, drown your cares in wine. Understand that all these things are given you by God for your enjoyment. Dress yourself in white robes and sally forth, pour perfumes on your hair. Give yourself to the embraces of whatever woman pleases you; match this short and empty life with pleasures that are likewise vain and passing. Apart from these you will have nothing else to enjoy; so whatever delights you, snatch it quickly before it disappears. Nor should you turn from artificial frivolities for fear that you will have to give account of every deed, good or bad, down below. There is no wisdom in death, no understanding lingers after this life is dissolved.'

He claims that this is how an Epicurus would speak, or an Aristippus and his Cyrenian followers, or the other philosophers who preach animal pleasures. But when I diligently reconsider the question, I find nothing to support such vile conclusions that everything happens by chance and that fortune has free rein in human affairs. Rather the truth is that everything is under God's judgment. The fleet of foot ought not to think that the footrace is his, any more than the strong man should confide in his brute strength. Nor should the wise man reckon that wealth and opulence go with prudence, nor should the learned orator reckon that he can find favor with the crowd because of his learning and eloquence. Rather, everything happens by the disposition of God, and except he govern everything by his will, and build the house, they labor in vain who build it. And unless he guard the city, they keep watch in vain who set a guard over it (cf. Ps 126:1).

Life is not then, as these people think, a simple issue, and the condition of this existence is not subject to chance. At a time they have not reckoned on they will be seized by sudden

[47]Text: CCL 72.325

death and brought to judgment. Just as fish are caught by the hook and in the net, just as the birds of the air in their freedom are taken unawares in the snare, so men according to their deserts will be brought down to eternal punishment when death suddenly overtakes them; a judgment comes upon those who thought that everything evolved in an indiscriminate way. It is in this sense, by which we have sought briefly to grasp the entire order of things, that we must interpret each of these statements. The prophet is citing not the fool's statement but his own: 'Go then and eat your bread with joy, and drink your wine with a glad heart, because your works are pleasing to God' (Eccl 9:7). As you have learnt that everything comes to term at death, and that there is no patience in hell, nor may recourse be had to virtuous conduct, hasten to do penance while you are in this world, work while you have time. God lovingly welcomes the penitent."

48. Augustine

St. Augustine (no. 4 above), in a characteristically brilliant exposition, stresses that we are journeying as pilgrims to a land unknown; our Christian hope in it is based on faith in the Jesus Christ who in the Incarnation became our Way.

Sermon, 262:4[48]

"We are still pilgrims in this life; we aspire in faith to the native land unknown to us. We are citizens of it, so why is it unknown? Because in our long pilgrimage we have forgotten it, and so we can label our native land unknown. The Lord Christ drives this forgetfulness from our hearts. He is the King of that land, and he visits us pilgrims. By embracing our flesh his divinity becomes our way, so that we may proceed through Christ Man and abide in Christ God. So with what words am I to explain to you, with what eye are

[48]Text: PL 39.1613

we to behold the secret 'which eye has not seen, nor ear heard, nor has it entered into the heart of man'? We can sometimes be aware of something which we cannot express; sometimes we are unable to express something because we do not know it. Even if I knew the things of heaven, it is possible that I could not explain them, so how much more difficult is it for me to speak when I walk with you in faith, and cannot yet behold them? Yet it is Paul and not Augustine who says this. He consoles our ignorance, and builds up our faith with the words: 'Brethren, I do not consider that I have apprehended it. But one thing I do, forgetting what lies behind and straining forward to what lies ahead, I press on towards the goal for the prize of the higher calling' (Phil 3:13f.). By these words he shows that he is on the way. And in another place he says: 'We know that while we are at home in the body we are away from the Lord, for we walk by faith not by sight' (2 Cor 5:6f.). And again: 'In this hope we were saved. Now hope that is seen is not hope. For who hopes for what he sees? But if we hope for what we do not see, we wait for it with patience' (Rom 8:24f.)."

49. *Augustine*

> In *The City of God* Augustine refuses to idealise the human reality of death in the interests of edification. He stresses its harsh and unnatural nature, and suggests that we console ourselves with the prospect of the glory of rebirth, and the hope of rendering satisfaction for our past sins.

The City of God, 13:3ff.[49]

"We must state that the first human beings were in the situation that had they not sinned they would have experienced no form of death. But as the first sinners they were punished with death, and the result was that all that issued from their stock were held subject to the same penalty; for all those born from them were to be identical with them-

[49]Text: CSEL 40, 1.617

selves. Their condemnation changed their nature for the worse, as was appropriate to the heinousness of their sin. So what came as punishment for the first sinners followed naturally in all other men who were born...

Physical death, the separation of soul from body, is not good for dying people when they experience it. The violence that prises apart the two elements which had been joined and intertwined in a living person is a harsh unnatural experience for as long as it lasts, until all the feeling resulting from the embrace of soul and flesh is removed. All this discomfort is sometimes cut short by a single physical blow, or by the soul's being expelled with such speed that this does not permit it to be felt.

But whatever deprives dying people of their feelings, and causes deep distress, increases the merit of their patience if it is endured in a devoted and faithful way; the label of punishment still adheres to it. Though death is undoubtedly the punishment of every man born, since he is descended directly from the first man, it becomes his glory when he is born again. And since death is his repayment for sin, it sometimes obtains for him exemption from the future repayment for sin."

50. Ps-Augustine

> The following passage, which is found amongst the spurious works which were attributed to Augustine, is written to a nephew suffering from an incurable illness; it offers the twin consolations of the prospect of future blessedness and deliverance from the afflictions of this world.

On ministering to the sick, 2ff.[50]

"Beloved nephew, you are hastening on the way of all flesh, and soon you will see your forebears the holy patriarchs, and also the greatest blessedness of all. So you have need of that special provision, the viaticum, for this impor-

---

[50]Text: PL 40. 1147-52

tant journey, lest you fail on the way. You are to become a living stone in the wall of the heavenly city, which rises without the sound of the hammer. In this life we must endure the clatter; here the mason's mallet must be applied to the stone; here the stones must be squared by chipping off the edges. Let that din signify the rehearsal of your sins as you confess them humbly in whispering into the ear of a priest; as scripture has it, 'Confess your sins to one another' (James 5:16). The stroke of the hammer can represent your conversion of heart rather than the beating of your breast, though both are to be measured during the little time left to you here in life, so that they will not be necessary when you become a part of God's building.

For where is it that you are going? To life. And by what road? Listen to the Lord as he tells you: 'I am the Way, the Truth, and the Life' (John 14:6). You cannot lose your way, for Christ is the Way. You cannot go astray, for Christ is the Truth. You cannot lose your life, for Christ is your life. Through Christ the Way you will pass to Christ the true Life. Christ is the Way; you are the wayfarer. Take Christ the Viaticum and he, the Way and the Truth and the Life, will lead you to himself. Where will you find this way? Where will you find this Viaticum? Christ is God, and God is everywhere. If God is everywhere, then he is in you, behind you, in front of you, all around you. Everything is full of God. Do not think him far away; wherever you seek him, you will find him. If you ascend to heaven, he is there; if you go down to hell, he is there. If you wing away at the dawn to dwell in the furthest parts of the sea, even there his hand will lead you and his right hand hold you (Ps 138:8). So you have God as your guest everywhere. Make your house ready for your important Guest and welcome him with untroubled mind, so that when he comes he may lead you out, become your Guide, and in guiding you give you hospitality. I tell you that if you show him kindly hospitality, he will afford you still more kindly and free hospitality. How happy you will be if you become God's guest and take up your dwelling in his city the heavenly Jerusalem, and if you receive his gratitude and he says: 'I was a stranger, and you received me as guest; as long as you did this for the least of my little ones, you did it for me. Come, blessed of my Father, receive the kingdom' (Matt 25:35-40). I was wrong to promise you God's hospitality in return for your own; I was wrong to call you his guest. You will be his enrolled citizen, or rather his fellow-ruler one day. God promises you more than a guest-house; he promises a kingdom. You will reign with Christ, you will be God's heir and Christ's fellow-heir (cf. Rom 8:17)...

So, dearest nephew, you are soon to leave this world. Do not turn your back on such ineffable goodness of the Lord God, but receive his correction with joy. He is correcting something of which you are unaware, but not unjustly; his judgments are ever just. This bodily disease is a spiritual medicine. Moreover, remember that the doctors have declared your sickness to be incurable. Ask yourself whether you have presumed to blame it on God. You must endure it willy-nilly; grumbling will never heal you. In fact you will only be weakened in soul by murmuring against your God, your Father and your Physician, the mildest and most serene of masters, who even as he disciplines you is the harbinger of peace, who is never angry, whose apparent anger shows him mindful of his mercy. So follow my counsels, and instead of suffering a twofold evil by grumbling, be at peace. Let your bodily burden be a spiritual antidote. For if you are unwilling to recognise God in your chastisement, you will be afflicted in body and soul alike; it is not God who punishes twice over. With what gladness and joy in your heart should you look forward to the divine visitation! Certainly if you were in the best of health you ought to have asked God for some medical infirmity with all your heart, and to fear that bodily health might bring sickness of soul. I am convinced that because you are sick you should rejoice to good effect. The divine roll is about to be called, and you should be glad with a full heart to reply 'Present'. See now, if God had granted you a bishopric or some similar honour as desirable as good health to the sick, would you not receive that gift with great joy? Certainly you ought to treat this special chastisement of God with even greater exultation, with more devoted will and with thanksgiving, because it is a most profitable gift from God. Moreover, if you thought of the shipwreck of this life, and of trading it for an advantageous death, your disdain of life and your longing to hasten to death in the Lord would be indescribable. 'Blessed are the dead who die in the Lord' (Apoc 14:13).

Let us make a brief comparison. Let us, if you like, draw a contrast with the present life which is the beginning of pains. Let us have a friendly disputation on which is better to seek after, living badly or dying well. Now no one can live a good life here and now, for 'every man is a liar' (Ps 105:11). And Paul, who above all others recognised one law in his members warring on another law in his heart (Rom 7:3), wanted to be delivered and to be with Christ (Phil 1:23). We know too that every creature is groaning and in travail until it can be freed from the servitude of corruption through him who made it subject in hope (Rom 8:20-22). Then too the troubles of this present life are numberless, like hunger, thirst, pain, heat, fatigue; they are countless, but we are so familiar with them that they are household words. Yet they are but the beginning of sorrow. If we ponder the passions within us — greed, possessive love, hatred, fornication, adultery, killing and being killed, rapine, theft — are not all these our enemies? Is anyone immune or free from them all? And who will be free from sin when he is exposed to so many furious passions? Who will live well under threat of sin like this? So every man lives badly because sin is an evil.

In short, I presume to say that the beginning of life is the beginning of pains. There have been philosophers well acquainted with this, who mourned the birth of children and rejoiced in their deaths. What they meant is that man is born to toil, and dies unto rest. Holy David was so saddened by the birth and life of his son by Bathsheba that as long as the child was alive he mourned and fasted; but when his son died he rejoiced and broke his fast (2 Kings 12:16ff.). O death desirable, term of all present evils, end of labour and beginning of rest! Who can reckon the advantages of your blessedness? To die badly is not the Christian's lot. To die well is to live with Christ. Who can properly unfold death's benefits? It fastens a man to Christ; it is, as was said, the end of evils, the source and nurse of sure happiness. All hail, my most beloved death! I confess that if I could I would welcome you with open arms, taste your joys with delight, willingly go to meet you...

And now you must pray, and (unless your disposition be otherwise) speak to God as one who relies on him:

My God, my God, my mercy and my refuge, I long for you and am in haste to come to you. Do not despise one who finds himself in such dire straits, but be merciful to me in the time of my great necessity. I cannot redeem myself by my own deeds; it is you who must redeem me and have mercy on me. I have no confidence in my own merits, but I rely on your compassion. My confidence in your compassion is greater than my distrust in my own evil actions. You are my hope, my God; against you only I have sinned through my own fault. Since I was dear to you when you ransomed me, let me not be so worthless as to be thrown away. Now I come to you who fail no man; I long to die and to be with you. Into your hands, Lord, I commend my spirit. Look kindly upon me, Lord God of truth. And grant to me, my God, to sleep in peace and find rest. You are God and you live and reign in the perfection of the Trinity for all eternity. Amen."

51. Eucher of Lyons

St. Eucher, who was bishop of Lyons c. 434-449, is one of those who believe that the world is gradually reaching its close, and that little joy will await those who survive in it. All the more reason, therefore, to rest our Christian hope in the secure knowledge of the eternal life to come.

Exhortation to his kinsman Valerian[51]

"'Do not love the world,' says the Apostle, 'nor the things which are in the world' (1 John 2:15), for all these things flatter our gaze with their deceptive show. Let the power of the eyes be focussed on the light, not given over to error; and

[51]Text: PL 50. 722-24

since that power is available for the enjoyment of life, let it not receive what causes death. As the Apostle well observes, 'The desires of the flesh make war upon the soul' (1 Pet 2:11), and all their preparations are aimed at our ruin and disaster. Upon arising they keep a watchful look-out against us just like external enemies. The more strength they draw from us the more they gain for themselves.

Up to now I have spoken about the irresistible allurements of this enticing world, of its honours and wealth, as if the world so pleasing in its blandishments were in full vigour. But whatever its appearances, no matter how dazzling its manifestations, all its painted splendour is doomed to perish. The world now hardly has the power to deceive. That image of reality with its beguiling comeliness is finished. It first thought to seduce us with its glitter, but could not; and now it is virtually incapable of corrupting us in its reality with false and vulgar display. Before it lacked the permanence of goodness; now it lacks even the transience. It is no longer adorned with temporary beauties, nor with qualities abiding in the future. So, unless we deceive ourselves, the world is no longer capable of deceiving us.

But why should we refrain from expressing matters of greater significance? We speak of the wasting resources of the world when the world itself is on its last legs and moving towards its end. How much more serious and important it is that the world is not going to last long! Why do we recount its enfeebled properties and appurtenances? It is deservedly faltering, its powers oppressed with age; it is robbed of its supports, for it now succumbs under its tottering burdens to old age. This end-time of the world is so to say its old age replete with evil maladies. In the era of its gray hair we have seen and still see famine, plague, devastation, wars, affrights. These are the illnesses in its final years. Hence frequent portents from heaven and earthquakes are experienced, rapid changes in the weather, and animals' monstrous offspring. All these are the prodigies of advancing age already failing. This conclusion is confirmed not by the words of my feeble self, but by the authoritative eloquence of the Apostle. In his epistles we read: 'Upon us the ends of the ages are come' (1 Cor 10:11).

Since this has already been said, why do we delay, what are we waiting for? The day that presses upon us is not only our own but the world's last day. Every hour warns us that the time of its fateful dissolution is passing, since there is an end which threatens alternately with twofold peril, a hazard which menaces all with a single death from a double source. The world's mortality weighs heavily on my personal wretchedness, as though my own mortality were not enough to terrify me. Why is it that we coddle our fears? There is no place for optimism when the end of every single thing with- out distinction hangs over us. The human condition is all the more pitiable now when the world, if not ending, is at any rate failing. Men do not store up hope of future joys when they do not enjoy any present delights. They neither obtain pleasure from a shorter life nor have they hopes of everlast- ing joy. Ephemeral blessings are not for them, nor will they enjoy eternal ones. Present possessions are too few, and there is no hope in what comes after. Man's condition is indeed one of tears and misery, unless perchance in the midst of the harshest conditions he can make a virtue of necessity, unless in this respect he can shape for himself a more powerful remedy for his own use, and after his urgent desires strive for wiser counsel; especially when the condi- tions of the present time are in shreds, so that whoever loses the advantage appertaining to the future loses that of the here and now as well.

The whole force of the spirit must be concentrated on hope for the future. And so that you may reach out for it as wholeheartedly and straightforwardly as possible, it will be my pleasure to disclose it to you by means of an example. Suppose someone were to make a person an offer here of five bronze coins, but also a promise to give five hundred gold coins tomorrow, and the option were given of having the bronze coins today or the gold tomorrow. Would there be any doubt that his preference would be for that greater prize after a short delay? So you yourself, if you looked at the circumstances of this short life and of eternity, would never choose the worthless when you could hope for the precious. The value of grabbing the small sum is less than the expectation of the great sum. But if we eye and lay hold of everything perishable in this world, clearly we cannot possess hope here where we enjoy the things we see. 'Hope that is seen is not hope. Who hopes for what he sees?' (Rom 8:24). Hence whatever the hope is that is involved in human affairs, it is to be sought for the future. Unless it is hoped for it cannot in any wise be called hope.

We therefore, for the future, follow a plainer substance of hope than that which we experience in the present world. Observe how we do not totally see the things which pass before our gaze, for our sight seems blurred; we look with more focussed gaze at more distant objects as though our eyes were lightened. Undoubtedly the same sort of thing has happened about the present and the future. Present things when pushed upon our eyeballs are not seen for what they are, whereas future things less close to our eyes are perceived more clearly. We do not ground this confidence in the future on any uncertain source but on our Lord Jesus Christ, the most faithful Guarantor of the truth, who promises to the just an everlasting kingdom and the splendid prize of a most blessed eternity. He is both Man and God, and he has reconciled man to God through the inexplicable mystery of his taking human flesh. He has also absolved the world of its criminal guilt by the great and secret mystery of his passion. So 'He was manifested in the flesh, vindicated in the spirit, seen by the angels, preached among the nations, believed in the world, taken up into glory' (1 Tim 3:16); and for this reason God has exalted him, so that all should now confess in heaven and on earth, in the sea and in the abyss, that the Lord Jesus Christ, King and God before all ages, is in glory (cf. Phil 2:10f.)."

52. Peter Chrysologus

St. Peter Chrysologus, who preached the following inspiring sermon on death and resurrection, was bishop of Ravenna in the first half of the fifth century; he died in 450.

Sermon 118[52]

"Since the whole hope of the Christian faith is grounded in resurrection from the dead, and so that no one should dare to cast doubt on it, we have recited to you today an extended passage from St. Paul in which he declares this truth with his authority, with the facts, and with examples; and we could find nothing to add to it. But because your charity always demands the service of our office, we are fired with the ardour of the resurrection to repeat what Paul has said, and to bring it home with greater force. My brothers, it is always a joy to speak of the resurrection, a constant delight to hear it mentioned, because there is never any pleasure in dying, but only in living. Let our voices be heard chanting the music of the resurrection, and let it always vibrate in the ear of our heart, so that death which ever lays siege to the gate of the senses may be driven off with its terror and lamentation. Just so the farmer sings of his abundant harvest and loaded table, and no longer feels the crushing labour and sweat of the plough. So too the sailor intones the profit won in reaching harbour, lest he fear the destructive force of the waves and the perils of the sea. So too the soldier recites his spoils and triumphs to avoid becoming fearful at the sight of wounds and trembling at the sword. In like manner should the Christian feast his eyes on the sight of the resurrection, let his tongue sing it, his heart dwell on it, so that he can despise all manner of fears of death and tread them underfoot.

Death, my brothers, is the mistress of despair, the mother of unbelief, the sibling of corruption, the begetter of hell, the wife of the devil, the queen of all evil. She invests the whole of the human race with her array of forces which are never replete. First she sends forth her child Despair with her seductive whisperings: 'Man, why do you waste your time? See, your mistress death is upon you, reducing to nothing your spirit, wasting your body with disease, consuming your bones with old age. Before birth you did not exist, and she will see to it that you are in the same case after death. Pay

[52]Text: PL 50. 522-23.

yourself and your youth their debts, then, before death comes. Surrender your childhood to play, your adolescence to delights, your manhood to pleasure, and your old age to me, so that when downcast you do not entertain hope fruitlessly.'

After this Death sends her daughter Unbelief in threatening vein: 'Is this how you order your life, as though you are not going to die, as though you are to escape death? Dear man, faith is deceiving you. You are trusting faith which promises you the future to rob you of the present, which holds in store for you benefits unseen to deprive you of what you have before death. Who has ever returned from there? What sage believes in promises undelivered for so many ages? Why not eat and drink? 'Eat and drink, for tomorrow you are to die' (Isa 22:13).

Death directs the third sister in wickedness, Corruption, with such intensity that she attacks men's very countenances, tugs at them and lays hold of them in their graves. There she reveals her final prisons, where those she has taken lie bound and immobile. In order to overthrow our human senses with complete horror and fear, she pours on them her rottenness, belches forth her poison, douches them with her decaying matter, sprays them with foul odours, and proclaims that she has bestowed innumerable worms on the body of a single man as so many executioners. Why should not the Christian believe in despair and unbelief? These are the wars of death which she conducts through these commanders, stratagems and conflicts. She imprisons, ravages and slays all whom nature ushers into the present life. She escorts kings, drags off peoples, compels nations. She cannot be bought off with riches, swayed by pleas, softened by tears, or overcome by any show of strength.

My brothers, those who have tried to write anything good about death have been mistaken. This is hardly surprising. The wise of this world consider themselves great and marvellous if they can persuade the simple that what is the greatest evil is in fact the highest good. Scripture appropriately says of them: 'Woe to them that call good evil, and evil good' (Isa 5:20). Woe to them that put darkness for light, and light for darkness. Indeed, whom would they not deceive, whom would they not make blind? They have brought the heedless to believe that life is an evil and death a good. Yet, my brothers, the truth dislodges such views as these, the light puts them to flight, the faith confronts them, the apostle censures them, Christ destroys them; for while he restores the good which is life, he dooms, damns and casts out the evil which is death.

So the apostle begins: 'Now I make known to you, my brothers, the gospel I have preached to you, which also you have received, and on which you too take your stand, and by which you are also saved. You must hold fast to the tenour of my preaching, unless you have believed in vain. For I passed on to you first of all what I myself received, namely that Christ died for our sins, and that he was buried, and that he rose again on the third day according to the scriptures' (1 Cor 15:1-4).

The divine largesse enriches him who is to live, not him who is to die. Otherwise what good does he receive if he does not obtain it? 'On which you too take your stand.' He who stands is he who lives forever; the dead is forever prostrate. 'By which you are also saved.' If anyone dies, he perishes; but he who lives forever is saved. 'You must hold fast to the tenour of my preaching, unless you have believed in vain.' He who has believed that he was born only for death has not only believed in vain but also lived in vain. What, O man, do you see rise which does not fall? And does not what falls rise again? The day rises in the morning, and again the following morning; it is buried late at night, but in the morning it rises again. The sun is born each day and dies each day; it rises again every day. The seasons perish as they pass, and return to life as they reappear. So even if you do not believe God, if you do not bow to the Law, if you do not assent to what you hear, then trust the evidence of your eyes or defer to the elements around you as they constantly declare to you your resurrection.

Certainly if the things under your control and far inferior to you are roused from death by your action, they should teach you that you can be raised up by God's action. Take the dry, lifeless, inert grain of wheat. Turn over a furrow, dig up the earth, make a grave, bury the grain. See how it dies the death, swells with moisture, putrefies and disintegrates. When it sinks to the level at which despair, unbelief, and corruption earlier assailed you, then suddenly life appears in its shoots, it clothes itself with green blades, it puts forth a youthful stalk, it ripens into an ear; the grain at whose passing you wept begins to resume its form and features. So, man, let the wheat teach you not so much eating as wisdom, let it force you not so much to toil as to believe. On the rest we need not speak, for the blessed apostle tells us in his lucid, clear and heavenly style wherefore, when, how and through whom death has come. O man, receive the faith, for it is freely given. Believe in the resurrection, for he who promises it asks no price."

53. Columbanus

St. Columbanus, the celebrated Irish missionary who was responsible for the monastic foundations at Luxeuil and Bobbio, lived from 543 to 615. Amongst his extant writings are thirteen sermons, one of which is a meditation on life to be considered as a journey and preparation rather than a resting-place and an end in itself.

Sermon 5[53]

"Life, how many have you deceived and seduced and blinded! When you flee, you are nothing. When you appear, you are a shadow. When you are raised up, you are smoke. Every day you flee away, and every day you come. As you flee, you come; and as you come, you flee. Your end varies, but your beginning is the same. You vary in the degree of luxury, but you are uniform in fluidity. The foolish find you sweet, the wise bitter. Those who love you do not know you; those who despise you understand you. So you are not truthful but deceitful. You posture as genuine, but show deceit in departing. So what are you, human life? You are

[53]Text: SLH, Dublin, 1970, ed. Walker, 84.

not life but men's journey. You begin with sin, and end with death. You would be genuine if only the sin of man's first transgression had not interrupted you; then you became transient and mortal when you assigned all your travellers to death. So you are the path to life and not life itself, for you are not true life. You are a path which is not level. For some you are long, for others short; for some broad, for others narrow; for some joyful, for others sad. But for all alike you hasten on, and cannot be summoned back. You are a journey, yes, a journey, but not clear-cut to all. Many see you but few realise that you are a journey; you are so crafty and seductive that only a few realise that you are a journey. So you are to be questioned rather than believed or claimed; you are to be traversed, not dwelt in, wretched human life! We do not dwell on a road, but walk on it, so that by walking on the road we may come to dwell in our fatherland.

So, mortal life, why are you dwelt in, loved, claimed? You are loved and claimed by fools and criminals, but despised by men of sense and suspected by those who are to be saved. So you must be feared and greatly suspected, because you are so fugitive, slippery, dangerous, short, uncertain. You are like a shadow or ghost or cloud. You are nothing or you dissolve into emptiness. So since you are nothing, mortal life — a shadow, fleeing like a bird, unsubstantial as a cloud, or frail like a shadow or dream — all who understand you must journey through you anxiously, carefully, quickly, to hasten as travellers to our true native land. You must not worry what lies behind, but be anxious about what is to come. It is of no avail to have climbed thus far unless you complete the rest, for this life is to be considered as a kind of road and ascent. On the road we must not seek what will be in the fatherland. On the journey is toil and weariness, in our native land rest and untroubled life are stored up for us. So we must beware not to be complacent on the way in case we do not arrive at our true land. There are many indeed on this journey who are idle, untroubled, malicious; they think themselves to be not so much *en route* as already home. They do not advance voluntarily but unwillingly towards their native land which they have assuredly forfeited. For they have anticipated the joys of that land on the way, and from their brief life they have purchased eternal death. Those unhappy ones rejoice in their empty exchange; they have loved what is foreign and transient, and neglected what is native and eternal. So let us avoid the foreign things of earth, however pleasant, alluring and comely, so that we may not lose our own eternal possessions. Let us be found faithful in foreign fields so that we may become heirs in our own. This is what our Lord Jesus Christ bestows on us. To him be glory for ever and ever. Amen."

54. Anselm

> St. Anselm (1033-1109), successor of Lanfranc as Prior of Bec and later Archbishop of Canterbury, was the greatest of the earlier scholastics and the most imposing theologian between Augustine and Aquinas. His vision of the future life is notable for its two-sidedness; the descriptions of the grim separation of sheep from goats at the last judgment and of the sufferings of the damned are reminiscent of the more repellent poetry on the Judgment (e.g., that of Peter Damian); the account of the glories and consolations of heaven are equally enthusiastic and rhetorical.

Anselm, Meditation 17, *Future Blessings*[54]

"Does any man provide for his family here and now as much as God preserves for his own in the future? The beginning of the future and the end of the present is death. All nature abhors it, all feeling trembles before it. Even the beasts ward off death, and seek to preserve their lives in a thousand ways; they flee, they hide. So pay careful attention to what your own awareness is saying to you, what your faith anticipates, what hope promises, what your feelings desire. If your life is a burden to you, if you have a loathing for the world, if the flesh is a sorrow, then you will have a desire for death; for death lays down the burden you are

[54]Text: PL 158. 795

carrying, it takes away your nausea, it takes to itself your bodily suffering. This one thing, I believe, surpasses all the delights, honours and wealth of this world, if in the tranquility of your conscience, the strength of your faith, the certainty of your hope, you are not afraid of death. What more exquisite experience is there for him who for a time has breathed this atmosphere of slavery than to emerge into the freer air of the consciousness? These are the first fruits, the security of your future blessedness, that when death comes your natural terror before it is overthrown by faith, tempered by hope, and routed by a clean conscience.

So in a sense death is the beginning of rest, the end of toils, the destroyer of evils. So scripture has it: 'Blessed are the dead who die in the Lord' (Apoc 14:13). The prophet distinguishes the death of the reprobate from that of the elect: 'All the kings have fallen asleep in glory, everyone in his own house. But you are cast out of your grave as unprofitable issue, defiled and covered over' (Isa 14:18-19). Those whom a good conscience commits to death sleep in glory, because 'the death of his saints is precious in the Lord's sight' (Ps 115:15). They indeed sleep in glory whose falling asleep the angels attend, and whom the saints meet so as to lend assistance to their fellow-citizens, and give them their comfort. They confront the enemies of the new arrivals, drive off those who block their path, refute those who accuse them. They escort their blessed souls to Abraham's bosom, and gather them into the place of rest and peace.

Not so with the wicked, not so! They are dislodged from the body like wicked spirits from a fetid tomb, with hellish instruments. Stained with lust and cloaked in greed, they are cast into the fire for burning, to be ripped open by vultures, and suffocated by the eternal stench. 'Truly the expectation of the just is happiness, but the hope of the wicked will come to naught' (Prov 10:28). But experience does not teach, nor can the pen express, what this quiet is, this peace, this gladness in Abraham's bosom which is promised to those entering on this rest, the happiness awaited. The joyful are waiting until the number of their brethren is complete, so that on the day of the resurrection they may enjoy perpetual happiness clothed in the twofold robe of body and soul.

Let us now contemplate the terror of that day when the powers of heaven will be moved, when the elements dissolve in the conflagration's heat, when the nether world will gape open, when all that is hidden will be revealed. The wrathful judge will come down from on high, his anger smouldering, and 'his chariot like a tempest' (Jer 4:13), so that in his rage he may wreak vengeance and destruction in flames of fire. Blessed is the one who is ready to meet him. But what shall happen to the souls in misery? What wretched lot shall be theirs who are besmirched with debauchery, shot through with avarice, highflown with pride? 'The angels shall go out and separate the wicked from the midst of the just' (Matt 13:49), setting the first on the left and the others on the right.

And now imagine yourself standing before the tribunal of Christ between both these groups, not yet consigned to one side or the other. Turn your eyes to the left of the judge and contemplate that wretched throng. What terror there is, what shame, what a stench, what fear, what grief! There they stand, wretched and full of gloom, gnashing their teeth, breasts heaving, horrible to behold, faces deformed, heads hanging down in shame, in confusion because of their nakedness and foulness. They wish to hide, and there is no place. They try to run, but they are held. If they lift up their eyes, they are menaced by the anger of the judge. If they look downwards, they are overcome with the horrors of the eternal pit. No excuses occur to them for their crimes; they will not be able to complain against God of an unjust sentence, for whatever is decided its justice will not lie hidden from their awareness. See then how much he is to be loved by you, for he has decreed in advance that you be sequestered from this crowd of the damned; he has separated you from them by calling you, he has purified you by justifying you.

Turn your eyes now to the right, and observe those whom you are to join and whose glory you are to share. What grace is there, what honour and happiness, what freedom from all care! Some are lifted high in the seat of judgment, others are resplendent with the martyr's crown, some are decked in the floral wreaths of virginity, others abound in the largesse of almsgiving, and yet others are adorned with the splendor of their teaching and their learning; yet all of them form one unity of love. The glory of Jesus' face shines upon them, a loving rather than awe-inspiring glance; nothing stern or terrifying there, only the gentle and encouraging.

And now stand in between, not knowing to which group the judge's sentence is to consign you. How hard the time of waiting! 'Fear and trembling are come upon me, and darkness has covered me' (Ps 54:6). If he puts me with those on the left, I will have no cause for just complaint. If he sets me amongst those on the right, this will be due to his grace, not to my deserts. Truly, Lord, my life is in your hands. So you see how your soul must be confided to the care of his love; he could have sentenced you to share the lot of the wicked, but instead he has chosen to save you and put you among the innocent. Consider now that you are listening to his voice as he joins you to the company of the saints: 'Come you, blessed of my father, take possession of the kingdom which was prepared for you from the foundation of the world' (Matt 25:34). It is then that the wretched hear that wrathful, dread word of the Lord: 'Depart from me, you cursed, into everlasting fire.' Then he says: 'They will go into everlasting punishment; but the just into life eternal.' O savage separation, O wretched fate! The wicked are carried off lest they see the glory of God. As for the just, they have been set among the choirs of angels according to rank and merit, when the glorious procession will begin led by Christ our head, with all his members following. Then the kingdom will be handed over to God the Father, that he may reign in them and they in him, when they take possession of that kingdom which was prepared for them before the foundation of the world. What it will be like we cannot even conceive, let alone speak or write of it. I only know that nothing will be missing that you would like to have there.

There will be no mourning, no weeping nor sorrow nor fear; no sadness nor dissension nor envy, no tribulation nor temptation; no bad weather nor corruption; no suspicion nor ambition, no flattery nor detraction, no sickness, old age or death; no poverty, night or darkness; no need for eating or drinking or sleeping, no tiredness. In what then will its goodness consist? Where there is no grief nor tears, no pain nor sadness, what can there be except perfect joy? Where there are no trials or tribulations, no change of climate, no alteration in the air, no extremes of heat, no severe winters, what can there be but perfect weather, and the truest possible tranquillity for body and mind? Where there can be nothing to fear, what can there be but absolute security? Where there is neither dissension nor envy there can only be a love that is wholly pure and sincere. Where all deformity is banished, there can only be the perfection of beauty. Where poverty is banished, there can only be plenty. Where there is no toil and nothing wanting, there will be perfect rest and strength. Where nothing is irksome or burdensome, there can only be perfect happiness. Where old age cannot creep in, nor the slightest suspicion of sickness, there can be nothing but perfect health. Where night and darkness do not exist, there can be nothing but perfect light. Where death and mortality are wholly swallowed up, there is nothing except eternal life.

What else should we be looking for? Surely what is more excellent than all the rest — the sight, knowledge and love of the Creator. He will be seen in himself and in all his creatures, ruling all things without anxious care, sustaining everything without effort, giving himself to every creature in his fullness, without slackening or breaking off. We shall look upon his face, most lovable and desirable, on which the angels are eager to gaze. Who can describe its perfection, its brilliance, its sweetness? The Father will be seen in the Son, and the Son in the Father; the holy Spirit in them both. God will be seen as he is, and the promise will be fulfilled by which he says 'Whoever loves me will be loved by my Father, and I will love him and will show myself to him' (John 14:21). From this vision flows that knowledge of which he himself says: 'This is eternal life, to know you, the only true God' (John 17:3). From this vision and knowledge such great love will be born, such a fire of familial affection, such sweetness of charity, such abundance of enjoyment, such a profoundity of desire, that to be satisfied impedes in no way the longing, nor the longing the satisfaction. What then is this? It is 'what eye has never seen, nor ear heard, nor has it entered into the heart of man what God has prepared for them that love him' (1 Cor 2:9).

I have sought, my sister, to sow some seeds of spiritual meditation which I have taken from memory's storehouse of the past blessings received from Christ, from experience of present blessings and from certain hope of future ones. From these fruits of divine love may other, richer blessings spring up and grow, so that meditation may prompt feelings, and feelings produce desire, and desire squeeze out the tears, and tears be your bread day and night (cf. Ps 41:4), until at last you appear in his sight and presence, and are taken up into his embrace, and you can say what is written in the Canticle: 'My beloved is mine, and I am his; he shall linger between my breasts' (Cant 2:26, 1:12). God himself grant you this, who lives and reigns for ever and ever. Amen."

Appendix I

THE PAIN OF THIS WORLD*

'Without any doubt, the mystery of our religion is very deep indeed' (1 Tim 3:16). Paul is referring to the mystery of Christ's incarnation and ascension into glory, and he is exploiting this hymn as instruction in catechetics. 'The point of all our toiling and battling is that we have put our trust in the living God, and he is the saviour of the whole human race, but particularly of believers. This is what you are to enforce in your teaching' (1 Tim 4:10-11). The depth and imponderability of the mystery is nowhere so evident as in the phenomenon of human suffering.

Paul was emphatic that his mission was to preach the good news, but not 'in terms of the philosophy in which the crucifixion of Christ cannot be expressed' (1 Cor 1:17). Yet in the first century, as in succeeding centuries, the teaching recommended by Paul had to be addressed to an audience rightly suspicious of instant saviours. If the sweeping Pauline claims were to be accepted as a satisfying rationale of our life on earth, they had to be underpinned by a perennial philosophy which could explain — or if not explain, help men to accept — the hard problems of human living. Hence the series of christian apologies in the Fathers, which culminate with Augustine's *City of God*, concern themselves with much more than the preaching of Christ's living presence in

---

*Reprinted from *The Way* (October 1981), pp. 261-269.

the world. Augustine has to enunciate his christian vision in the uncomfortable climate of a Rome lately humbled by the barbarian; he begins his defence not by evangelical proclamation but by grasping the nettle of recent famine, torture and death.

So begins a long tradition of christian witness based on that combination of rational enquiry and revealed truth which is dignified with the label of christian humanism. This double approach to the problems of living in the world develops most notably in the schools of the twelfth and thirteenth centuries, when biblical and secular spokesmen each have their authoritative status as guardians of revelation and reason respectively. St. Thomas is rarely content with citation of biblical and patristic teaching, but seeks support for his theological positions from Aristotle, Cicero and Seneca as well.

Such patient reconciliation of received truth and rational analysis can be epitomized in the words of the late T. S. Gregory as 'Trying to understand everything God means by everything he does'. It lies at the root of much of the contemporary liberation-theology; and a manful attempt was made to employ it as a controlling methodology at the recent bishops' synod on marriage and the family, when the 'inductive' principles of the anthropological approach were measured against the 'deductive' norms of the traditional teaching.

The problem of human suffering has traditionally been the sticking-point for many sympathetic enquirers into the truth of Christian claims, and our age of instantaneous pictorial reporting focuses the issue starkly. Can we 'put our trust in the living God. . . the Saviour of the whole human race' as we contemplate in rapid succession the dazed victims of Caribbean typhoons, the emaciated children doomed to die in Uganda, the corpses of Italian worshippers killed at the Sunday liturgy by earth-tremors? Or, to pass from such communal suffering to the ordeals of individuals, what are we to reply to the mother of a Jacqueline Hill, Sunday-school teacher and victim of a 'Ripper' murder in Leeds, when she says 'It seems so unfair'? Or to the old lady of eighty who stumbles, has a cerebral hemorrhage, loses her sight, and sits forlornly asking, 'What shall I do now?' Or to the mother of the deformed baby, unable to work her way through to acceptance of her changed life?

Thomas Blackburn's poem, *Hospital for defectives*, depicts four patients at work in the vegetable-garden, and asks the inevitable question:

> ...and two men pick the turnips up
> and two men pull the cart;
> and yet between the four of them
> no word is ever said,
> because the yeast was not put in
> which makes the human bread.
> But three men stare on vacancy
> and one man strokes his knees;
> what is the meaning to be found
> in such dark vowels as these?
> Lord of the images, whose love
> the eyelid and the rose
> takes for a metaphor, today
> beneath the warder's blows
> the unleavened man did not cry out
> or turn his face away.
> Through such men in a turnip-field
> what is it that you say?

The traditional 'deductive' teaching is that suffering is to be accepted as an indispensable part of the Christian's life. It exists as a result of Adam's fall and the presence of Satan in the world. The classic exposition of this teaching lies in the drama of the book of Job; God allows Satan to play havoc with the family and possessions of one 'perfect and upright, that feared God and eschewed evil'. Suffering is an integral part of the witness of the prophets down to John the Baptist; Christ renews the message when he emphasizes that following him entails the taking up of the cross.

Scripture offers two reasons within the design of providence for the existence of suffering. First, it can be a testing and a training, a discipline imposed by a loving father. 'My son, do not scorn correction from Yahweh; do not resent his rebuke, for Yahweh reproves the man he loves as a father checks a well-loved son' (Prov 3:11-12). The theme is resumed in the Letter to the Hebrews and in Paul: 'The Lord punishes the one he loves: he whips the one whom he accepts' (Heb 12:6). 'When the Lord does punish us, it is to correct us and to stop us being condemned with the world' (1 Cor 11:37). But such suffering will not be beyond our capacity to endure. 'You can trust God not to let you be tried beyond your strength, and with any trial he will give you the way out and the strength to bear it' (1 Cor 10:13). The Pauline view, therefore, is that suffering can be imposed by God as formative training, but such punishment will never become intolerable.

The second reason offered by scripture for the existence of suffering is more mysterious and profound. Suffering if shouldered willingly lightens the burden of others. Christ's role is foreshadowed by the prophecy of the suffering servant in Isaiah: 'Ours were the sufferings he bore, ours the sorrow he carried. *But we thought of him as someone punished, struck by God and brought low.* Yet he was pierced through for our faults, crushed for our sins....On him lies a punishment that brings us peace, and through his wounds we are healed' (Isa 53:3-5). Christ himself came 'to give his life as a ransom for many' (Mk 10:45), and his followers must aspire to the same role (Mk 8:34-35). We identify ourselves with Christ by being willing to share his sufferings undertaken to redeem all men; this service undertaken for others will entail sacrifice and perhaps death itself. 'If you refuse to love, you must remain dead....This has taught us love, that he gave up his life for us; and we too ought to give up our lives for our brothers' (1 John 3:15-16).[1]

These are the main strands of the 'deductive' teaching of scripture on suffering: that it is an inevitable part of man's condition, that it can be used by God to school us, that it will not be intolerable, and that if shouldered willingly it relieves

[1] There is a good analysis of this 'deductive' teaching by M. Tripole, 'Suffering and Christian Growth', in *Supplement to The Way*, 39 (1980), pp. 35ff.

in a mystical way the sufferings of others. The Fathers constantly stress that we are not to challenge or resent its presence, which we must attribute to the incomprehensible nature of divine wisdom.[2] Many of us who confront this problem from within the frontiers of christian adhesion know of people like Mary Craig[3] who have had the strength to live out the implications of the biblical teaching. In her case one can virtually draw the map of how shouldered suffering can bring relief to others, for the painful acceptance of her own handicapped children led her into dynamic participation of the work of the Sue Ryder homes. The profundity of the biblical teaching clearly offers sufficient inspiration and strength for exemplary characters like these.

Inevitably, however, the fact that many Christians have experienced peace of mind and acceptance of the biblical precepts will seem to some enquirers to beg the question. They will reasonably say that what works for some may not — apparently does not — work for others. More fundamentally they will insist that such precepts should not fly in the face of rational analysis, that we should use our God-given reason to ask God 'What is it that you say?'

The first and most basic contribution which reason makes is to distinguish between the sufferings which are the norm of human life (toothache or indigestion, anxiety about teenagers' whereabouts, breakdown through overwork and the like) and those which are intense and protracted. The former are a necessary part of a rational world; they regulate behaviour, signal the need for medical treatment, and enhance the joys of human living by their absence. It is surely this category of less intense suffering of which Paul thinks when he envisages God punishing us as a father punishes his sons (Heb 12:6-9).

Such intense and protracted sufferings as being maimed by a typhoon, suffering starvation through drought, or the degree of anguish which destroys the human personality cannot be considered in the same light. Though the line may

---

[2]John Chrysostom, *De providentia*, 12 (*Sources chrétiennes*, vol. 79).

[3]See her moving book, *Blessings* (London, 1978).

be sometimes difficult to draw, we have to maintain that objectively such experiences are an evil, and that accordingly God cannot be the author of them. He may countenance them, as in the case of Job, but he cannot originate them. This fundamental principle can serve as an important corrective to mistaken interpretations of the 'deductive' teaching. We have probably all heard sermons which have sought to glorify such suffering as an objective good; but reason cries out that a God who is loving and good cannot have willed such things. It seems blasphemy to suggest that the children dying of starvation in Uganda, or the blinded old lady in the hospital-bed, are being punished by the christian God.

As all know, Augustine wrestled with this problem for half his thinking life before finally adopting the Neoplatonist solution that evil must be that corruption which is the privation of good.[4] However heartless it may sound, the rational perspective offers insights which help to make the witnessing of even hideous sufferings less intolerable. Such pains are to be visualized as aberrations or deficiencies in the proper order of the world, and not as integral to the grand design of creation. It is at this point that the Christian must have recourse to the myth of Adam's fall — that radical misdirection of the human will which we call original sin.

It is much easier for the enquirer of our generation to concede the fundamental flaw at the heart of mankind than was the case fifty or sixty years ago. The history of Buchenwald and Hiroshima has left its mark on much of the significant fiction of our day. Those who have read Saul Bellow's *Mr. Sammler's Planet* will recognize the novel as a parable of our times. Arthur Sammler, a Polish Jew from Cracow, had lived for several years in London on nodding terms with H. G. Wells, and had thus become attuned to the scientific humanism which optimistically visualized the world as the oyster of *homo sapiens*. Then by a dreadful irony he returns to Poland, to be imprisoned in a concentra-

---

[4]See especially, *Confessions* 7:3-16 (*Supra*, 25f).

tion camp from which he escapes only by murdering his german guard. Living with jewish relatives in New York, he casts his one sound eye over the anarchy of New York society: the pickpocketing, the violence, the obsessive preoccupation with sex, the avarice of near relatives. And as he sits over the treatises of Meister Eckhart, he contemplates the possibility of a fresh start for man on the moon. This is the kind of candid camera which encourages the theologian to preach the myth of original sin; man fell by desiring to decree good and evil for himself, and redemption is the only remedy for this canker in the human race. We are 'chronically ill patients',[5] and the suffering which we experience is a part of our condition of alienation from God.

Two consequences follow from this flawed condition. First, our bodies are overtaken by a progressive material corruption and by death. All the sufferings concomitant with the gradual process of dying (even including such harrowing examples as the old lady overcome with blindness) are acceptable to the reason as a consequence of our being human. Secondly, we are vitiated not merely by material corruption but also by moral corruption. Much of the suffering in the world is inflicted by ourselves upon ourselves or upon each other. But it is not merely a matter of our own sins and omissions catching up with us, nor a matter of innocents (like Jacqueline Hill) becoming victims of a neighbour's spite. Our sins in this generation attack or handicap those who succeed us, just as the sins of the fathers (the phrase inevitably recalls the tragedy of Ulster) rebound on us.

It is therefore rational to accept the existence of many forms of suffering as the consequence of our corrupted material and moral nature. But we cannot claim that there is any visible logic in the allocation of suffering to particular individuals. Divine scripture claims that God punishes those whom he loves, but many of the Fathers are in no doubt that there is no apparent consistency in the trials which individuals undergo. 'Not only are good men found in

[5] I take the phrase from Peter Geach, *Providence and Evil* (Cambridge, 1977).

evil fortune and evil men in good fortune, which seems unjust', says Augustine, 'but in many cases evil men experience evil fortune and good men good fortune, so that the judgments of God become even more inscrutable, and his ways more unsearchable'; Augustine concludes that what good and evil men share — the blessings and sufferings of this world — are not to be accounted important.[6]

To the eye of reason, then, immoderate and protracted suffering may strike at random; but can its very existence in the world be justified? It is possible to argue that such suffering, even if apparently undeserved, is 'inevitable in the best possible world'.[7] A world which is to enable man to achieve the highest realization of his potential must contain within it trials and hazards to be overcome; moreover there must exist in that world fixed laws to allow men full play to act as free moral agents. As Peter Geach remarks, such virtues as those of Thomas More or Maximilian Kolbe could never have emerged except in a world where extreme villainy was permitted to exist.

The 'best possible world' must have not only fixed moral laws but also fixed physical laws to allow man to achieve his full potential of inventive genius. Perhaps the most memorable literary expression of this basic truth is (in John Dryden's famous formula) 'the best poem of the best poet', the *Georgics* of Virgil. Here is presented a powerful picture of a planned and ordered world in which the divine dispensation sets before men a series of trials and difficulties which he has been given the mental and material equipment to overcome. Has it not become the cliché of our century that man can tread the moon, but has failed dismally to feed the starving? Is not the solution to the hazards of typhoons in the Caribbean, earthquakes in Algeria and Italy, and drought in Uganda precisely the application of human intelligence, hard work, vigilance — all combined with a sense of community and piety — such as Virgil proposed? And the

[6]*City of God*, 20:2.

[7]See C. A. Campbell, 'Reason and the Problem of Suffering', in *Philosophy* 10 (1935), pp. 154ff.; John Collins, 'C. A. Campbell and the Problem of Suffering', in *Religious Studies*, 16 (1980), pp. 307ff.

reward would be a world of plenty, of which the 'glorification of Italy' in the *Georgics* presents such a splendid poetic
vision. This awareness of the beneficence of God's creation,
which appears to require nothing more from men than
sustained ingenuity and effort in order to create a paradise,
has led poetic thinkers from Isaiah to Teilhard to foresee an
earth of blessedness; we need not succumb to this seductive
'millenarist' prospect to accept that man has been endowed
with the capacity to master his environment and to obliter-
ate the hazards of typhoons, earthquakes and droughts if
only he is willing to apply himself to the problems which
should concern him. The divine dispensation has left a
world of fixed physical laws for man to exploit for the good
of his species, and the responsibility for failure is man's, not
God's.

For many Christians, however, this is too chilling a
vision, with its overtones of the 'death of God' thesis, or the
sense of an Epicurean divinity who leaves man to his own
devices. Christians cannot subscribe to the notion of a frigid
god who ignores the cries of the weak, the poor, the distressed. Our God is the God of the psalms, 'who hears the
cry of the poor' (Ps 33:7), the defender of widows and
orphans (Ps 67:5). Our God cannot contemplate with equanimity the starving child in Uganda or the Vietnamese
crippled by a Russian or an American bomb. The noble
notion of man grappling with the difficulties of his environment and aspiring to full moral and spiritual maturity has to
be complemented with the vision of an all-compassionate
Father who knows our limitations and sustains us in our
trials. We are not mere cyphers in a grand cosmic development, but set on earth for the love, knowledge and service of
God.

It is therefore reasonable to infer that a balance will be
struck between what we bear in this life and what we experience in the life to come, that those who suffer grievously
here will have their compensation in heaven. This is a theme
which recurs repeatedly in the fathers. Augustine states that
since death itself is the outcome of our first parents' sinning,
it is an evil which we must endure. 'Whatever it is which

deprives dying people of their senses and causes deep distress, increases the merit of their patience if it is endured in a devoted and faithful way.... Since death is man's repayment for sin, it sometimes obtains for him exemption from the future repayment for sin.'[8] John Chrysostom asks: 'How did sickness, sores, poverty and the absence of men to tend him harm Lazarus? Was it not through these hardships that he won more splendid crowns to wear?'[9] The parable of Dives and Lazarus, the distillation of the scriptural teaching that there will be a just balance between our experiences in this world and in the next, haunted the consciousness of many of the fathers of the Church, as it did of Paul (cf. Rom 8:18).

We may summarize the arguments from reason in this way. Intense and protracted suffering is an evil; God cannot be the author of it. Such suffering is an aberration in the order of the world which God did not will; it is the result of our flawed humanity. The material decay in our bodies entails suffering in the course of nature. The moral flaw or canker within us causes us to inflict suffering upon ourselves, or upon our neighbour, or upon generations still to come. But beyond these self-inflicted pains lie sufferings for which man cannot be made directly responsible; but he has been granted the intellectual, physical and material means by which to cope with these hazards. Many of the calamities which we suffer are the outcome of his failure to use these resources. Even so, the loving Father does not remain indifferent to the sufferings which as individuals men must endure with no logical pattern or allocation; the notion of justice suggests that those who suffer harshly here will be compensated in heaven.

It is clear that however manfully we try to reconcile these 'inductive' arguments with the 'deductive' biblical teachings, there remains much which we cannot explain or begin to understand. The pauline verses which must always be at the forefront of the Christian's mind, 'How incomprehensible

---

[8] *City of God*, 13:6.

[9] John Chrysostom, *Quod nemo laeditur*, 4 (*Sources Chrétiennes*, vol. 103).

are his judgments, and how unsearchable his ways. For who hath known the mind of the Lord, or who hath been his counsellor?' (Rom 11:33-34), are in fact the culminating argument which the reason must accept. Man's finite mind cannot plumb the depths or heights of the infinite mystery. There is a twelfth-century allegorical poem, the *Anticlaudianus* of Alan of Lille, in which human wisdom mounts to heaven in a spacecraft drawn by the five senses, and steered by reason; reason can take her only to the limits of the firmament, and theology conducts her onwards towards heaven. But even under theology's guidance, wisdom is blinded by what she sees; faith has to be summoned to revive her, and to lead her onward into the presence of God the Father. The reason must acknowledge and be content with her own partial vision, admitting with Job that man cannot comprehend the ways of God.

Scholastic argument rarely survives the shattering impact of emotional experience. It happened that while I was gathering my thoughts for this paper with the deadline looming, I was invited to talk to a local discussion-group, and I cold-bloodedly chose this subject to clarify the pattern of the argument. The man who had to give the vote of thanks almost broke down; I was told afterwards that the week before his small niece had fallen from a balcony and killed herself, and that he had spent the week trying to console her mother. I went away cursing the glibness with which I had rehearsed the arguments for human responsibility for suffering, for the need for suffering in the best possible world; the glibness with which I had spoken of the faith which enables us to believe that God 'orders all things sweetly'. In such circumstances it must be enough to ask: 'what is it that you say?'

P.G.W.

Appendix II

APOSTOLIC LETTER OF POPE JOHN PAUL II ON THE CHRISTIAN SIGNIFICANCE OF HUMAN SUFFERING

I
Introduction

I. There is a suffering which is effective unto salvation; and St. Paul proclaims its power when he says: 'I bring to completion in my own flesh what is still wanting to the sufferings of Christ with regard to his body, the Church.'[1]

These words of the apostle Paul appear to present us with the final term of the long drawn-out pilgrimage of pain which runs like a filament through man's history, suffusing it with the light of God's word. The epigram carries with it the value of a saying newly-minted, and a gladness besides, which is why he begins, 'Now I rejoice in my sufferings on your behalf.'[2] For the gladness has its source in the suffering's significance, when this is rightly understood; and this perception is also shared by the rest of us, though it first touched the mind of the blessed Paul of Tarsus, who is the author of the saying. What the apostle conceived he was glad to pass on to others. For he knew that they would be

[1]Col 1:24.　　　　　　　　　　[2]*Ibid.*

helped by it, as he had been himself, to penetrate the meaning of this suffering which saves.

2. The theme of suffering, in this precise context of its relation to salvation, would seem to insert itself very aptly into this year consecrated to the Redemption; which is being celebrated by the Church as an extraordinary jubilee. It provides us with an excellent opportunity to examine the matter with the greatest care. And even if this Holy Year were not being celebrated, the question about the phenomenon of pain would still affect humankind at every level and in every corner of the earth. The distress it causes is, so to speak, born into the world with humanity, and is a subject that constantly provokes our attention. For although Paul in his *Letter to the Romans* writes that 'Every creature, as we know, has been groaning and is in travail up until now',[3] and we are aware that the animal kingdom as a whole experiences pain, nevertheless the term 'suffering' properly and uniquely applies to humankind. The idea is as profound as humanity itself in that it reveals the depths of a human soul, and in a way reaches beyond it. It seems to belong to that environment where man transcends the material, one of the elements in which he finds that it is his destiny to exceed his own capabilities, to which in some dark and secret way he is called.

3. If an examination of suffering and all its scope seems to be fitting during the Holy Year of Redemption, it is because through Christ's cross, through his torments, the Redemption was accomplished. Similarly during this year, that truth comes to mind, as was stated in the Encyclical Letter *Redemptor Hominis*, 'the way of the Church is everyman in Christ.'[4] It may be said then that everyman, whenever suffering enters his life, becomes the way of the Church. Obviously this can happen in a person's life at various times, for a variety of reasons, and will assume different forms. Yet however it comes, it would seem true to say that suffering is inseparable from human life here below.

Granted, then, that during this earthly life a person must

---

[3]Rom 8:22   [4]14:18, 21, 22.

pass through afflictions of one kind or another, the Church must always meet humankind along this road, and perhaps most fittingly during this Year. Because she finds her origin in this sacred mystery of the Redemption on Christ's cross, the Church must strive to come face to face with humanity, especially in those places where it is acquainted with grief. For it is there in this confrontation that humanity truly becomes the way of the Church; a highway which takes precedence over all others.

4. During this holy year of Redemption, then, these factors lead us to our meditation. When we reflect on human suffering, it inclines us towards compassion; it gives birth to reverence, and also brings with it its own kind of fear. For it has in it a special wealth of mystery. The awe-inspiring nature of any and every form of human suffering must take pride of place in all that we intend to say here, moved as we are by the deepest affections of the heart and the commandment of faith. In reflecting on suffering, these two reasons seem to come together and find a special unity. The first is insistent that we overcome any fear; the second provides us with the human material (an example might be the above citation from St. Paul) because of and through which we may dare to reach out after what would appear to be altogether unattainable in every man. For man in his suffering is clothed in the most sacred and inviolable of secrets.

II
The field of human suffering

5. If we look at suffering from a subjective point of view, as something highly personal and inherent in the human spirit which of its nature is substantial and unique, it would appear that we can neither define it nor offer analogies for it. Furthermore, if we look at it objectively, it may be that there is nothing else demanding so much reflection and meditation, and the sort of treatment owed to a serious enquiry where the right questions and answers are asked and given. And clearly it is not just a matter of giving a description. For

along with any definition we may give of suffering, there are other criteria which must be applied if we are to get the true measure of human suffering.

It is evident, first of all, that medicine, as the science and art of healing, has as its field of investigation in the vast area of human suffering whatever is most familiar: the matters, that is, which can be most accurately identified and diagnosed, and are of a kind which can be dealt with by established methods of healing — therapy which works by opposing the suffering. Medicinal healing is only part of the picture. Human suffering covers a much wider area and has many more strands. The human person suffers in ways that the art of healing cannot always reach, not even with its most advanced techniques. The skein of human suffering always stretches wider than disease. It is more intricate and tends to thrust its tangled roots down into humanity itself. We shall begin to comprehend this more easily by making the distinction between physical and moral suffering, which is based on the two parts of man, the corporeal and spiritual elements, as the direct and proper object of suffering. Although passion (or pain) and suffering are to a certain extent synonymous, physical suffering denotes that the body is in pain, whereas moral suffering denotes mental anguish. Here we are dealing with suffering of a spiritual kind, not merely the mental ingredient of suffering which is present both in moral and physical affliction. The extent and diversity of moral affliction is in every sense the equal of those denoting physical pain, and the former would appear to be more difficult to identify and less amenable to therapy.

6. Sacred scripture might be called the great book of suffering. It is worthwhile citing some examples from various places in the Old Testament in which the marks of human suffering, particularly its moral aspects, are especially noteworthy. There we find suffering in the form of danger of death,[5] in the death of children,[6] most poignantly

---

[5]Cf. Isa 38:1-3 — the experience of Hezekiah.

[6]Cf. Gen 15:16 — the fear of Hagar; Gen 37:33-35 — as Jacob imagined; cf. 2 Sam 19:1 — David's experience.

where it concerns the death of a first-born and only son;[7] again, in the form of childlessness,[8] the nostalgia of the exile,[9] persecution and hostility,[10] the contumely and mockery of those who are suffering,[11] loneliness and abandonment;[12] in the form also of remorse of conscience,[13] the difficulty of understanding why evil men prosper whilst the good are molested,[14] the infidelity and ingratitude of friends and relatives,[15] and the misfortunes of one's people.[16]

The Old Testament also looks at the human person as a composite of the corporeal and the physical, and often links the moral afflictions of the spirit with the pains of various parts of the body: the bones,[17] the kidneys,[18] the liver,[19] the entrails,[20] the heart.[21] Certainly moral sufferings flow over into the corporeal or somatic, and frequently extend themselves to the whole complex of the human person.

7. These examples show that the bible provides us with a full list of situations in which human beings are pursued by diverse sufferings. In spite of its diversity, this index is in no sense exhaustive of the sufferings already assembled in the unwritten book of human history, the history of the whole

[7]Cf. Tob 10:1-7 — the fear of Anna, Tobias' mother; cf. also Jer 6:26; Amos 8:10; Zach 12:10.

[8]Cf. Gen 15:2 — Abraham; Gen 30:1 — Rachel; 1 Sam 1:6-10 — Anna.

[9]Cf. Ps 137 [136] — the lamentation of the Babylonian exiles.

[10]Cf. Ps 22 [21]:17-21; Jer 18:18.

[11]Cf. Job 19:18; 30:1-19; also Ps 22 [21]:7-9; Ps 42 [41]:11; Ps 44 [43]:16-17; Jer 20:7; Isa 53:3 — the Suffering Servant.

[12]Cf. Ps 22 [21]:2-3; Ps 31 [30]:13; Ps 38 [37]:12; 88 [87]:9-19; Jer 15:17; Isa 53:3.

[13]Ps 51 [50]:5; Isa 53:3; Zach 12:10.

[14]Ps 73 [72]:3-14; Qoh 4:1-3.

[15]Cf. Job 19:19; Ps 41 [40]:10; Ps 55 [54]:13-15; Jer 20:10; Sir 37:1-6.

[16]Cf. Ps 44 [43]:10-17; Ps 77 [76]:3-11; Ps 79 [78]:11; Ps 89 [88]:51; Isa 22:4; Jer 4:8; 13:17; 14:17-18; Ezek 9:8; 21:11-12; Dan 3:31-40; 9:16-19.

[17]Cf. Isa 38:13; Jer 23:9; Ps 31 [30]:10-11; 42 [41]:10-11.

[18]Cf. Ps 73 [72]:21; Job 16:13; Lam 3:13.

[19]Cf. Lam 2:11.

[20]Cf. Isa 16:11; Jer 4:19; Job 30:27; Lam 1:20.

[21]Cf.1 Sam 1:8; Jer 4:19; 8:18; Lam 1:20-22; Ps 38 [37]:9, 11.

human race, as it continues to offer cases of suffering in the life of every man.

In fact, it can be said that the human person suffers whenever any kind of evil is experienced. In the language of the Old Testament, the relationship between suffering and evil is such that they come to mean the same thing, and there is no separate word to express suffering. When a person suffers in any way, it is called evil.[22] Only the Greek tongue — and therefore the New Testament and the Greek versions of the Old Testament — employs the word πάσχω, which means, 'I am affected by something,' 'I have a feeling,' 'I suffer.' It is by means of this verb that suffering is differentiated from objective evil, and denotes the condition in which man experiences evil, and suffers pain in that experience. So it is that suffering has a twofold character: it is active and passive (from the Latin word *patior*, 'I suffer'); so that even when a person is the cause of his or her own suffering, this is still something passive, something which 'happens', according to its essential nature.

Nor does it follow from this that mental anguish, in its psychological aspect, does not possess its own special activity. In fact we can distinguish out, subjectively, many separated 'actions'; pain, sadness, hope confounded, discouragement, despair even, depending on the sensitivity of the persons, whether they tend to be moved more superficially or more deeply, whether that is, it goes down deep or remains on the surface. Here we touch the whole psychological structure of the one who is suffering, the unique complex of his faculties for experiencing. Here, in every psychological manner of affliction, there is always an experience of evil in which the pain is felt.

---

[22]It will be helpful to remember that the Hebrew root *r"* means in general evil as opposed to the good (*ṭōb*), and makes no distinction between the physical, psychological or moral sense of the word. It occurs in the substantival form *ra'*, *ra'a*, and again makes no distinction between what is evil in itself, the evil action or the evil agent. With regard to verbal forms, besides the simple *qual* which indicates variously "something is evil," there is also a reflexive passive form *niphal* — "to undergo evil," "to be afflicted by evil," and a causative form *hiphil* — "to inflict evil," "to impose evil on someone." The Hebrew lacks a word corresponding to the Greek *pascho* (I suffer) which is probably why this word occurs rarely in the Septuagint.

It is not surprising, then, if suffering itself leads to a further question about the nature of evil: what is evil?

It would appear that this question cannot be separated from the one about suffering; and the Christian answer differs from those given by the traditions of other religions and cultures, where human existence is itself believed to be an evil, from which each person has to be freed. Christianity, however, proclaims that existence is essentially good, which applies to all things that have existence. It acknowledges the goodness of the Creator and declares that all creatures are good. So one is afflicted with suffering because of evil, which is a kind of privation or corruption of good. One might say that the human person suffers through not sharing in a good, by being cut off from it, or from which one has excluded oneself. The human being suffers maximally when in the normal course of events, he or she ought to be a participant in a particular good, and this is not what is happening.

According to the Christian understanding, then, the truth of suffering is to be found in evil, which in some sense or other always corresponds to a good.

8. So it is that human suffering is to be regarded as a particular environment which coexists with humanity, appears and vanishes there, but sometimes, on the other hand, consolidates and roots itself there. This ambience of suffering is as it were breathed in by many individually, even by the majority, for it is scattered abroad at random. And everyman by his own personal suffering constitutes a small fragment of this environment; and not only that, but the same atmosphere is breathed and given definite dimensions in each one, in a way that is unique to the individual. There is also a reciprocal and social dimension of this ambience of suffering, which gives it its own structure. Those who suffer begin to become like one another, because of similar living conditions, the experience of what happens to them, their longing for kindly treatment and care and, perhaps most of all, because of their ceaseless questioning about the meaning of their suffering. Hence, though this environment of suffering is experienced piecemeal, it also invites to fellowship and

to bonds of intimacy: a challenge that we shall try to bear in mind as we offer these reflections.

When we look at this environment of suffering according to its social as well as its personal aspects, there emerge times and moments in human life when the climate becomes as it were more opaque: for example, when natural calamities occur, such as plagues, catastrophes and disasters and the various kinds of shared calamity, one thinks of a ruinous harvest and the dreadful hunger and other evils that flow from it.

Finally there is the dread spectre of war; and here specific events come to mind: the ravages of the last two world wars, the second of which wreaked a much more frightening havoc in the shape of the huge numbers of those who died and with it such a mass of human suffering. And the second half of our century in its turn — as though in payment for the deviations and crimes consequent on the lifestyle of our present civilisation, is sowing the terrible seeds of nuclear conflict, to the extent that we can hardly contemplate these times of ours except in terms of suffering piled upon unimaginable suffering. There is even a distinct possibility that the human race will destroy itself. Here is the reason why this environment, which beyond doubt makes every human being its subject, would appear to be converting itself, in our time more than ever before, into a special world of suffering. It is also a world which has equally been transformed by the advance of human technology and brought to the edge of destruction by the mistakes and crimes of humankind.

III
Searching for an answer to the question:
what is the significance of suffering?

9. In every kind of pain, in the whole ambit of suffering endured by humankind, is inevitably involved the question 'Why?' It concerns the cause of the pain, its reason, purpose and in particular its meaning. All these questionings are the companions of human suffering, and also, it seems, define

its very humanness, underlining the fact that it belongs to our very nature — a suffering that is nothing else but human.

Though pain, and especially physical pain, afflicts the animal world in general, it is only the human being, when stricken by affliction, who knows that he or she is suffering, searches for the reason why, and humanly speaking suffers even more acutely until a likely answer is forthcoming. The really difficult question, and others akin to it, concerns evil. Why does evil exist? Why is there evil in the world? When we formulate it thus, we are, in one way or another, including a question about suffering.

Both questions are problematic, whether they are put by one individual to another, or one group to another; and it is the same when the person puts them to God. It is not from the world that one demands the answer, even though one's suffering often comes from the world. It is from God, as Creator and Lord of the World. We know well enough that in this matter people reach a point where they become wholly devoid of guidance and enter into conflict with God and are even brash enough to deny his existence. For if the world's existence opens up to the gaze of human intelligence God's existence, power, wisdom and magnificence, it also happens that evil and suffering sometimes totally blur this image, most specially in those daily occurrences of innocent suffering and of the many crimes which escape condign punishment. These situations, perhaps more than anything else, show how crucial is this matter of suffering's meaning, and with what insight we need to proceed in examining the question and whatever answers can be given to it.

10. It is indeed possible for a person to put the question to God with troubled heart, bewildered mind and impassioned concern. And God indeed awaits and listens to the question as we learn from revelation in the Old Testament. It is in the book of Job that the question receives its most profound treatment.

The familiar story is of a just man who, without being guilty of any fault, is put to the test through countless sufferings. His material possessions, sons and daughters are lost to him, and at the last he himself is stricken by a dire sickness. Whilst he is suffering these dreadful circumstances, three of his old companions come to visit him, and each of them in different ways tries to persuade him that he must have committed some grievous misdemeanour, since he is stricken with so many distressing pains. For suffering, they say, only afflicts a person as punishment for sin. It is inflicted by God who is perfectly just, and it happens only in the divine order of justice. These old acquaintances wish to convince Job that the evil he suffers is morally justified; their purpose is to defend the position, to their own satisfaction, that suffering has a moral significance. It is their belief that suffering is intelligible only as the punishment for sin, inasmuch as it falls within the ambit of God's justice who recompenses good with good and requites evil with evil.

So they rehearse the teaching contained in other books of the Old Testament which demonstrates that suffering is meted out by God because of sin. The God of revelation is Legislator and Judge who is above all human jurisdiction. This God of revelation is first and foremost the Creator from whom the essential good of creation flows forth within the very act of existence. Thus the conscious and free violation of this good as perpetrated by the human person is not simply the transgression of a law; it is an offence committed against God, the supreme Lawgiver. Such a violation bears the true mark of sin according to the precise meaning of the word in biblical and theological parlance. The punishment is made to fit the moral evil of the sin; and it maintains the moral order in giving it that transcendent value imparted to it by the will of the Creator and supreme Legislator. This is the source of one of the fundamental truths of religious faith, also based on revelation, which affirms that God is the just Judge, who rewards good and punishes evil: 'You, Lord, are just in all that you have done to us and all your works are true and your ways right, and all your judgments are truth. For you have carried out true judgments in all that you have brought upon us...for in truth and justice you have brought all this upon us because of our sins.'[23]

The view of Job's comforters reveals a belief often found in the moral consciousness of the human race: the objective moral order demands a sanction for its violation, for sin and crime. Hence suffering is revealed as an evil rightfully approved. The belief of those who explain suffering as punishment for sin is supported by the order of justice and corresponds to the opinion put forward by one of Job's comforters: 'I speak of what I have seen; those who work iniquity sow suffering and reap its harvest.'[24]

11. However, Job repudiates the principle that suffering is the punishment for sin as untrue. His judgment rests on his own belief, for he is conscious that he has in no way deserved this punishment. In fact, he sets out the good deeds he has performed during his lifetime. And at the last, God himself reproves Job's comforters for their accusations and avows that Job is not guilty. His suffering is that of the innocent, and this is to be accepted as a mystery which no one can succeed in fully understanding by the power of human intelligence.

Nor does the book of Job do damage to the transcendent moral order whose foundations rest upon justice and are determined by the whole of revelation as set forth in the Old and New Testaments. This book also emphatically teaches that the principles of the moral order cannot be interpreted in any selective or arbitrary fashion. It is true that there is an aspect of suffering that identifies it with punishment, when the punishment is connected with a sin; but it by no means follows that all suffering is due to sin and has the character of punishment. In the Old Testament, Job as the type of the just man is striking proof of this. Revelation, as the word of God himself, manifestly states the problem of the suffering of the innocent, of one who is suffering though guiltless. Job is not being punished; there is no reason at all that he should be visited with punishments, no matter how severe his trials.

---

[23]Dan 3:27-28; cf. Ps 17 [18]:7-10; 36 [35]:7; 48 [47]:12; 51 [50]:6; 99 [98]:4; 119 [118]:75; Mal 3:16-21; Mt 20:16; Mk 10:31; Lk 17:34; Jn 5:30; Rom 2:2.

[24]Job 4:8.

From the beginning of the story it is clear that God has permitted him to be tested at the instance of Satan, who stood before the Lord and questioned Job's righteousness: 'Job does not fear God for nothing, does he?...you have blessed the work of his hands and his earthly possessions have increased. But stretch out your hand just a little and touch all that he has, and see if he continues to bless you to your face.'[25] So, when the Lord agrees to try Job with suffering, it is to demonstrate his rightfulness. The suffering has the character of a test.

The book of Job does not exhaust all that revelation has to say on the subject. It is in some respects a foreshadowing of the passion of Christ. In its own right it provides an adequate reason for the view that problems about the meaning of suffering are not to be solved by reference to the moral order simply, which is based on justice alone. Such a solution has a fundamental and transcendent explanation and virtue, but this is not applicable to suffering experiences like those of Job. Equally and most vitally, it would seem to limit and water down the whole idea of justice and justification such as we find in revelation.

12. The book of Job sets out the problem of suffering in a very pointed manner. In showing that the innocent also suffer, it does not solve the problem. However, what we do notice in the Old Testament is a certain way of seeing things, a tendency to set aside the view that suffering can be explained only as a sanction for sin, while at the same time emphasising the efficacy of suffering as a corrective. In the sufferings which God inflicted on the chosen people we find the stimulus of his mercy which is itself a corrective and leads to conversion: 'These punishments are not for the destruction but for the correction of our nation.'[26]

In this way the reason for the individual's punishment is assured; and its potency is seen not so much as the compensation of the objective evil of the transgression by another ill, but as leaving the way open for restoring the goodness of the one who is suffering.

---

[25] Job 1:9-11.   [26] 2 Mac 6:12.

This aspect of suffering is of the highest importance in the whole of revelation. It is deeply rooted in the Old Testament, but more especially in the New. Suffering should lead to conversion, that is, to the restoration of what is good in a person, who can recognize the divine mercy in this call to penitence. The commitment to penitence is to the conquering of evil which lurks in a person in many different forms: and to the strengthening of what is good in the person, as well as in neighborliness to others, and above all in relationship with God.

13. Yet if we are to divine the real answer to the question which asks the reason for suffering, we must examine the revelation of divine love wherein ultimately we shall find the meaning of all things that are. For love is still the all-abundant source of suffering's meaning; and it remains a mystery, since we know that none of our explanations can be adequate or equal to our task. Christ leads us into the mystery and sees to it that we find a reason for suffering's existence, insofar as we are capable of touching the height and depth of the divine love.

If we are to rediscover the profundities of suffering's meaning, we are to follow the Word who is revealed by God, opening our hearts to all that is human and taking account of the whole range of human powers. Above all we must welcome the light of revelation, certainly in its expression of the transcendental order of justice, but more importantly in the light that love sheds on this order: the love which is the supreme and certain origin of all that is. Here is the abundant source which aids us to discover the answer to every question about suffering. God has given this answer to man in the Cross of Jesus Christ.

IV
Jesus Christ, the Bearer of all human sufferings

14. 'For God so loved the world as to give his only begotten Son, that whosoever believes in him may not

perish but have eternal life.'[27] These words which Christ addressed to Nicodemus lead us into the heart of God's work of salvation. They are declaratory of the very stuff of Christian soteriology, the theology of salvation. Salvation means being set free from evil, and it is thus closely related to the problem of suffering. The words to Nicodemus inform us that God gives his Son to the world so as to free humanity from evil, which itself holds the last and definitive explanation of suffering. At the same time, the words 'to give' indicate that this act of setting free must be achieved by the only-begotten Son through his own personal suffering. Here love is shown, the infinite love of this only-begotten Son and of the Father who gives his Son for this purpose. Humankind is the object of this love, love given to the world: a love effective unto salvation.

Here we enter a new phase in our argument, and this we must unfold before the eyes of our mind as we proceed with our common reflections on our general theme. This particular aspect is different from the one which was set out above, circumscribing as it did our search and limiting the meaning of suffering to the bounds of justice. This new aspect is that of the redemption which the Old Testament statement of Job the just man already seems to anticipate (at least according to the Vulgate text): 'I know that my Redeemer liveth...and at the last...I shall see God.'[28] So far, our meditation has primarily and almost exclusively concerned itself with suffering in its many finite forms: the sufferings of Job the just were of this kind. But the words cited above from the conversation of Jesus with Nicodemus look at suffering according to its principal and definitive meaning. For God gives his Only-begotten so that humankind 'may not perish', and the meaning of this statement 'may not perish' is more exactly defined in the words that follow: 'but may have eternal life.'

Man does indeed perish when he loses eternal life. It is not so much temporal suffering, any kind of suffering which is

---

[27] Jn 3:16.　　　　　　　　[28] Job 19:25-26: the Vulgate text.

opposed to eternal life, but that specific and unchangeable suffering — the loss of eternal life, being rejected by God, damnation. The only-begotten Son has been given to humankind above all to protect them from this evil, from a suffering that is fixed and immutable. In accordance with his salutary task, Christ must lay his hands on the roots of suffering which transcend time; for it is thence, in the history of humankind, that suffering proceeds. These transcendent origins of suffering are to be found in sin and death; they underlie the loss of eternal life. The mission of the only-begotten Son is precisely to conquer sin and death. His obedience unto death defeats sin and death itself by the force of his resurrection.

15. When we say that Christ in his mission takes hold of evil by its roots, we mean not merely evil and suffering as fixed and immutable, its eschatological aspect — 'so that man may not perish but have eternal life'; we are referring as well to evil and suffering from the temporal and historical point of view, at least obliquely. For evil is the associate of sin and death. And though we must not reckon human suffering to be the consequence of actual sins except after using great prudence — and the example of the just man Job is our cautionary tale in this respect — yet it cannot be divorced from the sin of our ancestors, from what St. John calls 'the sin of the world,'[29] the sinful state, that is, of individuals in their actions and of social movements in human history. And though it would be wrong here to apply a narrow concept of direct responsibility, as did Job's three comforters, we cannot at the same time put aside the conclusion that human suffering derives from a manifold involvement in sinfulness.

It is much the same when we turn our attention to death. Often enough it is awarded as a deliverance from the sufferings of this life. Yet no one can overlook the fact that it puts a final conclusion to the deadly work of suffering, whether in the make-up of either body or soul. Principally death brings with it the dismemberment of the entire psycho-

---

[29] Jn 1:29.

physical personality of the whole man. The soul is separated from the body and continues to exist so. But a progressive decomposition overtakes the body, according to the word of the Lord God, the sentence pronounced when man first sinned at the beginning of his earthly history: 'Dust thou art, and unto dust thou shalt return.'[30] So, although death is not a suffering in any temporal sense, because up to a point it transcends all torments, yet the evil which the human person experiences in death has a finality which is all-pervading. Now the only-begotten Son by his salutary activity frees all humankind from sin and death. Above all he deletes sin and its dominion from the page of human history, that domination which implanted its roots under the impact of the wicked Spirit out of original sin. Then he gives to us the capability of living under the influence of sanctifying grace. After his victory over sin he also overthrows the dominion of death, and there by his own rising from the dead opens the way to the future resurrection of our bodies. The one and the other are necessary conditions for eternal life which is the unchangeable blessedness of those who are brought into union with God. This means, for those who are saved, that suffering, in the light of the end-time, is entirely destroyed.

Because of Christ's salutary activity, all live here below in the hope of life and holiness eternal. Even though the victory which Christ has won through his cross and resurrection over sin and death does not take away the sufferings of this present time, nor set free from pain the historical complex of human life, it does, however, shed new light on the whole historical dimension and thus on all suffering. This light is the light of salvation, and also of the gospel, the good news. In the very radiance of this light is to be found the truth uttered in the words to Nicodemus: 'God so loved the world that he gave his only Son.'[31] It is a truth that changes human history from top to bottom and the human condition here below. For though sin survived, rooted in the historical process as an inheritance from the beginning, and

[30]Gen 3:19.   [31]Jn 3:16.

as the sin of the world as well as the summation of all individual sins, God the Father loved his only-begotten Son and loves him always. In time, then, and because of this love which is all-conquering, the Father 'gives' the Son, that he may touch the very roots of human evil, and by this salutary activity reach out to the whole environment of suffering which is shared by humankind.

16. In his messianic activity amongst the people of Israel, Christ moved directly into the ambience of human suffering. As 'he went about doing good',[32] his actions were directed primarily to those who were suffering and seeking help. He healed the sick, comforted the afflicted, fed the hungry, freed human beings from deafness, blindness, leprosy, diabolic possession and a variety of physical ailments. And three times he brought back the dead to life. He was sympathetic to every kind of human suffering both of body and spirit. He was also teaching, and right at the centre of his doctrine are the eight beatitudes, directed to people who were a prey to various kinds of adversity in their lives. There were those who were 'poor in spirit', those who 'mourned', who 'hungered and thirsted after justice', who 'suffered persecution for justice' sake, in Christ's name, when others reviled and persecuted them, spoke all kinds of evil against them and lied about them.[33] So Matthew; but Luke mentions expressly those 'who are hungry now'.[34]

In any case, Christ entered into the vale of human suffering principally by taking this suffering on himself. During the time of his public life he experienced extreme tiredness and had no fixed abode; he was misunderstood even by his closest relatives; whilst his greatest suffering was to be overshadowed more and more by a miasma of envy and the open conspiracies of those who would cut him off from the land of the living. His consciousness of this was such that he often spoke to his disciples of the torments and death which lay in store for him: 'Behold, we are going up to Jerusalem, and the Son of man will be betrayed to the chief priests and to the scribes, and they will condemn him to death and deliver

---

[32]Acts 10:38.   [33]Cf. Mt 5:3-11.   [34]Cf. Lk 6:21.

him to the gentiles; and they will mock him and spit upon him, and scourge him and kill him, and after three days he will rise again.'[35]

Christ goes out to meet his passion and death with full awareness of his mission and of the manner of its necessary fulfilment. It is through this passion of his that 'man must not perish but have eternal life'. Through the cross he must come down and lay his hands on those roots of evil planted in human history and flourishing in the human spirit. Through his cross it is for him to achieve the work of salvation, whose redemptive character is determined by the design of everlasting Love.

So Christ will severely rebuke Peter who seeks to have him cast aside the idea of suffering and of death on a cross.[36] And when the same Peter struggles to defend him with a sword in the moment of his arrest in the garden of Gethsemane, Christ replies: 'Put your sword back in its place... How otherwise will the scriptures be fulfilled so that it might be done?'[37] He also says: 'The chalice which my Father has given me, shall I not drink it?'[38] This answer, no less than others which appear in various places in the gospel, shows how deeply Christ was imbued by the idea already expressed in the conversation with Nicodemus: 'For God so loved the world as to give his only-begotten Son, so that all who believe in him may not perish, but have eternal life.'[39] Christ sets himself to proceed in his pilgrimage to his own passion, fully conscious of its saving power. He goes forward in obedience to the Father; but he is especially the companion with his Father in this love wherewith he has loved the world and humankind. So Paul was to write of Christ: 'He loved me and delivered himself for me.'[40]

17. The scriptures must needs be fulfilled. There are many messianic texts in the Old Testament which proclaimed the sufferings of the Christ, the anointed One of God who was yet to come. The most moving of all these is the one called *The Fourth Song of the Servant of Yahweh* in the Book of

---

[35]Mk 10:33-34. [36]Cf. Mt 16:23. [37]Mt 26:52, 54.

[38]Jn 18:11. [39]Jn 3:16. [40]Gal 2:20.

Isaiah. The prophet, who has been deservedly called the fifth evangelist, draws in this Song a picture of the Servant's sufferings in such vivid colours that he would appear to be seeing them with his own eyes: not only an intellectual sight but a corporeal one. These verses of Isaiah shed such light on Christ's passion that it is thrown into greater relief and touches our hearts more effectively than the narratives of the evangelists themselves. See how the Man of Sorrows truly stands before our very eyes:

> There was no beauty, no comeliness in him, that we
>   should look on him.
> He was despised and the most abject of men,
> A man of sorrows and acquainted with grief,
> Like one from whom men hide their faces,
> He was despised, and we esteemed him not.
> Surely he has borne our sicknesses
> And has carried our sufferings;
> We considered him as one wounded,
> Stricken by God and afflicted.
> He was pierced for our transgressions,
> He was bruised for our iniquities.
> The chastisement that made for our peace was on him
> And with his stripes we have been healed,
> All we like sheep have gone astray,
> Everyone has gone his own way;
> And the Lord has laid on him the iniquity of us all.[41]

The Song of the Suffering Servant offers a description of Christ's Passion in which we can identify its separate moments down to the smallest detail: his arrest and humiliation, the slaps and the spitting, the contempt against the human dignity of the Prisoner, the unjust sentence and the scourging, the crown of thorns pressed down on his head, the mocking, the way of the cross, the crucifixion, the last agony.

What makes our spirits tremble even more than this

[41]Isa 53:2-6.

description of the passion is the all-pervading quality of Christ's sacrifice as communicated in the words of the prophet. See how in his innocence he takes upon himself the sufferings of all humankind because he assumes the sins of us all. 'The Lord has laid on him the iniquity of us all:' every single human sin in all its abundance and intensity is now portrayed as the true reason for the sufferings of our Redeemer, and if the pain is to be reckoned in proportion to the evil carried, then the prophet's words help us to understand the magnitude of the evil and the suffering which Christ took upon himself. This suffering may be called vicarious; but it is first of all redemptive. The Man of Sorrows of this prophecy is truly 'the Lamb of God who takes away the sins of the world'.[42] Sins are taken away by his suffering because he alone, as the only-begotten Son, could take them upon himself and accept them with that love for the Father which overcomes the evil inherent in every sin. In fact, he reduces this evil to nothing in what may be called the spiritual space of the relationship between God and the human race; and he fills that space with goodness.

Here we look at the twofold nature of the one person who is the subject of redemptive suffering. By his passion and his death on a cross, he achieves the redemption — he, the only-begotten Son whom God handed over. At the same time, he, the Son who is of one substance with the Father, suffers as a man. For his suffering is human in its condition; but it also has — and this is unique in the history of the human race — a profundity and a power which, whilst remaining human, can also be, in depth and intensity, incomparable to any other suffering; and this is because the Man who suffers is the only-begotten Son in person — 'God from God'. He alone, the Only-begotten, is competent to assume the whole weight of evil to be found in the sin of man; in every actual sin and in the universal sin corresponding to the circumstances of the historical existence of the human race on earth.

18. The considerations examined above lead us by the

[42] Jn 1:29.

straight path to the garden of Gethsemane and to the place of Calvary, where the Song of the Suffering Servant surviving in the book of Isaiah was finally fulfilled. Before we make our pilgrimage thither, let us read the verses which follow in the Song, proclaiming in prophetic prediction this passion in Gethsemane and on Golgotha. This Suffering Servant himself puts on these sufferings to which we have already referred, and he does so willingly and totally: points which we must take into full account if we are to give the rightful explanation of Christ's passion:

> He was afflicted and he submitted to it
> And never opened his mouth;
> Like a lamb that is led to the slaughter,
> And like a sheep that is dumb in the presence of its
>   shearers;
> So he did not open his mouth.
> By oppression and judgment he was taken.
> And as for his generation, who will care?
> For he was cut off from the land of the living;
> He was stricken down to death for the crimes of my
>   people.
> And they made his grave with the wicked,
> And his tomb with the rich,
> Even though he had committed no wrong,
> And there was no deceit in his mouth.[43]

Christ suffered willingly, and he was an innocent sufferer. In his sufferings he accepts to answer the question so often asked and set out in so extreme a fashion in the book of Job. The question also belongs to Christ himself, and much more properly, for he is not only a man like Job, but the only-begotten Son of God. Hence he can give the fullest possible solution to this problem. Both question and answer have the same source. Christ responds to the question concerning suffering and its meaning certainly by his teaching which is the good news, but more especially by his own suffering

---

[43]Isa 53:7-9.

which is linked organically and intrinsically to the teaching of the gospel. Here is the last and definitive word of his doctrine, 'the word...of the cross', as Paul was to say later on.[44]

This 'word of the cross' has within it the ring of perpetual truth. It is the fulfilment of the ancient prophecy. The many places and discourses of his public life and teaching testify to the manner of Christ's acceptance from the very beginning of this passion, which is the Father's will for the world's salvation. The final step here proves to be the prayer in the garden of Gethsemane, and in the words: 'My Father, if it be possible, let this chalice pass from me; nevertheless, not as I, but as you will,'[45] and later on, 'My Father, if it cannot pass unless I drink it, may your will be done.'[46] The words are rich and powerful, and demonstrate the truth of the love whereby the only-begotten Son lives out his obedience to his Father. They also bear witness to the reality of his suffering. This prayer of Christ in the garden of Gethsemane establishes his love's truth through the reality of his suffering. His words have a limpidity which succeeds in conveying the human quality of his suffering to the very end. Suffering means undergoing evil, in the face of which a person trembles and says, 'O, may it pass!', just as Christ cried out in the garden of Gethsemane.

His words are also witness to a unique and incomparable depth and power in this suffering which only the Man who is the sole-begotten Son could experience. They testify to a profundity and vehemence which the prophetic utterances cited above assist us in understanding, though this can only be in part; to grasp it all would mean to penetrate to the heart of the mystery, at once divine and human, of the Incarnate Word. Yet at least we can perceive the differences and also the similarities between every imaginable suffering proper to man, and the passion of the One who is both God and man. Gethsemane is the place where this suffering is revealed in its final form before Christ's inner gaze, according to the truth which the prophet has discovered and

---

[44]Cf. 1 Cor 1:18.   [45]Mt 26:39.   [46]Mt 26:42.

revealed concerning the evil embedded in it.

Besides the words spoken in the garden of Gethsemane, there are those which follow on Calvary. These do indeed bear witness to the absolute profundity of the evil in the suffering there experienced; it is unique in the history of the world. When Christ cries out, 'My God, my God, why have you forsaken me?', his words express that dereliction of soul which is quite often heard in the Old Testament, especially in the Psalms, and in particular in Psalm 22(21), where these words occur.[47] This cry of abandonment can be said to have its origin in the inseparable union of the Son with the Father; it comes into being in that the Father 'has laid upon him the iniquity of us all'.[48] Such expressions of dereliction will be echoed by Paul: 'For our sakes God made him into sin who had no experience of sin, so that he might become in him the justice of God.'[49] Along with this terrifying burden, Christ takes full account of evil in its entirety — the evil harboured in sin whereby God is rejected. It is in the depths of the Godhead that the Son experiences his union with the Father; and now in an ineffable manner that is still human he also feels this suffering which is alienation, repudiation by the Father, the breaking of the bond of relationship with God. But it is through this very suffering that he accomplishes the redemption; and now, as he dies, he is able to say, 'It is finished.'[50]

It can be said that scripture is fulfilled and the words of the Suffering Servant's Song have indeed been accomplished once and for all. 'It was the will of the Lord to bruise him in his weaknesses.'[51] Human suffering has reached its ultimate in the passion of Christ. The passion has taken upon itself new circumstances; it has moved on to a new level. It has been linked with love, the love of which Christ spoke to Nicodemus, the love which begets goodness, which produces it even from evil, begetting it through suffering, even as that supreme good which is the world's redemption is drawn from the cross of Christ and constantly flows from

[47]Ps 22 [21]:2.   [48]Isa 53:6.   [49]2 Cor 5:21.
[50]Jn 19:30.   [51]Isa 53:10.

that cross. Christ's cross has become the fountain from which the living waters stream.[52] To the cross then we must turn to ask again the question concerning the meaning of suffering, and to examine it in depth in order to find the answers.

V
Partners in Christ's Suffering

19. The same song of the Suffering Servant in Isaiah leads us into the question and its answer in the verses which follow:

> When he makes of his life an offering for sin
> He shall see his seed and his days prolonged,
> And the will of the Lord shall prosper in his hand.
> In return for his soul's labour he shall see the light,
> He shall brim over with knowledge.
> The righteous one, my servant, shall justify them all,
> And he shall carry their iniquities.
> I will in consequence distribute them all to him,
> And he shall divide the spoils with the mighty,
> Because he gave his life over to death
> And he was reckoned with the wicked.
> He carried the sins of all,
> And made intercession for the transgressors.[53]

With Christ's passion, then, we can say that all human suffering enters a new environment. Job, it would seem, had a premonition of this when he said: 'I know that my Redeemer is alive.'[54] It was as though he had relocated his own suffering to the same effect. He could hardly have known it in this completeness without the Redemption. In Christ's cross it is not only that the redemption is completed through the passion; but human suffering is itself redeemed. Christ,

---

[52]Cf. Jn 7:37-38.   [53]Isa 53:10-12.   [54]Job 19:25.

without any guilt on his part, took to himself the whole evil of sin. It is according to the experience of evil itself that the incomparable abundance of Christ's sufferings is measured: the sufferings which became the price of the redemption. It is of this that the Suffering Servant sings in Isaiah; and the witnesses of the new covenant, itself sealed with the blood of Christ, would, in their own times, witness to the same. So we read in the *First Letter of the Apostle Peter*: 'You know that you were ransomed from that useless way of life inherited from your forebears, not with any perishable commodity like silver or gold, but with the precious blood of Christ, as of the Lamb without stain or blemish.'[55] In his *Letter to the Galatians*, the Apostle Paul writes: 'He gave himself for our sins that he might rescue us from this present age of evil;'[56] and in the *First Letter to the Corinthians*: 'You were ransomed at a price, so glorify God in your body.'[57]

In these, and words like them, the witnesses of the new covenant speak of the great marvel of the redemption which was made perfect in Christ's passion. The Redeemer suffered on behalf and in place of all humankind. Everyone has a part to play in the redemption, and is called to share in the passion by which the redemption was accomplished, and by which all human suffering was also redeemed. When Christ achieved the redemption in his passion, he also raised human suffering to the level of the redemption. So it is that every human being in his or her suffering can become a sharer in the redemptive passion of Christ.

20. There are many places in the New Testament where this opinion is expressed. In the Second Letter to the Corinthians the Apostle writes: 'We suffer hardships in everything, but are not hemmed in; we are often at a loss, but never forsaken; we are persecuted, but never deserted; we are stricken down but not done to death; we always carry about in our bodies the death of Jesus, but so that the life of Jesus may show itself in our mortal flesh. . . . We know that he who raised up the Lord Jesus will raise us up with Jesus.'[58]

[55] 1 Pet 1:18-19.   [56] Gal 1:4.   [57] 1 Cor 6:20.   [58] 2 Cor 4:8-11, 14.

Paul speaks of a variety of sufferings, and especially those in which the first Christians shared 'for the sake of Jesus'. It was these which enabled the recipients of Second Corinthians to play their part in the work accomplished through the suffering and death of the Redeemer. At the same time the import, force and weight of Christ's cross and dying are to be completed by the parallel significance of the redemption. In the resurrection, humanity sees everything in a totally new light, by the help of which we can continue our pilgrimage through the near-impenetrable darkness of humiliations, doubts, desperation and persecution. So the Apostle wrote in the same letter: 'For as the sufferings of Christ are multiplied in us, so through Christ our consolation is equally abundant.'[59] In other letters, too, he encourages his converts when he writes: 'May the Lord direct your hearts in the love of God and the patience of Christ.'[60] In his Letter to the Romans we read: 'So I appeal to you, brethren, through the mercy of God to present your bodies as a living sacrifice, holy and pleasing to God, your spiritual worship.'[61]

These communications on Christ's passion in the Apostle's writings carry with them a twofold meaning. If we become sharers in Christ's sufferings, this is because Christ makes his passion available to humanity, in that he himself somehow participates in all human suffering through his own saving passion. In addition, when we find through faith that Christ's passion is redemptive, then we also discover our own sufferings there; and we also see them enriched through our faith with a new point and a new meaning.

It was when pregnant with this understanding that Paul wrote these persuasive words to the Galatians: 'I have been nailed with Christ to the cross; now it is no longer I who live, but it is Christ who lives in me. The life I now live in the flesh, I live in the faith of God's Son, who loved me and handed himself over for me.'[62] Faith brings it about that the writer of these words comes to recognise this love which led Christ to his cross. And if he loved thus by suffering and dying, then he lives by his passion and death in the one he

---

[59]2 Cor 1:5.   [60]2 Thess 3:5.   [61]Rom 12:1.   [62]Gal 2:19-20.

has so loved: that is, he lives in this man, Paul. And while Christ lives in him, in the measure in which Paul, aware in his faith of what is happening, repays love with love, Christ in this extraordinary way is united through the cross with this man Paul. It is this union which led Paul to write in similarly weighty vein in the same letter: 'Far be it from me to glory save in the cross of our Lord Jesus Christ, through whom the world is crucified to me, and I to the world.'[63]

21. Christ's cross sheds a light that is effective unto salvation on human life, and especially on human suffering. And this it does with such power that it touches the human person through faith with the resurrection as well: the mystery of the passion has its place in the whole paschal mystery. So the witnesses of Christ's passion are equally witnesses of his resurrection. Paul will write: 'that I may know him (Christ) and the power of his resurrection and have communion with him in his passion, becoming conformed to him in his death, if I might somehow attain that resurrection which is from the dead.'[64] The Apostle did indeed experience the power of Christ's resurrection, first of all on his journey to Damascus; only later, in this Easter light, did he come to that communion with him in his passion, as we read, for example, in the Letter to the Galatians. Paul's road is clearly paschal. Communion in the cross happens through the experience of Christ risen, through a specific sharing in the resurrection. So it is that in the Apostle's statements on suffering the theme of glory is often dwelt upon; for this finds its beginnings in Christ's cross.

The witnesses of the cross and resurrection were fully persuaded that 'we must enter the kingdom of God through many tribulations.'[65] Writing to the Thessalonians, Paul says: 'We ourselves glory in you...because of your patience, and your faith in all the persecutions and afflictions you are sustaining. This is an indication of God's just judgment, so that you be found worthy of God's kingdom for which you are suffering.'[66] Communion, then, in Christ's

[63]Gal 6:14.   [64]Phil 3:10-11.   [65]Acts 14:22.   [66]2 Thess 1:4-5.

passion is the same as suffering for God's kingdom. As they stand before the judgment seat of the God of justice, those who share in the sufferings of Christ are found to be worthy of God's kingdom. Through their afflictions they restore to Christ a measure of that infinite cost of our redemption, which is his passion and death. It is by these payments that the Kingdom of God is compacted anew in human history, and so becomes the prospect that waits at the end of earthly existence. It is through sufferings that Christ introduces us into this kingdom. Furthermore, through affliction humanity reaches the maturity necessary for establishing the kingdom; all are wrapped around with the mystery of Christ's redemption.

22. To this expectation of God's kingdom is related the hope of that glory which finds its beginnings in Christ's cross. It is the very last glory which is shown forth in the resurrection, though it was hidden completely on Christ's cross through the immensity of his pains. Those who share in the torments of Christ are called by their own afflictions to share in his glory. Paul makes this point in various places. To the Romans he writes: 'We are co-heirs with Christ, as long as we suffer with him in order to be glorified with him. I reckon that the sufferings of this time are not worth anything alongside the future glory which is to be shown forth in us.'[67] And we read in Second Corinthians: 'The light burden of tribulation which is our present lot is preparing us for the sublime reward of eternal glory beyond measure; for we contemplate not the things that are seen, but those that are unseen.'[68] The apostle Peter expressed the same truth in his first letter: 'In so far as you have communion in Christ's sufferings you must rejoice, so that you may rejoice and exult when his glory is revealed.'[69]

This theme of passion and glory is wholly characteristic of the gospel. This is manifest and is clearly illuminated because it points directly to the cross and resurrection. The resurrection is before everything the manifestation of that glorious transformation which corresponds to the lifting up

[67]Rom 8:17-18. [68]2 Cor 4:17-18. [69]1 Pet 4:13.

of Christ as this was achieved on the cross. For, while to the mere human vision the cross appeared as the despoilment of Christ, before God it was his exaltation. On the cross Christ worked for and carried out his mandate; and by fulfilling the will of the Father he at once affirmed his own existence and brought it to perfection. His power he showed forth in weakness; in humility the fullness of his messianic magnificence. All the words he spoke on Golgotha surely testify to this magnanimity, as he breathed his last, and particularly what he said about those who brought about his crucifixion: 'Father, forgive them, for they do not know what they are doing.'[70] These words provide a supreme example of this power for those who share in Christ's passion. Suffering, it would seem, provides the stimulus for the human person to demonstrate that magnanimity of behaviour, that spiritual maturity. Certainly Christ's martyrs and confessors of the faith have exemplified these qualities across the ages, relying on his words, 'Do not fear those who kill the body but cannot kill the soul.'[71]

Christ's resurrection has revealed 'the glory of the age to come' and has established 'the glory of the cross': that glory which is carried in Christ's passion itself, and often has been, and still is reflected, as its image, in human suffering. It is the manifestation of spiritual excellence. This glory needs to be acknowledged not only in martyrs for the faith but in countless others who sometimes, even if they do not believe in Christ, suffer evils and spend their lives for the truth or other righteous cause. In the afflictions of all these, the greatness of human dignity finds its true affirmation.

Suffering is the test — often a very severe one — to which the whole of humanity is subject. The pages of Paul's letters often speak to us of that marvellous gospel-paradox which brings together power and weakness. It is the paradox which the Apostle experienced himself along with all those who have found a share in the sufferings of Christ. So Paul says in Second Corinthians: 'I will all the more willingly glory in my weaknesses, that the power of Christ may dwell

[70] Lk 23:24.   [71] Mt 10:28.

in me.'[72] We read in Second Timothy: 'It is on account of this that I suffer; but I am not thrown into confusion. For I know the One in whom I have believed.'[73] And this is certainly what he says in the Letter to the Philippians: 'I can do all things in him who strengthens me.'[74]

Those who share in Christ's sufferings are contemplating the paschal mystery of the cross and resurrection. It is here that Christ first of all stoops to the very depths of human weakness and helplessness. He dies nailed to a cross. But if his exaltation to glory is achieved in such weakness, and this is confirmed by the power of the resurrection, this very fact demonstrates that the weakness inherent in every human affliction can be permeated by the power of God revealed in Christ's cross. In this context to suffer means to become particularly sensitive, and with all one's defences down, to the operation of God's saving power which is offered in Christ to humankind. In Christ, God has confirmed his pre-eminent will to act through a special kind of suffering: that is, through human weakness and despoilment in which he has decreed to reveal his power. It is in this sense that the exhortation in First Peter can be interpreted: 'But if it is as Christians that we suffer, we are not to be ashamed, but rather in that name to glorify God.'[75]

In his letter to the Romans, the apostle Paul speaks more at length of weakness as the source of power and of this spiritual renewal of a person in the midst of temptations and affliction, which is the proper vocation of those who share in Christ's passion: 'We glory, then, in our afflictions, because we know that affliction begets patience, and patience makes for proving, and proving for hope; nor does hope put us to shame, because the love of God is poured out in our hearts by the holy Spirit who is given to us.'[76] Suffering contains within itself an attraction to the virtue which human beings must cultivate on their own account. This virtue is perseverance in putting up with annoyances and wrongs. When one acts in this way, hope is aroused, as is the conviction that

[72] 2 Cor 12:9. [73] 2 Tim 1:12. [74] Phil 4:13.
[75] 1 Pet 4:16. [76] Rom 5:3-5.

one will not be overcome by affliction, nor ever be robbed of that human dignity which belongs to the consciousness of life's meaning. This is revealed in the working out of God's love, itself the sublime gift of the holy Spirit. In proportion as the human spirit participates in this love, it discovers itself in the depths of affliction. It is here that one's very soul is found again which was thought to have been lost in suffering.[77]

24. Now the Apostle progresses even further, as his experience of sharing Christ's suffering expands. In the Letter to the Colossians we read the sentiments which mark the final end of the spiritual pilgrimage in its relation to tribulation: 'Now I rejoice in my sufferings for you, and I fill up in my flesh what is lacking in Christ's sufferings for the sake of his body, that is, his Church.'[78] Elsewhere he asks those to whom the letter is sent: 'Do you not know that your bodies are Christ's members?'[79]

In the paschal mystery Christ initiated his union with humankind in the community of the Church. The mystery of the Church may be described as follows: when baptism is conferred, the human person is configured to Christ; then, through Christ's sacrifice — sacramentally, in the Eucharist — the Church is continually built up as the spiritual body of Christ. It is Christ's will to be joined in this body with the whole of humankind, and pre-eminently he unites himself with those who suffer. The above citation from Colossians testifies to the singular character of this union. Whoever suffers together with Christ — as does the apostle Paul when in his adherence to Christ he carries his afflictions — not only draws that strength from Christ already mentioned, but fills up by means of his own pains 'what is lacking to the passion of Christ.' This is a gospel revelation which is especially illuminative of the creative character of suffering. It was the passion of Christ which achieved the good of the world's redemption, itself inexhaustible and infinite. No human ingenuity could ever increase its value. At the same time, in the mystery of the Church, his body, Christ has

[77]Cf. Mk 8:35; Lk 9:24; Jn 12:25.　　　[78]Col 1:24.　　　[79]1 Cor 6:15.

revealed his redemptive passion in all human affliction. In so far as a person shares in the passion of Christ, anywhere and at any time in human history, in that far, each fills up in personal fashion those sufferings through which Christ achieved the world's redemption.

Must one conclude from this that the redemption Christ effected was imperfect? By no means. What we are saying is that the redemption which was accomplished by the restorative power of love is open to every kind of love expressed in human suffering. In this environment of love, the redemption has already been brought to its perfection; and yet this perfecting still continues. Christ brought the work of the redemption to its final finish, and yet he did not stop its working.

By means of his redemptive suffering which effects a universal ransom, Christ embraced from the beginning all that mortals suffer; and he continues to do it. It is indeed so; it evidently belongs to the essence of Christ's redemptive passion that such suffering requires to be filled up without ceasing.

Thus it is that Christ in his own passion embraced all that humankind suffers and in this way redeemed the world. This redemption lives on in all its vigour across human time and space, although already brought to its fullness by the sufferings of Christ. This life and growth continues to flourish because it is the body of Christ, that is, the Church. It is here that all human suffering because of the communion in Christ's charity fills out the passion of Christ, just as the Church fills out his saving work. The mystery of the Church, that is, of the body which in itself brings to fullness Christ's own body which was crucified and is now risen from the dead, also shows forth the whole area in which human sufferings fill out the sufferings of Christ. In this spiritual environment of the Church as the body of Christ, which is continually growing everywhere and in every era, one may properly think and speak of 'what is lacking to the sufferings of Christ.' The apostle does in fact make this point clearly when he writes about 'filling up what is wanting to Christ's suffering for the sake of his body, that is, the Church'.

The Church herself constantly has recourse to the super-abundant riches of the redemption which she centers on the life of all humankind. She is the means whereby this redemptive suffering of Christ can be constantly filled up with human suffering. In fact, the divine and human nature of the Church is illumined by this truth. Suffering, it would appear, finds a mode of inhering in the Church's essential marks, as she sees in suffering an inestimable value. It is an excellence which the Church, with her unshaken belief in the power of the redemption, cultivates with all diligence; that is, with all the depths of her faith in the redemption, by which she embraces the everlasting and ineffable mystery of Christ's body.

VI
The Gospel of Suffering

25. The witnesses of Christ's cross and resurrection have passed on to the Church and to humankind a rare gospel of suffering. The Redeemer himself first wrote it when he accepted his own passion for love's sake, 'that man may not perish, but have eternal life.'[80] It is the passion which, enriched by the living word of his teaching, has provided such an abundance for all those who shared Christ's pains during the first generation of his disciples and confessors, and then among those who have followed him across the centuries. A first reason for consolation, and one established in gospel and history alike, is that in the first, most prominent place at Christ's side was always standing his holy mother, so as to give the most complete testimony —her whole life — to this unique gospel of pain. A great confluence of intense sufferings was so mingled in her life that they give proof of the steadfast faith and play a part in the universal redemption. Indeed, from the first intimate colloquy with the angel, she saw in her mission of mother-hood her destined task to share in the sending of her Son in a

---

[80] Jn 3:16.

way that was unique to her and which could never happen again. And in a very short time, what happened at the birth of Jesus in the town of Bethlehem confirmed it all, as did that certain and clear prophecy of the old man Simeon, when he spoke of the sharp sword that would pierce her soul. Finally, there were the anxieties and constraints of the flight into Egypt which had to be made in such haste because of the cruel design of Herod.

Next, after the historical events of her Son's hidden and public life, in which she undoubtedly shared with all her heart's affection, the sufferings of the blessed virgin Mary reached their culmination on Calvary. Their intensity can hardly be measured by any human understanding; but assuredly in their hidden and heavenly quality they were most profitable towards the achieving of universal redemption. Her going up to Calvary and her stance at the foot of the cross with the beloved disciple constituted a unique sharing in the redemptive death of her Son; whilst the words she heard him speak contained a formal mandate that this specific gospel of suffering be proclaimed to the whole community of believers.

The blessed virgin Mary, so totally present to Christ in his passion and a partner in it by her own suffering, makes a unique contribution to this gospel of suffering. One might say that she wrote the major part of it together with her Son. She certainly anticipated in her living those words of St. Paul which stand at the head of this letter. She has a special claim to having filled out in her flesh what was wanting to the sufferings of Christ.

With the light shed by the incomparable example of Christ which is also reflected appropriately in the life of his mother, this gospel of suffering becomes an ever-brimming fountain for the successive generations in the history of the Church through the witness and the writings of the apostles. The good news of suffering is not simply offered as one of the four evangelists' themes. It is the revelation of the saving power and purpose of suffering in Christ's messianic mission, and in the mission and vocation of the Church as well.

Christ never hid this necessity of suffering from those who

listened to him. His message was always clear: 'If anyone
would come after me...let him take up his cross every
day.'[81] And he gave to his disciples principles of morality
which could only be practised 'by denying themselves'[82]
The road which leads to the kingdom of heaven is 'a hard
and narrow one'; and then Christ contrasts it with the broad
and spacious ways which lead to perdition.[83] He also said
many times that his disciples and witnesses would suffer
many persecutions; and this happened, as we know, not
only in the first centuries of the Church's life under the
Roman empire, but during the various periods of history,
and in all parts of the world. It is still happening in our own
time.

Let us cite some of Christ's statements on this theme.
'They will lay their hands on you and pursue you, and hand
you over to the prisons and synagogues, and you will be
dragged before kings and governors for my name's sake.
This will be the time for you to give witness. Let it come into
your hearts now, that you are not to ponder ahead of time
what replies you are to give. For I will give you words and
wisdom which none of your enemies will be able to resist or
contradict. You will be given over by your parents even, by
your brothers, friends and relatives, and they will put some
of you to death. You will be hated by everybody for my
name's sake. But not a hair of your head will perish. By your
endurance you will gain possession of your souls.'[84]

This gospel of suffering first speaks in various places of
suffering 'on Christ's behalf' and 'on account of Christ', in
Jesus' own words or those of his apostles. The Master does
not hide from his disciples and followers the sort of occasion
on which they are likely to suffer. Rather he makes it abundantly clear, whilst at the same time revealing that the divine
assistance will sustain them during these persecutions and
tribulations 'for his name's sake'. These sufferings will also
establish to a high degree their likeness to Christ and their
union with him. 'If the world hates you, know it has hated
me before you...because you are truly not of the world,

---

[81]Lk 9:23.   [82]Cf. Lk 9:23.   [83]Cf. Mt 7:13-14.   [84]Lk 21:12-19.

rather I have chosen you out of the world; and so it is that the world hates you;...the servant is not greater than his master...If they persecuted me, then they will persecute you...But they will do all this to you for my name's sake, because they do not know him who sent me.'[85] 'I have spoken these things to you, that in me you may have peace. In the world you have distress, but have confidence, I have overcome the world.'[86]

This first chapter of the gospel of suffering, which deals with persecutions, that is, of being afflicted on Christ's account, carries with it its own call to that inner strength and courage of heart which is maintained by the glorious power of the resurrection. It is by his resurrection that Christ has overcome the world once and for all. However, because of its relationship with his passion and death, the world is also conquered by his suffering. Indeed, suffering is extraordinarily alive in that victory over the world which is signalized by his resurrection. Christ retains in his body, now risen from the dead, the marks of the cross's wounds in his hands, feet and side. His resurrection manifests the victorious power of suffering and fills the heart of those whom he chose as his apostles and of those whom he continues to choose and send with confidence in this power. As the apostle Paul said: 'All those who wish to live a filial life in Christ Jesus will suffer persecution.'[87]

26. If the first great chapter of this gospel of suffering is set down from generation to generation by those who endure persecutions on Christ's account, there is another one, equally important, which has been written across the events of history. The authors are all those who, by joining their own sufferings with Christ's saving passion, can be said to suffer with him. It is they who fulfill what the first witnesses of the passion and resurrection said or wrote about sharing Christ's pains. In them is fulfilled the good news of suffering. Each of them continues to write it and to proclaim it to the world in which they live, and to the people of our time.

We can be certain that an extraordinary power has

[85]Jn 15:18-21.   [86]Jn 16:33.   [87]2 Tim 3:12.

remained hidden in suffering through the centuries and in generation after generation of humankind. This is a special grace, intimately uniting a person with Christ. Many saints, such as Francis of Assisi, Ignatius Loyola and the like, owe their spiritual conversion to this grace. Its effects are to be found not simply in the fact that a person has discovered the salutary meaning of suffering. It is rather that he or she is transformed through it, and begins to live an altogether new kind of existence and a new way to perfect life's call. Such a discovery sets the seal on a person's spiritual magnanimity, which enables him or her to transcend entirely their physical limitations. When the body is severely ill and suffering from extreme weakness, and the person is almost entirely unable to go on living and acting, the inner maturity and greatness of soul find their full scope, so as to move the hearts of those who are normal and healthy.

Certainly these gifts of maturity and magnanimity discovered in suffering are achieved by a distinct conversion and by cooperation with the grace of the crucified redeemer. It is Christ himself who is at work in human suffering through his Spirit of truth and of consolation. In some sense he transforms the nature of the spiritual life, when he asks the sick to sit with him. He, too, as Master and Guide of souls, teaches his suffering brothers and sisters of this wonderful commerce which goes on in the mysterious depths of the redemption. Suffering of its nature is an experience of evil. But Christ has set in it the rock-bed of a perpetual good —the good of eternal salvation. By suffering on the cross he laid hold of the very roots of evil, sin and death. He conquered Satan, the artisan of evil, and his continual rebellion against the Creator. To his suffering brothers and sisters he opens up and gradually unfolds the territory of the kingdom of God; a world, that is, freed from sin and converted to its Creator; one which is gradually being built up on the saving power of love. So Christ slowly but surely introduces into such a world, into this kingdom of his Father, those who bear the burden of suffering, whom he finds in the heart of his own suffering. For suffering can hardly be transformed or altered by grace from outside; only from within. It is he who is fully present by his saving passion in all human suffering, and thus can operate from within it through the power of his Spirit of truth and of consolation.

Nor is this all. The divine Redeemer is anxious to enter the soul of all who suffer through the heart of his most holy mother, the first fruits and crown so to say of all the redeemed. Christ in the moment of death conferred on the most blessed and ever virginal Mary a new motherhood, in addition to and as it were a continuation of that by which he was brought into the world through the power of the holy Spirit. This spiritual and universal motherhood was to embrace all humankind, so that everyone, during their earthly pilgrimage in faith, might be one with her, and so be closely united with him even unto his death on the cross. Thus every kind of suffering would, by the power of the cross, be created afresh and be transformed from human weakness into the power of God.

This interior growth does not always take place in the same way. It is often hard to get it started and establish it. Beginnings differ; the spirit of a person afflicted with sufferings, the level of his or her tolerance: all this is relative. However one can say as a general rule that everyone to whom suffering comes will find that one instinctively cries out against it, asks 'why?'. The person wants to know what the suffering means, and seeks an answer to the question in the specific human context. Indeed the question is very often brought to God, to Christ. Sometimes it becomes clear that the one to whom the problem is brought is himself suffering and wishes to give his answer from the cross as from the heart of his own experience. Yet often there is need for a lapse of time; it may be long enough before the inward answer makes itself felt. Christ never answers in an abrupt or abstract fashion to a person's question on the meaning of suffering. It is only when, little by little, one becomes a sharer in Christ's pains that the truly saving answer is heard.

The answer which is given by such participation in the interior union with the Master is something more than a merely abstract reply to the question concerning the meaning of suffering. Christ's reply is first and foremost an invitation, an appeal. He explains the causes of the suffering in a very practical way, when he says: 'Come, follow me. Let your suffering make you a partner in this work for the world's salvation, which is achieved through my passion and my cross.' When someone takes up his cross, he finds union in spirit with Christ's cross. It is then that the salutary meaning of suffering becomes clear. Nor is this understanding revealed simply at the human level, but from within Christ's passion. At the same time, however, this salutary meaning of suffering comes down from Christ into the human condition, and so it becomes the human person's individual response. Then indeed the person discovers in the suffering interior peace and even spiritual joy.

27. The apostle writes about this joy in his Letter to the Colossians: 'I rejoice in my sufferings on your behalf.'[88] Its source is found in the victory won over the feeling of the uselessness of suffering, which often lurks in the shadow of human suffering. It is a feeling that can wither a person from within, and what is worse, seems to make one a burden to others. One feels driven to accept the help and care given by others, whilst seeming useless to oneself. Once the saving aspect of suffering in and with Christ is experienced, the feeling of utter desolation is banished. Belief that I am sharing in Christ's passion brings with it the inner surety that in my pains I am 'filling up what is wanting to the sufferings of Christ'; so that, in the spiritual context of the work of redemption, as Christ willed it, I am contributing to the salvation of my brothers and sisters. Nor is it simply a question of doing some good to others. It is the fulfillment of a task for which there is no substitute. In the body of Christ, which constantly finds its increase through the redeeming cross, it is the suffering imbued with the virtues of Christ's sacrifice which is the essential mediator and source of those goods which of their nature contribute to the world's salvation. It is the most powerful means to the grace which transforms souls, and makes operable in human history the virtues of the redemption. And when it comes to

[88]Col 1:24.

that cosmic struggle between the spiritual powers of good and evil mentioned in the Letter to the Ephesians,[89] human suffering, when allied to Christ's redemptive passion, is a special support for those influences for good and hastens the victory of these saving powers.

So the Church holds in reverence all Christ's suffering brothers and sisters as being the manifold instrument of his divine power. The shepherds of the Church must regularly turn to them to seek their support and stay. The gospel of suffering continues to be preached and written, expressing the same paradoxical sentiments, that the divine power springs up from the midst of human weakness. Those who share in Christ's passion have in their own sufferings that seed of the infinite abundance of the world's redemption and can communicate these riches to others. The more people are menaced by sin, and the more oppressive are the structures of sin in the modern world, the greater the influence wielded by human suffering; and the more the Church is driven to have recourse to its benefits for the world's salvation.

VII
The Good Samaritan: neighbour to the suffering

28. The parable of the Good Samaritan is an integral part of the gospel of suffering. Christ told it as an answer to the question, 'Who is my neighbour?'[90] There were three who travelled by the same road from Jerusalem to Jericho. But it was the Samaritan who showed himself to be the real neighbour to the man wounded and stripped and left half-dead by the robbers. The word neighbour points to the one who fulfilled the law of love towards the next person. Of the two other travellers, the first was a priest, the other a Levite. Both 'saw him and passed him by'. When the Samaritan 'saw him, he was moved with compassion, and he went up to him and dressed his wounds'. Then 'he brought him to an inn and

---

[89]Cf. Eph 6:12.   [90]Lk 10:29.

took care of him'.[91] And before he left, he arranged without hesitation that the innkeeper should take care of the suffering victim, and promised to pay any expenses incurred.

The parable is integral to the gospel of suffering because it shows why each of us should wait upon our suffering neighbour. We are not permitted to 'pass by' heedlessly; we must take our place beside him. The good Samaritan is every human being who takes his stand beside the one who suffers, whatever that suffering may be. This taking up one's stand has nothing to do with unmannerly curiosity; it is the spirit of readiness in one who is prepared to help. It is the disclosure of a quality which is lodged in the innermost recesses of the heart, and is also the expression of a compassionate heart. The good Samaritan is everyman who is overwhelmed by the sufferings of others, one stirred to compassion by the misfortunes which befall the neighbour. Since Christ, who can read one's inmost thoughts, proffers this compassion, then it must have a like effect on our whole attitude towards the sufferings of another. We therefore need to cultivate the same quality of sensitivity which will disclose a truly effective compassion for the sufferer. For it does sometimes happen that such compassion is the only or principal expression of our love for the afflicted and our union with them.

Yet the Samaritan in Christ's parable was not satisfied with the emotion of pity and the feeling of compassion. These sentiments became a stimulus for going to the help of the wounded man. The good Samaritan is the one who relieves the sufferer, who finds an efficacious remedy, insofar as possible, for the particular injuries. His whole intent is to bring all material help to bear. We might even say that he makes a gift of himself, of his own ego, to the other. This is one of the principal tenets of Christian anthropology. One cannot 'fully find oneself except through a sincere gift of oneself'.[92] The good Samaritan is one who is able to make this donation of himself.

---

[91]Lk 10:33-34.

[92]*Gaudium et Spes* (The Pastoral Constitution of Vatican II on the Church in the Modern World), 24.

29. In our reflection on this gospel parable, we may conclude that suffering, which dwells in our world in so many guises, is here amongst us in order to stimulate love in the human heart, to prompt us to that gift of self on behalf of others who are suffering, without counting the cost to our own well-being. The ambience of human affliction constantly demands another — that of human love. In some way or other the existence of suffering gives rise in the human heart and spirit to a completely unselfish love which translates itself into action. The human person who is neighbourly cannot let himself heedlessly pass by when he sees others suffering; and this because of basic human relationships and much more the love of the neighbour. He must take his stand and let his heart be moved with compassion like the Samaritan in the parable. This of itself reveals a deep Christian truth which is also universally human. And it is right that what is done for people who are suffering or in need of aid should be commonly designated as the work of the good Samaritan.

Such activity across the years has taken on institutional forms and is now well able to operate in the field of various professions. We can recognise the good Samaritan at work in the medical field, in nursing and other similar activity. And, if we look at the evangelical character of such work, we speak of fulfilling a vocation rather than a function. The institutions which for centuries now have performed a good Samaritan service have become more specialized in our times and increased their ministry. Undoubtedly this is proof that the men and women of our time are more aware of and concerned for the sufferings of their neighbour, seeking to understand them and provide more exactly for them. Here capacities and abilities are always on the increase with the development of specializations and techniques. When we review all this, we may rightly say that the gospel parable of the good Samaritan is one of the chief elements in our moral culture, and indeed in human society as a whole. And when we reflect on all the people who serve their suffering neighbour with their diverse knowledge and expertise, the least we can do is to offer them fitting words of gratitude with thankful hearts.

We would extend these thanks to all those who, without a thought for their own welfare, direct their services to their suffering neighbour, and, like the good Samaritan, freely spend themselves, devoting all their time and energy outside their own profession to such charitable work. These voluntary and charitable services going by the name of social work, may well be called apostolic, since they are often undertaken for evangelical reasons, and especially in connection with the Church or any Christian community. These voluntary services, under the title good Samaritan, are carried out in suitable areas and institutions set up for this purpose. The regularity and zeal which such works manifest is most impressive, especially the larger operations which demand careful organisation and modern equipment. This does not mean that individual efforts are of less value, particularly in those aspects of human sickness which need a more personal touch and can only be done on a one-to-one basis. Finally, there is family help — the acts of charity extended to members of the same family, or the mutual help between families.

It is hardly possible to enumerate here the various kinds of work and the different situations in which the good Samaritan activity is pursued in the Church and human society in general. It is obvious that they are very numerous, and it must be a source of joy for us that they point up the substantial moral values, such as human friendship and relationships, Christian love of the neighbour, the solid framework of life in society and its regular circumstances amongst people. They also keep up the struggle against all kinds of hatred, violence, cruelty, contempt for human dignity, heedlessness of the other's existence, the crass indifference towards one's neighbour and his or her sufferings.

Here we must stress the great importance of making provision in education. The family, the school and the other institutions for forming the right attitudes of mind, even if only on the humanitarian level, must persevere in their efforts to awaken and foster that gentleness towards the suffering neighbour, of which the Samaritan in the gospel has become the image. The Church, it is obvious, must become the same. Insofar as possible she must search out even more deeply the purposes which Christ made his own in this parable and in the whole of the gospel. The seriousness of both is evident. Everyone must feel personally called to give testimony to love in suffering as the most important task in the world. Though institutions are of great moment and even essential, none can of themselves replace the human heart or spirit in the matter of another's suffering. This is so of bodily suffering, but it is even more true of moral sufferings, especially when the spirit is afflicted.

30. The parable of the good Samaritan, as we have said, belongs to the gospel of Suffering and with it reaches across the history of the Church, of Christianity and of the human race as a whole. But saving suffering, as Christ's revelation testifies, has no truck with inertia. Rather the contrary. The gospel in respect of suffering is the enemy of inertia. Christ himself is here the mover *par excellence*, and fulfills the messianic purpose of his mission. As the prophet says: 'The Spirit of the Lord is upon me; therefore he has anointed me to preach the gospel to the poor, he has sent me to proclaim release to the captives and sight to the blind, to set at liberty the broken-hearted, to announce the acceptable year of the Lord.'[93] Christ is most careful to fulfill the messianic design of his mission. He goes about 'doing good',[94] and the beneficial results of his activity stand out particularly in relieving human suffering. The parable is in total agreement with Christ's own method of work.

Finally, the central argument of this parable has immediate reference to those very disturbing words concerning the Last Judgment which are recorded in Matthew's gospel: 'Come, you blessed of my Father, take possession of the kingdom prepared for you from the foundation of the world. For I was hungry and you gave me food, I was thirsty and you gave me drink, I was a stranger and you welcomed me, naked and you clothed me, sick and you visited me, in prison and you came to see me.'[95] To the just, who ask when they did all this for him, the Son of man will reply: 'Truly, I

---

[93]Lk 4:18-19. Cf. Isa 61:1-2.   [94]Acts 10:38.   [95]Mt 25:34-36.

tell you, as often as you did it to one of the least of my brethren, you did it to me.'[96] The opposite sentence will be meted out to those who behaved otherwise: 'As often as you did not do it to one of the least of these, you failed to do it to me.'[97]

One could certainly draw out the list of sufferings which have stimulated or failed to stimulate the fellow-feelings, the compassion and the practical help of humankind. The first and second parts of Christ's proclamation concerning the Last Judgment unambiguously witness to the need everyone has, in the context of eternal life, to take one's stand, as did the Samaritan, at the side of one's suffering neighbor, to have compassion on him and to minister to him. In Christ's messianic purpose, which is equally that of God's kingdom, sickness is in the world as a stimulus of charity, as a source of loving activity for the neighbor and thus to transform humanity into a culture of love. In such love, the meaning of suffering as leading to salvation is brought to its completion with all its questions answered. Christ's words on the Last Judgment illuminate all this with gospel clarity and simplicity.

What is said about charity and charitable activity in the context of human suffering, discovers for us again and again Christ's redemptive passion as the foundation of all human sufferings. 'You did it to me,' Christ says. He it is who experiences love in everyman, who receives the assistance which is given to the one who is suffering, without any distinction of persons. He is present in the one who suffers because his own saving suffering has expanded once and for all so as to touch every human pain. All those who suffer are driven once and for all to partake of 'Christ's passion'.[98] In the same way, all are urged to fill up with their own pains 'what is wanting in the sufferings of Christ'.[99] Christ has taught us both to do good by our suffering and to do good to those who suffer. Thus he has revealed to us the whole meaning of suffering.

[96]Mt 25:40.　　　[97]Mt 25:45.　　　[98]1 Pet 4:13.　　　[99]Col 1:24.

VIII
Conclusion

31. This, then, is the meaning of suffering, truly supernatural and also human. It is supernatural because it exists within the mystery of the world's divine redemption. It is at the same time fully human, because the human person discovers within it himself, his humanity, his dignity and his mission.

Undoubtedly, suffering belongs to the mystery which is human nature. It may be that suffering is not as obscured as is man himself in this mystery, which is particularly opaque. Vatican Council II has described this truth: 'Only in the mystery of the Word Incarnate does the human mystery shine forth with any brightness...For Christ, the last Adam, in the revelation of the mystery of the Father and of his love, fully reveals human person to human person and shows forth the heights of their vocation.'[100]

If these words relate to all that belongs to the mystery of humankind, then certainly they have to do in a special way with human suffering. For there it becomes absolutely essential that human beings should be open to one another and the heights of their vocation revealed. Experience also shows that such happenings are attended by extraordinary difficulties. But when they come to fruition and shine forth with the light of human life, they bring extraordinary blessedness. 'Through Christ and in Christ light is cast on the obscurities of suffering and death.'[101]

So we bring to an end our consideration on suffering in this year when the Church is celebrating the extraordinary Jubilee of the Redemption. It is wonderful how this mystery of the redemption of humankind is to be found in suffering, which itself has its deepest roots in the same mystery.

It is our desire to spend this Year of the Redemption in close union with all who suffer. So may all those who are in pain come together in mind and heart to the cross of Cal-

[100]*Gaudium et Spes*, (see #92), 22.   [101]*Ibid.*

vary: all those who believe in Christ, and especially those who are afflicted for their faith in the crucified and risen Lord, in order that they may offer up their sufferings and so hasten the fulfilment of the Saviour's own prayer that all may come together in unity.[102] May all people of good will achieve the same unity, since on this cross is the Redeemer of humankind. He is the Man of Sorrows who has taken upon himself the world's sufferings in body and mind in all times, so that the saving purpose of these sufferings may be fully grasped and all their problems solved.

We stand and look upon every human cross of suffering, together with Mary who stood by the cross of Jesus.[103]

We offer our prayers through the intercession of all the saints who through the course of the centuries have shared most closely in the sufferings of Christ. We beseech them to support us.

And we ask all you who are suffering to support us, and you who are ill to be a source of strength both for the Church and for humanity. In the fierce war between good and evil, whose theatre is this world of ours, may your suffering in union with Christ's cross prevail.

And to all of you, beloved brothers and dear children, we send our apostolic blessing.

Rome, St. Peter's, 11 February, Feast of our blessed Lady of Lourdes, 1984, the sixth year of our pontificate. John Paul II

John Paul II

---

[102]Cf. Jn 17:11, 21   [103]Cf. Jn 19:25.

SUGGESTIONS FOR FURTHER READING

D'Arcy, M.C., *The Pain of this World and the Providence of God* (London 1935).

Dougherty, Flavian, C.P. (ed.), *The Meaning of Human Suffering* (New York 1982).

Geach, Peter, *Providence and Evil* (Cambridge 1977).

Hick, John, *Evil and the God of Love* (London 1966).

Journet, Charles (tr. M. Barry), *The Meaning of Evil* (New York 1963).

Lewis, C. S., *The Problem of Pain* (New York 1944).

Russell, R. P. (ed. and tr.) *St. Augustine, Divine Providence and the Problem of Evil* (New York 1942).

Sutcliffe, Edmund F., *Providence and Suffering in the Old and New Testaments* (London 1955).

INDICES
1: SCRIPTURE

266

2: GENERAL